Singing of Birth and Death

Texts in Performance

Singing of Birth and Death

Texts in Performance

STUART H. BLACKBURN

University of Pennsylvania Press

Philadelphia

Printed in the United States of America

Library of Congress Cataloging-in-Publication Data

Blackburn, Stuart H.
Singing of birth and death.

Bibliography: p.
Includes index.
1. Tamils—Rites and ceremonies. 2. Tamils—Folklore.
3. Folk-songs, Tamil. 4. Folklore—Performances—Case studies. I. Title.
DS432.T3B57 1988 398.2′089948 87-30137
ISBN 0-8122-8097-0

For

Na. Vāṉamāmalai

(1917–1979)

and

Ku. Āṟumukam Perumāḷ Nadar

(1901–1983)

Contents

	Note on Transliteration	ix
	Plates	xi
	Maps and Figures	xiii
	Introduction: Texts in Performance	xvii
1	Nāñcil Nāṭu: The Shape of Place	1
2	The Bow Song as Oral Tradition	10
	The performing group	
	Delivery styles	
	Composition	
	Manuscripts and bards	
3	Narrative and Ritual in Performance	31
	The narrative world	
	The *koṭai* festival	
4	The Birth of Śāstā	48
	Introduction	
	Performance translation	
5	The Death of the Little Brothers	89
	Introduction	
	Performance translation	
6	The Marriage of Muttuppaṭṭaṉ	141
	Introduction	
	Performance translation	
7	Conclusions: Death and Ritual Narrative	214
	Notes	223

Appendix: Temple Plans 239
Glossary 243
Bibliography 249
Index 261

NOTE ON TRANSLITERATION

Tamil words are transliterated according to the scheme used by the *Tamil Lexicon* (Madras, 1926–1939); words common to Tamil and other Indian languages have been given in their Tamil forms (for example, Pārvati rather than Pārvatī). Certain words have been left in their usual English spellings (for example, Brahmin, Tinnevelly, raja, Nadar).

Plates

The plates appear between pages 30 and 31.

Plate 1 A typical bow song temple (center, rear) with associated icons.

Plate 2 Two *pītams* (the distinctive bow song icon).

Plate 3 A Piḷḷai priest performing *pūjā* to a bow song god.

Plate 4 A *pītam* dressed in flower garlands during a festival.

Plate 5 Clay icons of Icakki Ammaṉ in her two roles (left, maternal; right, destructive [eating a child]).

Plate 6 Close-up of Icakki Ammaṉ in her destructive role.

Plate 7 A male bow song deity, flanked by his large wooden clubs.

Plate 8 Bow song group in action (the woman to the left is the lead singer).

Plate 9 Singing the Muttuppaṭṭaṉ story (see Chapter 6).

Plate 10 The audience (mostly female) during a daytime performance.

Plate 11 The lead singer leans in to hear lines read from a palm-leaf manuscript during a "scripted performance."

Plate 12 Possessed dancer (right) stands while monitor asks for knife to open coconut requested by the dancer.

Plate 13 Possessed dancers carrying swords and staffs as emblems of their possessing hero-god.

Plate 14 Possessed medium (left) distributes sacred ash and speaks *kuṟi* in response to questions.

Maps and Figures

MAPS

1 India and the Bow Song Region xiv
2 Nāñcil Nāṭu and Vicinity xv

FIGURES

1 Bow Song Performing Group 12
2 Basic Unit of Bow Song Composition 22
3 Narrative Patterns of Birth Stories and Death Stories 32
4 Birth Stories and Death Stories as World View 36
5 Pattern of Narrative and Ritual in the *Koṭai* Festival 46

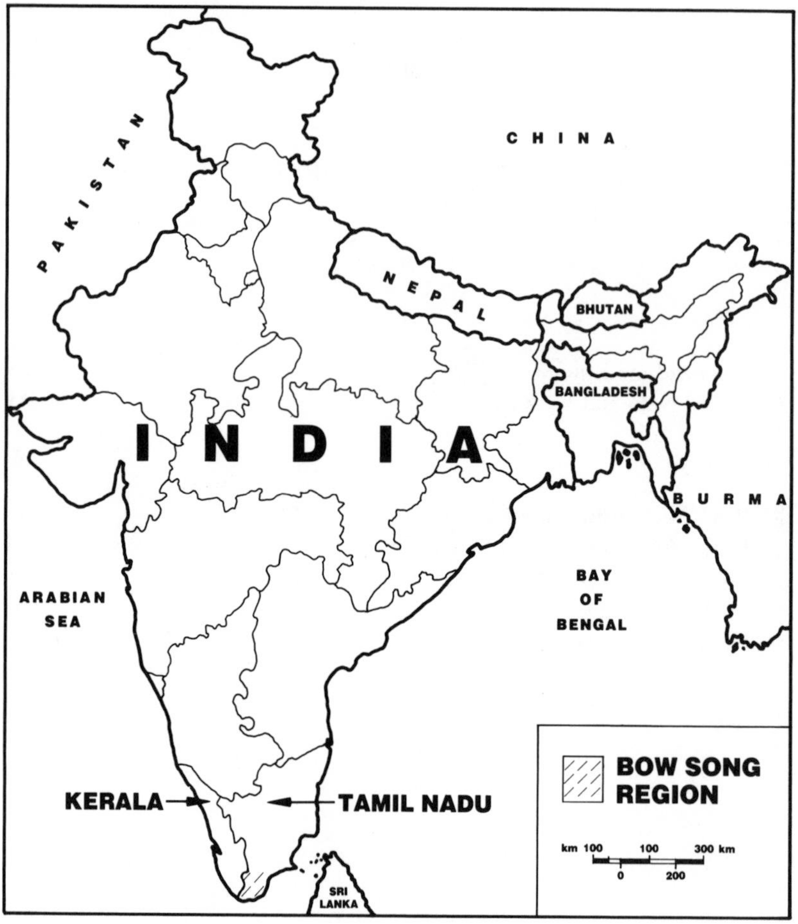

Map 1. India and the Bow Song Region

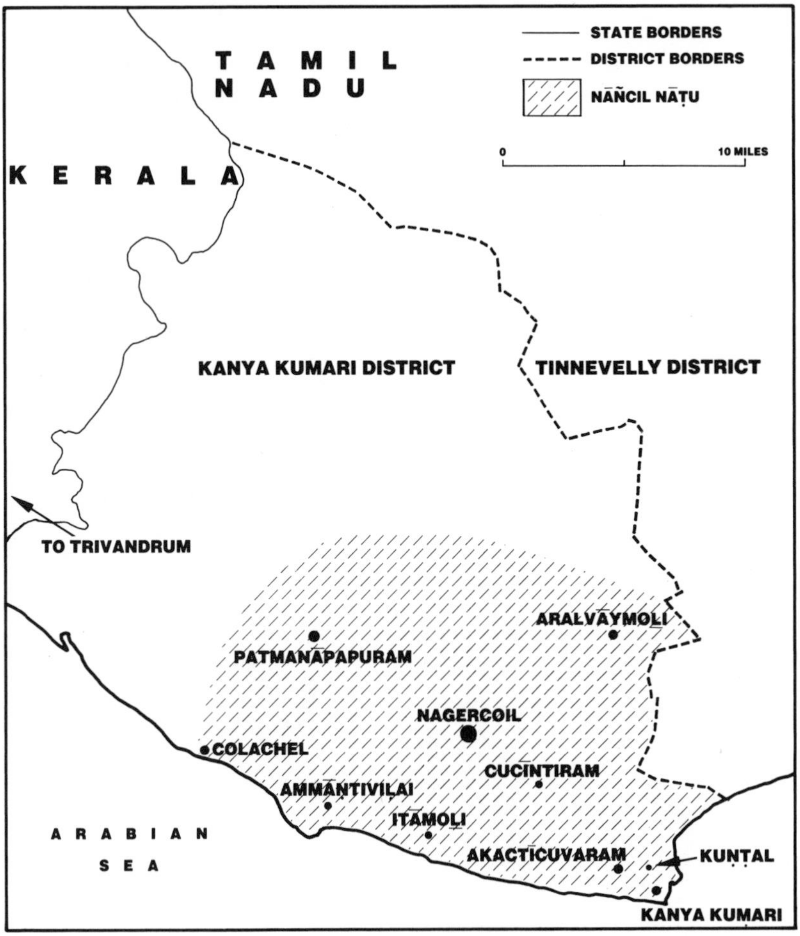

Map 2. Nāñcil Nāṭu and Vicinity

Introduction: Texts in Performance

This is a book about texts and oral performance in a Tamil tradition called the bow song (*vil pāṭṭu*). When I began writing several years ago, the focus was squarely on oral performance because both my own field experience and the new thinking in folkloristics had inspired me to look at bow song singing, rituals, spirit possession, and dance as performance events. As I studied my materials more closely, however, it became clear that the narrative texts were primary to performance. Reversing the direction that performance studies had charted, my thinking shifted from events back to stories—the end result is this book. In analyzing the relations between narrative, ritual, and performance, it centers upon the texts themselves. This approach I hope will prove useful to others working with oral traditions in which narrative plays a central role.

The study of performance, almost from its inception, has shown a mild allergy to texts. In part, this was a historical necessity. When that eclectic blend of performance studies (combining K. Burke's dramatology, V. Turner's processual anthropology, and E. Goffman's microsociology) first coalesced in the 1970s, it wisely downplayed textual issues.[1] Themes, types, and motifs gave way to frames, markers, and reflexivity in an exploration of the new concept of performance. Even in the anthropological study of oral narrative, text receded into a metaphor—everything except oral performance was approached as a text. As Bauman summed up this intellectual shift (Bauman 1977, 4), there was a move toward "artistic *action*—the doing of folklore—and artistic *event*—the performance situation . . . [a shift] from folklore-as-materials to folklore-as-communication." Narratives in performance were process not products, events not texts.

With hindsight, we can now say that this turn away from texts was as artificial as it was necessary. The event-centered approach generated ideas that lifted the study of performance to new levels of sophistication, but no approach can afford to downplay the narrative force that propels performance.

We have reached a point from which an advance in the study of oral performance can only be made by first reclaiming its narrative base.

A new approach is especially desirable for the study of extended narratives in performance. Whereas the event-centered approach worked well for the shorter, conversational genres (riddle, proverb, and toast),[2] it virtually abandoned the longer narratives either to structuralism or to the theory of the oral formula, both of which have blunted the original thrust of performance studies and returned to a decontextualized text. With its origins in formalism and linguistics, structuralism studies grammar not speech (Lévi-Strauss 1955);[3] and although the *Singer of Tales* (Lord 1960) broke new ground in performance studies, its derivative research has also focused on formulas as grammatical structures.[4] Clearly the study of oral performance should not retreat into this kind of oral textual formalism, but neither can it proceed without harnessing the full force of narrative.

Text and performance have begun to merge in recent studies of the oral epic in Africa and India; the concept of "segmentation," how performance organizes textual units, is one example.[5] Also, text was never totally abandoned in studies that continue the "ethnography of speaking" school of sociolinguistics (see Seitel 1981; Sherzer 1983; Bauman 1986). From this scholarship we learn how the text is performed and how performance affects text; what is rarely addressed is the reverse process—how texts affect their telling.[6] This is the question a text-centered approach asks. This book attempts to demonstrate that approach by discussing how bow songs structure their own singing.

In the Tamil bow song tradition, the narrative world controls virtually every level of performance. The key contrast between birth stories and death stories (see below), for instance, determines the sequence of performances in a temple festival. Individual performances are themselves segmented by certain narrative events (including birth and death), and singing those events induces spirit possession and dancing. Even outside the immediate performance event, in the wider context of bow song cults, the influence of narrative is apparent. Gods and goddesses enshrined in local temples, for example, are the main characters of bow songs; when their story is sung, they step out from the narrative and are worshiped in the temple festival.

A text-centered approach to performance thus starts with the narrative outside its enactment. It consciously rejects the claim that the meaning of a text lies only in performance, that the text is inseparable from its telling. In the bow song tradition, palm-leaf manuscripts carry cultural value before and after, as well as during, performances. Also, the narrative content of a bow song marks it (by an internal tag line) as either a "birth story" (*piṟanta katai*) or a "death story" (*iṟantappaṭṭa katai*), which in turn determines when and how it will be sung in a festival. The point is simply that a bow song carries meaning as it moves into performance. The target of analysis is then to follow this movement and to discover what kind of relation arises between the text and its performance.

When bow songs enter performance, they become ritual acts, and in this process lies the key to understanding how these narratives structure their performance. First, there is a degree of reciprocity: narrative and ritual help shape each other. On the one hand, and as the event-centered approach predicts, the ritual setting of performance alters story content (see Chapter 7). On the other hand, as a text-centered approach reveals, the ritual function of a bow song performance itself is dependent on its narrative content. The performance summons a god (to visit the festival, receive worship, and enter a dancer's body) by singing his story. Bow songs in performance are invocations because they are narratives.

Bow songs, in other words, are ritual language. Studies of ritual language have historically focused on the short, nonnarrative genres (prayers, mantras, and so forth),[7] but a text-based approach shows that extended genres, like the bow songs that are sung for five or six hours, are also ritual precisely because they are narrative. By presenting the full translated text, instead of the usual repetitious lines of a chant or analytic paraphrase of a myth, I hope to demonstrate the importance of narrative to the study of ritual.

The ritual role of bow songs leads this book into an important issue in the anthropology of religion. The bow song tradition stands in a long line of cults of the dead (including mortuary rites, afterlife cosmology, and ancestor worship) studied since the nineteenth century and prominent in recent research as well (Reynolds and Waugh 1976, Huntington and Metcalf 1979, and Parry and Bloch 1982). What has never been adequately examined, however, are the stories associated with such cults of the dead. Again, a text-centered approach encourages us to look back to the narratives about the dead for an understanding of their cults. Following this cue, the concluding chapter of this book offers an explanation of the bow song cults; instead of the usual idea that such cults are based on a fear of death, I suggest that bow song performances are an attempt to contact the power of death.

As biographies of the deified dead, the death stories at the ritual center of the bow song tradition are also history. The stories that generate the greatest ritual intensity tell about royal intrigue in eighteenth-century Travancore (see Chapter 5); about a raja who brought the Nadar caste to Kanya Kumari; about Iravi Kuṭṭi Piḷḷai, who defended Travancore in the seventeenth century; and about other culture and caste heroes and heroines who died in struggles for social justice, and are now worshiped in small temples spread throughout the bow song region. Why do these stories elicit the greatest ritual response? As already mentioned, their performances name and summon the gods whose deaths have made them powerful. But the naming in death stories is broader: it reveals what happened and tells what is true. The death stories are the stories (to use Geertz's phrase [1973, 448] literally) that local people "tell themselves about themselves." Death stories thus transmit that collective identity known as history.

Social and political history may be gleaned from bow songs, but the act of performance reveals the local culture's self-images, too. Through the bow songs we see, for instance, that the two castes that dominate the tradition (Nadar and Piḷḷai) are set in opposition to each other. On the other hand, Brahmins and Untouchables, who do not participate in the tradition, are often conflated, as in the complex character of Muttuppaṭṭaṉ (see Chapter 6). Reflexivity in bow song performances also takes more unusual turns. The narrative is not only a metacommentary on society, but at times the border between story and society is erased and the audience becomes a character in the performance (see pp. 145ff.). Yet, even this reflexivity has a narrative base: it amounts to a skillful manipulation of the text, through which the singers gain leverage in their attempt to encourage further patronage.

Bow singers, however, do not control or compose their texts. A major finding of this book is that bow songs, even in performance, are largely fixed-phrase, often memorized. In fact, this Tamil tradition follows a method of composition not described in the literature. The two methods commonly described are simultaneous composition (oral formulaic) and prior composition. In the first, considered natural for long narratives such as epics, the singer creates the text as he performs it by fitting phrases into set metrical lines. Shorter genres, like Somali or Eskimo oral poetry, are generally composed by the second method, in which the singer creates his piece before performing it, memorizes it, and then sings it. Bow singers use a third method, which I call "prior preparation" (see Chapter 2); they prepare a story for performance by learning it, reading texts, repeating lines, rehearsing tunes, and fixing even a great deal of the spoken commentary. This bow song method is closer to prior composition than to simultaneous composition; the essential difference is that bow singers do not compose their songs, they only prepare them.

The most extreme example of textual fixity in the bow song tradition takes us back to the death stories sung as the ritual center of a festival. In certain temples, these performances are actually verbatim recitations from an official palm-leaf manuscript. The manuscript is held by one man and read line-by-line to the lead singer, who immediately turns each line into song. Such recitations are not conducted in every, or even most, temples, but they do remind us of a basic truth in the study of oral tradition: fixed, written texts are not necessarily inconsistent with oral performance. In the bow song tradition, they go literally hand-in-hand.

The textual basis of the bow song tradition also undermines the common assumption that in India the sacred is oral. Starting with the Vedas, the argument runs, religious literature was not written down because to do so would desacralize it; the illiterate priest has a higher ritual status than the scribe, and so forth. This may accurately describe ancient, Sanskrit culture, but not folk tradition. On the contrary,

> writing and the materials of writing, like palm leaves, have an almost magical, authoritative significance in oral societies (which corresponds to the mystique of the oral singer in print cultures). In India, traditional people worship books as deities. People in Andhra Pradesh pick up books or paper which they have accidentally hit with their feet and bring them close to their eyes to ask the goddess of learning (Sarasvatī) to forgive them for the sin of disrespecting her. (Narayana Rao 1986, 152)

When oral performance is a ritual act, its written text is a ritual object.

Nor is this ritual status of written texts a consequence of modern print media invading traditional India. In fact, the printed pamphlet has no ritual status in the bow song tradition. Only palm-leaf manuscripts, inscribed with an iron stylus (and sometimes handwritten, paper copies of them), are held as official temple texts, disseminated through certain channels, and therefore considered authentic and capable of summoning gods during a festival. Even when a printed pamphlet is a word-for-word reproduction of a manuscript (and some pamphlets are exact copies), it has no ritual efficacy because it is mass-produced and sold impersonally on the street. Ritual power, then, lies not simply in the fixity of the text, but also in the cultural control over the production and dissemination of the text.

These observations and interpretations are fleshed out in more detail over the chapters of this book, but even in their summary form I hope they signal the value of recovering lost narrative ground in the study of oral performance. Performance studies have tended to slight the role of texts, of fixity, and of memorization, especially in longer, narrative genres. This book has been written, in part, to tip the scales in the other direction and show that fixed, written, even memorized texts are well suited to play a central role (here a ritual role) in oral performance.

This is not to say that bow singers, or others like them, lack talent (to assume so would be to repeat the mistaken correlation between creativity and improvisation). The lead singers of the performances translated in this book, for instance, are extraordinary storytellers by any standards. They play the parts of many characters, often shifting voice and persona between three or four figures in a single scene; they synchronize their narration with the rituals conducted around them, and they are skilled comedians. Still, the stories they tell and the lines they sing are relatively fixed. This is the last lesson of the bow song tradition, and probably the most difficult to accept. The force of narrative, it suggests, is not the ability to transform the world, but to describe it. Some people think that power should not be left to chance.

The materials on which this book is based were collected during eighteen months of field research in Tamil Nadu, India (see Map 1).[8] What happened to launch that project has happened to others, but the story is true and deserves another retelling. When I first arrived in the research area in 1977, I knew next to nothing about bow songs (the "literature" totaled two bow song texts in Tamil and one article in English). My contacts in the universities were not encouraging either: few songs, they said, were sung today and no one knew where to find them. Fortunately, the independent folklorist Na. Vāṉamāmalai steered me to the town of Nagercoil, at the very southern tip of Tamil Nadu, and told me to contact Ratnam in the tailor shop across from the bus stand. I did, and within a few days the tailor shop had become a clearinghouse for information about bow singers, songs, festivals, and manuscripts. After a month I had learned enough to realize that the tradition was not only alive, but was the primary carrier of local culture.

By the close of my project, I had 175 hours of bow songs on casette tape. The total number of stories in the collection is sixty-one, with over one hundred versions. Only five stories, however, have versions that diverge sufficiently (by adding or omitting a key event) to form separate variants; these five, predictably, are the stories most widely performed in the tradition: Cuṭalai Māṭaṉ, Muttār Ammaṉ, Kāḷi Ammaṉ, Śāstā, and Muttuppaṭṭaṉ. Another four stories, collected in written texts, are no longer sung because the cult of their hero-god has disappeared (though cults are sometimes revived).

The great majority of the sixty-one stories were collected directly from their performance context, as they were sung in a festival. A few were collected only in written form: palm-leaf, handwritten pen-on-paper copy, or printed pamphlet; some were collected in both oral and written forms. As written texts, bow songs average about 3,000 to 5,000 lines; the longest I found is a palm-leaf manuscript of the *Rāmāyaṇa* (dated 1832) with 13,000 lines.

Let me briefly describe the organization of this book. Chapter 1 places us in the local setting of Nāñcil Nāṭu (see Map 2) where the bow song retains its ritual role. Emphasis is given to the geographical isolation of the region, which has contributed to a strong sense of regional identity, and to the social divisions that surface as themes in the narratives. Chapter 2 examines various aspects of the bow song as oral tradition—singers, their training, delivery styles, composition—and finds more fixity than improvisation. The narrative world, with the crucial contrast between birth and death stories, is introduced in Chapter 3, which then lays out the sequence of a festival and concludes with the correlation between narrative and ritual patterns.

The translations in Chapters 4, 5, and 6 take the reader through three performances in a standard bow song festival. Although the performances I have translated were originally sung in different festivals, their sequence in these chapters (from birth to death to birth story) replicates the sequence of a bow song festival. Each translation is preceded by a brief discussion of how the performance illustrates various aspects of the bow song tradition. The final chapter takes a step back from actual performance and analyzes two conclusions of the book as a whole: the ritual center on death and the ritual role of narrative.

Although they are integral to the argument in this book, the translations are also intended to be read as stories in their own right. Like any translator, my aim has been to bring the reader as close as possible to the original work, here singing on the bow. Some license has been taken—words and phrases have sometimes been added or omitted to achieve a smoother reading. In some instances, which are noted, a refrain that would have been burdensome in print has been left out entirely; otherwise, each phrase in the performance has been matched by one in translation. Also, song lines in translation do not always follow the line breaks (see the discussion of prosody in Chapter 2) in the original. In order to retain some of the pace and echo effect of the singing, however, key words are occasionally repeated. Finally, music and rhythm, not to mention the singers' gestures and laughter, have been lost.

Translating from oral performance has imperfections, but it has also one distinct advantage: by working directly with the vocal record (not from a written transcription), it is possible to maintain close contact with the singer's words and moods. For this reason, I believe, one is able to bring into English the meaning and intention of an oral performance more easily than that of a written work. In any case, the translations are my attempt to imitate the original voice of bow song performance.

Finally, a brief note on the format of the translations may be helpful. To indicate changes in delivery styles (see Chapter 2), I have used the following conventions: lines in formal speech begin at the left-hand margin; those in informal speech or in dialogue (indicated by quotation marks if spoken by a story character, or by a dash if spoken as the singer's own comment) begin at the first indentation; lines in song style are placed at the second indentation.

Many individuals and organizations have supported the work that lies behind this book, and I thank them all. Field work in India was funded by grants from the Social Science Research Council, the American Institute of Indian Studies, the Office of Education (Fulbright Program), and the Smithsonian Institution. Typing the manuscript in several revisions was made possible, in part, by monies from a faculty grant at Dartmouth College. From the very beginning of this project, George Hart, Alan Dundes, and A. K. Ramanujan have, in their very different ways, given me encouragement and advice. I owe special thanks to both Peter J. Claus and Margaret Mills whose perceptive comments guided revisions of the manuscript. Kausalya Hart also gave me invaluable help in clarifying difficult passages in my tape recordings.

Those persons who assisted me in India are too numerous to list, but I would like to mention two. Na. Vāṉamāmalai, the late Tamil folklorist and political activist, gave birth to this book by first directing me to the tailor shop in Nagercoil and later nourished it by critical comments on my findings; he was the kind of scholar and friend one does not forget. Ku. Āṟumukam Perumāḷ Nadar, a bow song bard now deceased, shared his extensive knowledge of the tradition and argued with my observations, giving much of himself to a project whose purpose he never fully understood.

1

Nāñcil Nāṭu: The Shape of Place

It is the best of lands,
a land where three rains fall.[1]

At the southernmost tip of the Indian subcontinent, a long bow (*vil*) is used to perform bow songs (*vil pāṭṭu*) in hundreds of temples every year from January to May. During these festival months, the bow is a conspicuous presence, protruding from the window of a crowded bus, carried down a village road by a singer, or standing upright against a temple wall. This Tamil bow is unique among the musical bows of India, and perhaps of the world, yet when it was first played or even whence it came is unknown. Some local people say the epic hero Rāma was the first to play the bow; others smile at this and say only that their bow is special because it is a weapon of war used to play music. Tamil scholars, pointing out references in ancient Tamil poetry (c. A.D. 100–300), have claimed an early history for the bow;[2] however, not until the sixteenth century do we have a certain reference, in a semicourtly poem that describes the bow exactly as it exists today—played in a festival to invoke local gods.[3] The tradition is very likely much older than the 1500s, but there is no other evidence.

The first descriptions of the bow appeared about three hundred years later, written (somewhat paradoxically) by the Protestant missionaries in southern Tamil Nadu who sought to destroy it.[4] Although evangelical zeal pushed many to learn something of the local "devil worship," few missionaries actually witnessed any bow song performances because, as one explained, "the devils are supposed to shrink before the presence and superior power of the European."[5] One missionary who did see performances was the Reverend Robert Caldwell, a famous scholar of Dravidian languages, who left this detailed portrait:

> The musical instruments, or rather the instruments of noise, chiefly used in the devil-dance are the tom-tom, or ordinary Indian drum, and the horn; with occasionally the addition of a clarionet, when the parties can afford it. But the favourite instrument, because the noisiest, is that which is called the "bow." A series of bells of various sizes is fastened to the frame of a gigantic bow; the strings are tightened so as to emit a musical note when struck, and the bow rests on a large empty brazen pot. One strikes the string of the bow with the plectrum, another produces the bass by striking the brazen pot with his hand, and the third keeps time and improves the harmony by a pair of cymbals. As each musician kindles in his work, and strives to outstrip his neighbour in the rapidity of his flourishes, and in the loudness of the tone with which he sings the accompaniment, the result is a tumult of frightful sounds, such as may be supposed to delight even a demon's ear. (Caldwell 1849, 19–20)

Caldwell's description is valuable because it enables us to state that the elements of a bow song performance have changed very little over the past 150 years. From his and other reports we know also that the geographical spread of the bow song has remained stable.[6] The bow was and still is played only in the Kanya Kumari and Tinnevelly districts of Tamil Nadu, and some contiguous areas in Kerala.[7] In Kanya Kumari district, in particular, the missionaries were zealous. Having burned or otherwise destroyed several bow song temples around Nagercoil, they claimed to have eliminated the tradition. Fortunately, that claim proved premature.

In fact, in a portion of Kanya Kumari district called Nāñcil Nāṭu, the bow song is stronger, more traditional, and more ritualistic than elsewhere. The remainder of this chapter will present an overview of this local setting, highlighting features that have shaped the broad contours of the bow song tradition there.

Nāñcil Nāṭu is one of the oldest geo-cultural regions in South India. Its approximately 350 square miles fan out from the "land's end," the sacred bathing site of Kanya Kumari known to early Greek and North Indian sources. When it was first settled is unknown, but even the ancient Tamil sangam poems (c. A.D. 100–300) contain references to a chieftain from the region.[8]

Circumscribed by natural boundaries on nearly all sides, Nāñcil Nāṭu is a well-defined geographical region (*nāṭu*). To the north are the Western Ghat mountains, which climb to 5,500 feet; along both flanks is the ocean, the Bay of Bengal on the east and the Arabian Sea on the west. Travel in and out of the region is along these coasts—east to the Tamil country, or west to the Malayali country—but movement in either direction has not been easy. The westward passage is along a narrow, hilly tract only seven miles wide and across several rivers. Until 1900 transportation along this strip was slow, and Trivandrum, the administrative capital farther west, was not connected by rail to the rest of India (lest the temple town be polluted) until 1918.[9] Movement to the Tamil east was even more restricted because it was funnelled through two narrow gaps in a hilly wall that extends from the mountains to the sea. Even these gaps were sealed off by military fortifications from about 1600 to 1800, when the British tore them down.[10] A rail link to the Tamil east, furthermore, was not completed until 1984. Isolated and defined by these natural boundaries since ancient times, Nāñcil Nāṭu has shaped its own distinct local culture, including a highly ritualized bow song tradition.

The geographic position of the region, specifically its location between Malayali and Tamil country, has also had an impact on local culture and history. The region's strategic value is evident even in myth; both Tamils and Malayalis claim the tip of Kanya Kumari as the origin of their respective coastlines. In the Malayali myth, Paraśurāma (an avatār of Viṣṇu) threw his axe to reclaim the land from the sea, and it stuck in the soil at Kanya Kumari; in the Tamil myth, the world was submerged by three oceanic floods until the waters receded and left Kanya Kumari as the coastline.[11] Indeed, Nāñcil Nāṭu is extremely fertile (*nāñcil* means "wetlands"). A high water table, an active monsoon, and three rivers provide two good rice crops per year, sometimes three; coconut, areca nut, banana, and the less profitable but immensely useful palmyra tree are also abundant.

Continuous struggle to control these rich agricultural resources marks the history of Nāñcil Nāṭu up to modern times. A very brief overview would be that the Malayali kings of Vēnad (ancient Travancore) held the dominant position and that the Tamil kings of the Pāṇṭiyaṉ and Cōḻa dynasties invaded and established suzerainty. It was Tamil patronage that built the great temple centers of Cucīntiram and Kanya Kumari (which supported Tamil Brahmins, artisans, temple servants, and peasants who came to work the temple trust lands), and amid all the warring these temples remained Tamil centers.

By A.D. 1600, when the Travancore capital was moved inside Nāñcil Nāṭu to Patmanāpapuram, the region had come under the direct rule of the Malayali kingdom. Over the next two hundred years Travancore expanded to become a dominant power in South India and defended Nāñcil Nāṭu's rice bowl against Tamil, Muslim, Portuguese, Dutch, English, and even fellow Malayali invaders.

Although Portuguese influence was confined to the coast, entire fishing villages did convert to Christianity. The tall spires of ornate, stone churches that dot the coast, the Christian (or Hindu) fishermen with names like Rodrigo Fernandez, and the Portuguese loan words in Tamil and Malayalam are reminders of this initial contact with Europe. By the mid-seventeenth century the Dutch had driven out the Portuguese, but like them could not penetrate the interior of Travancore. Their naval invasion near Kanya Kumari turned into a siege resulting in an eventual surrender by the Europeans, an event much celebrated by local historians. Meanwhile, the English had quietly been pursuing a different policy, exchanging their military protection for Travancore's permission to build factories on the west coast near Trivandrum. This special relationship continued after the British took control of most of South India around 1800 when Travancore was made a Princely State and allowed to retain much of its palace bureaucracy and court culture. Nāñcil Nāṭu remained part of Travancore State until 1956 (nearly a decade after Indian independence) when it was ceded to Madras State (later Tamil Nadu) and became part of Kanya Kumari district.

Despite the fact that the influence of Tamil kingdoms on Nāñcil Nāṭu (especially since the watershed mark of A.D. 1600) had been reduced to plunder raids, local village society became increasingly Tamil. Spreading out from the large temple centers and migrating in from Madurai and Tinnevelley, Tamils soon owned most of the fertile land; economic and military power, however, was ultimately in the hands of the Malayali rajas at the Patmanāpapuram court who extracted heavy taxes from their Tamil subjects. Thus, for at least the past four hundred years, Nāñcil Nāṭu has been a two-tiered society—a Tamil village culture beneath a Malayali court culture. Census figures for 1900 clearly show the disparity: Malayalis comprised only five percent of the local population, but fully thirty-three percent of its literates.[12]

Nor, despite four hundred years of interaction, have the languages of Tamil and Malayalam moved toward a merger. Instead, they have stood apart as markers of different and unequal status. Tamil was spoken in villages (and used for temple inscriptions), but Malayalam was the official, administrative language whose obvious Sanskritic influence gave it a cultured quality.[13] Except for some bilinguals in towns, the great majority of Tamils did not read, write, or speak Malayalam, and no hybrid form of the languages ever evolved. Tamils and Malayalis in Nāñcil Nāṭu shared few kin or religious networks; their temple architecture, house architecture, and village settlement plans were all visibly different.

Perhaps the most divisive element between Tamil and Malayali cultures has been their different systems of inheritance. Most local Tamil castes follow the *makkatāyam* system in which descent is patrilineal and assets devolve to the deceased's wife and sons; most Malayalis, on the other hand, follow the *marumakkatāyam* system in which the property of the deceased goes primarily to his sisters and their children. Thus Tamil women rarely married Malayalis because as wives they would receive little or no property if widowed, and as sisters (unlike Malayali women) they would receive no inheritance from their natal families.[14]

Not surprisingly, this social tension has pressed its stamp on the bow song tradition. (It may not be coincidental that the bow song tradition can only be dated from about A.D. 1600, the point from which Nāñcil Nāṭu was dominated by Malayali court culture.) The story of Tōṭṭukkāri Amman̲, a goddess worshiped in several small temples in and around the town of Kanya Kumari, is a case in point. She is born a princess in a minor Tamil court on the seacoast; visible only a few miles down the shore is a Malayali fort in which a young prince is born. After he sees her bathing, the prince asks to marry her, but the girl's father refuses because marriage into the Malayali court would deprive her future children of inheritance and status. A war ensues and the Tamil fort is destroyed, but the princess is unharmed. Later, however, she climbs a hill to escape capture and jumps into a deep pool, killing herself. Śiva then intervenes, takes her to Kailāsa (his mountain heaven), names her Tōṭṭukkāri Amman̲, and sends her back to earth to receive worship.

The abstract quality of this story reflects the peculiar relation between Tamils and Malayalis in Nāñcil Nāṭu; the spatial and cultural distance between them gives their conflict a symbolic nature. A sharper, more volatile tension existed between two Tamil castes who were in constant contact and whose stories, therefore, are told in graphic detail. They are the Piḷḷais, tax collectors for the Travancore maharajas, and the Nadars, the dominant peasant group; significantly, these castes are the backbone of the bow song tradition in Nāñcil Nāṭu today.

The Piḷḷais (also called Veḷḷāḷa) owned most of the land although they comprised only five percent of the local population.[15] They also controlled the local governing council (*nāṭṭār*) and served as the raja's liaison in official interactions with Tamil peasants. Certain sections of the Piḷḷai community actually served at the Travancore court, and some held high posts. Many assimilated Malayali culture—adopting the dress and hair style, language, and eventually the matrilineal inheritance of the court—leading to a schism between them and the Tamil-speaking, patrilineal Piḷḷai families who had a slightly inferior status.[16] As a whole, the Piḷḷai caste held a high ritual status, second only to that of Brahmins; other castes (the Malayali Nāyar and the Tamil Taṭṭaṉ [goldsmiths]) had a roughly equal status, but the more numerous Piḷḷai were conspicuously at the center of local society, particularly as patrons of religious activities at the large and wealthy temples (which do not sponsor bow song performances).

Nadars, on the other hand, are a thoroughly Tamil caste. Much the largest caste in Nāñcil Nāṭu (more than half the population, by recent figures),[17] they have been squeezed into a narrow strip of arid land between the sea and the fertile rice fields owned by Piḷḷais. Their traditional occupation (and one source of their low status) was climbing the tall palmyra, which abound in the sandy tracts around their villages, to extract its juice and prepare toddy, coarse sugar, and other products. Few Nadars owned these trees; they held them on rent, just as they leased garden and rice plots from other castes. Many Nadars worked along with the Untouchable castes (Cāmpavar, Cerumāṉ, and Paṟaiyar) as agricultural laborers on the Piḷḷais' rice fields. Until recently, Nadars were treated little better than Untouchables: Nadar men and women were forbidden to wear anything beneath the knee or above the waist while in the presence of a high-caste man; they were not allowed to wear sandals, a head covering, long hair, or gold ornaments; they could not use high-status names like Perumāḷ, Mārttāṇṭa, or Nākamaṇi (names of Viṣṇu); and they were barred from riding a horse, building a house above one story, or passing within eighteen paces of a Brahmin.[18]

Such tremendous tension between Nadars and Piḷḷais has left its mark, a deep and violent mark, on the bow song tradition. A vivid illustration is the story of Nāṭāṉ Cāmi, a young Nadar man. One day he discovers a burning funeral pyre on which lies a Brahmin woman who had been bitten by a snake and then left to burn by her relatives. He quickly realizes by a supernatural power that she is not dead, cools the flames, extracts the venom, and brings her back to life. Awaking as from a dream, the Brahmin woman claims him as her husband, but he is shocked and refuses since no one would accept a marriage between a Brahmin and a Nadar. The woman insists, they do marry, and their families accept their bond as a fait accompli, but the Piḷḷais in the woman's village are outraged. Eventually they convince her family and the other Brahmin families to send a petition to the Travancore maharaja asking for permission to kill the presumptuous Nadar. Although the maharaja decides to pardon the Nadar, the Piḷḷais, who have meanwhile tied him to a stake, willfully misinterpret the message and hack Nāṭāṉ Cāmi to death.

History also records the violent confrontation between Nadars and Piḷḷais, as groups, in the famous "breast cloth controversy" of the nineteenth century. Protestant missionary work in Nāñcil Nāṭu had extraordinary success and by 1870 could boast of 30,000 converts; most of these new Christians came from the three Untouchable castes and from the Nadars. For women, conversion meant they were expected to wear a cloth to cover their breasts, a privilege traditionally held only by higher caste women. With the church's sense of decency fueling the social aspirations of an exploited caste, the breast cloth became a symbol of equality and by mid-century Nadar women, both Hindu and Christian, took to wearing it in increasing numbers. Orthodox factions of Piḷḷais and other castes responded with protests, then litigation, and the matter landed on the desk of the British Governor in Madras. In the end, a compromise was reached that allowed Nadar Christians to wear an upper cloth different from that worn by higher caste women, but not before tensions burst into a wave of violent attack and counter-attack that destroyed several Christian Nadar settlements.[19]

All women in Nāñcil Nāṭu now wear an upper cloth (or its equivalent), but the struggle to gain that privilege is remembered in oral tradition. One local legend (not a bow song) describes the humiliation suffered by a Nadar woman when she went to pay her taxes to Piḷḷai officials who forced her to remove the cloth and put iron clamps on her nipples. And even if the specific issue of the breast cloth has disappeared, the conditions that led up to the controversy have not. Personal indignities to Nadars are less public and violent than before, and the caste has raised its status through business and education (Hardgrave 1969a), but most Nadars are still crowded in the sandy land near the sea and most still work fields and climb trees they do not own.

Modern Nāñcil Nāṭu is likewise changed yet fundamentally the same. Since incorporation into Madras State in 1956, it has become a clearly Tamil region. Its new capital, the growing urban center of Nagercoil, supports a provincial, educated elite in universities and government offices that has replaced the court culture of the maharajas. There is some intellectual life: a new Ramakrishna Mission institute, a small circle of writers and artists, and the major city of Trivandrum is now only two hours away by bus. The land remains fertile, and the city of Nagercoil has attracted more commercial prosperity. Yet, local society is still insular and traditional.

In particular, the region's self-image as the distinct, traditional land of

Nāñcil Nāṭu remains strong. Local people refer to the region only by that term, and not by the modern name Kanya Kumari district; in local speech, "Kanya Kumari" refers only to the famous temple site. Partly from habit, partly from a backlash against modernization, and partly for the commercial value of local color, one frequently sees signs advertising "Nāñcil Press," or "Nāñcil Tailors," and so forth. In recent years, a local man stood for election to the State Legislative Assembly in Madras by styling himself "Nāñcil Vaḷḷuvaṉ," after the chieftain who ruled the region some sixteen centuries ago; he was elected.

The clearest indicator of continuity in Nāñcil Nāṭu, however, is the vital presence of the bow song tradition itself. Today, as in the time of the missionaries' reports, the heart of the tradition is the Nadar caste, whose enclaves (clusters of villages, each eight to ten thousand strong and often ninety percent or ninety-five percent Nadars) mirror the insularity and traditionalism of the region as a whole. Most of the singers in Nāñcil Nāṭu are Nadars, and most of the temples where they sing are controlled by Nadars. Other low or middle level castes do produce singers and patronize festivals, but not with the same consistency or in the same large numbers as the Nadars.[20] The only relatively high caste to support the bow song tradition is the Piḷḷai, but only those families still tied to the village agrarian system; many urban Piḷḷais have severed links with the folk tradition to avoid loss of prestige; Brahmins and other high castes never had any links to sever. Castes lower than the Nadars, the Untouchables and a few others, participate in the tradition only marginally for lack of money.[21] Since a caste will not invite a singer of a lower caste to sing at its temple, groups at the very bottom of the hierarchy have no other patronage than their own.[22]

Perhaps the bow song once had a wider appeal and was supported by those groups (like the Piḷḷai) who have left it for "higher ground." The evidence, however, is to the contrary. The bow song tradition seems always to have occupied a place just below the middle level of local society—that large space between the high castes who shun it and the poorest castes who are financially unable to maintain a folk tradition of such complexity.[23] And if the tradition once lost ground to the missionaries' concerted efforts to eradicate it (propaganda and conversion did take their toll), it now loses the same ground to other groups who wish to leave behind any trace of the old-fashioned, unsophisticated, and sometimes vulgar aspects of village life that the "devil-worship" and animal sacrifices of the bow song tradition must represent. From this particular position, between the lowest and middle levels of society, bow songs present themes of conflict (Malayali versus Tamil; Piḷḷai versus Nadar) from the vantage point of the disadvantaged.

The ground that the tradition has indeed lost in recent years are the temples that used to sponsor bow song festivals (*koṭai*) and now support festivals of another kind (*viḻā, utcava*).[24] The latter are dedicated not to local, but to more pan-Indian gods; they feature not singing on the bow, but more widely known Tamil entertainments—pot dancing (*karakam*), standard temple music (*mēḷam*), "modern" drama, and South Indian classical singing and music. Even the performances in bow song festivals have changed with changing times: some groups have added the harmonium (*śrūti* box) to the ensemble, and many lead singers are now women. But such losses and changes are negligible compared with the healthy condition of the bow song tradition in Nāñcil Nāṭu today; nearly every village contains at least one temple that holds an annual festival, and most villages contain several such temples. Even more significant, bow song performances in these temples retain a firm ritual grip on the festival.

A description of these performances must await a later chapter. For the present, we have seen only how the broad contours of the tradition in Nāñcil Nāṭu are shaped by this special setting. Local history, itself conditioned by the geographical position of Nāñcil Nāṭu, has left a thematic impress on the bow songs. A deeper layer of influence is the relative isolation combined with a historic sense of place that have given the local bow song tradition the strength of self-identity. The local folk tradition is also shaped by other, more internal factors and they are the subject of the next chapter.

2

The Bow Song as Oral Tradition

> I will never forget my *aṇṇāvi,*
> who put the *vīcukōl* in my
> hands.

Oral tradition has been accused of many things: preserving culture, corrupting literature, legitimizing political power, structuring consciousness, and more. Obviously it holds the same fascination for print cultures as written texts do for oral cultures. However, real advances in the study of oral tradition have been made only when the monolith is broken down into its primary processes: composition, transmission, and performance. Once delineated, each of these processes may be examined in greater detail and in terms of specific questions. Is the medium of transmission written or oral? Is composition improvisational? Are texts fixed?

Pursuing these questions with respect to the bow song tradition, this chapter offers answers to most of them. While none of the answers is absolute in itself, in aggregate they do point to a generalization—realms of improvisation exist in the bow song, but fixity plays the greater role. The bow song is not a collection of individual performers; it is a tradition whose fundamental concern for accurately reproducing texts sets the bounds within which patterns of narrative and ritual unfold.

The emphasis in this chapter is on composition and transmission. Performance is touched upon, especially as the discussion opens with the structure of the performing group and the performers' training and social status; but the performance event, in which all these other aspects cohere, is deferred until the chapter that follows.

The Performing Group

One of the basic structures of the bow song tradition is its performing group. Minimally, the group has five persons, each of whom both sings and plays an instrument; on occasion, one or two others are added (Fig. 1). This group is divided into two subgroups: the lead singers (called *valampāṭi* or "right-hand singers") include the lead singer, the cymbals player, and the *aṇṇāvi* (guru) when present; the choral singers (*iṭampāṭi* or "left-hand singers") include the pot player, the drummer, and the wooden blocks player. This division structures the antiphonal singing of the bow song and its speech styles as well. Before discussing these, however, let us look first at the bow song instruments, their performers, and the performers' training.

The Tamil bow (*vil*) is unique among musical bows for its extreme length (ten, sometimes fourteen, feet) and its presence in a group of several instruments.[1] Made from hard palmyra wood (infrequently from bamboo), and preferably from the female tree, it is shaped like a hunting bow. For performance, the bow is wrapped with colorful paper or cloth (often silk) and fitted with brass or bronze animal figures on each end; several, usually nine, variously pitched cow bells hang from the frame. The bow is held in place, ends pointing up, by lashing its center to the mouth of the pot instrument (Plate 8); one end is held under the arm of the pot player, the other by a string tied to it and then looped around the lead singer's big toe. The bow is played by striking its cowhide string with a pair of slim wooden sticks (*vīcukōl*); in the center of each stick are affixed two small concave discs turned face-to-face to create a cavity that holds a number of tiny metal balls. When the sticks strike the string, these balls jingle and the bells, hanging from the frame, ring. The sticks are usually handled by the lead singer, but sometimes by the aṇṇāvi to allow the lead singer greater freedom to animate his or her presentation with gestures. Although the bow gives the tradition its name and spatially orients a performance, it is musically insignificant, adding only decorative flourishes to the other instruments.

The leader of the choral singers is usually the pot player, who also keeps the main rhythms of performance and provides the response to the lead singer. The pot (*kuṭam*) is made of clay reinforced with iron filings and extra thickness at the mouth to withstand the beating it receives from a paddle made from the sheath of the areca nut tree and toughened by leather strips sewn into it. By covering more or less of the pot's mouth when he slaps down

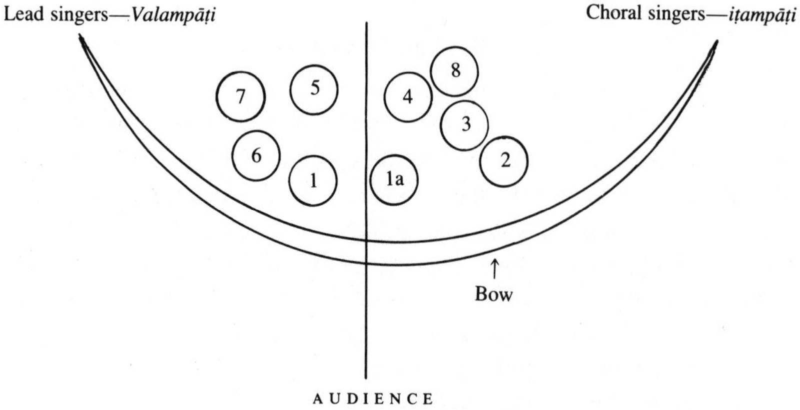

Key:

basic group

1. lead singer (playing bow)
2. pot player
3. drummer
4. wooden blocks player
5. cymbals player

optional performers

1a. woman (when lead is woman) with blocks
6. *aṇṇāvi* (playing bow or blocks)
7–8. extra blocks or cymbals players

Figure 1. Bow Song Performing Group

the paddle, the player can produce either a deep resonating or a high flat sound; he also creates a counter-rhythm with a small wooden spool that he clicks against the side of the pot.

The rhythms controlled by the pot are supported by both the wooden blocks (*kaṭṭai*) and the cymbals (*jālra*). The blocks are small (1/2″ × 3″ × 5″) and are made from the Indian redwood tree; the cymbals are also small (about 3″ in diameter) and are made of bronze or brass. The primary rhythms or *tāla* of the bow song are cycles of three or four beats; cycles of five or seven are used, but less commonly.

Variations and sometimes cross-rhythms are played on the drum (*uṭukkai* or *tuṭi*), a small version of the hourglass-shaped drum played all over India.[2] At the ends of the drum's brass body are cowhide heads held on by a network of leather thongs; a cloth band is wound around these thongs and held in the drummer's left hand. Tension on the heads is thus controlled by tightening or loosening the grip on the cloth band. By varying the tension, the fingers that hit the head, and the places where they strike, several tones are possible. The drum also can produce beats at an extremely fast pace. In recognition of this virtuosity, each performance traditionally begins with a solo by the drummer, who is the performer (after the lead singer) most critically evaluated by audiences.

The music of the drum is also important ritually. Not only in the bow song tradition, but throughout India and elsewhere in the world, it is used by specialists to contact dangerous powers.[3] It produces an eerie and ominous sound, and a special rhythmic effect (*tuṭukku*, "urging on") at the highly charged points of performance that bring spirit possession.[4] No wonder local people call it the "demon drum" (*pēy paṟai*).

As a public performance tradition, the bow song is dominated by men; only the lead singer may be female. Although today nearly half the leads are women, I was told that this was a development of the last two decades. Almost without exception, the women singers are young, aged sixteen to about twenty-five, because after marriage most will not be permitted to sing; even when a woman is the lead, she is chaperoned by another woman who sits to her left and plays a minor instrument. Some of the women singers (including the singer of the performance translated in Chapter 4) are the most talented in the tradition, but as public performers they are the objects of cheap fascination by some men in the audience.

The other performers are always men, aged about twenty to fifty. When a male lead singer loses his voice or is no longer physically able to sing throughout the night, he often retires to become the group's aṇṇāvi, and lets a younger man or woman take his place. Most of the performers are only minimally literate, although the lead singers and aṇṇāvi are often self-educated in the Tamil versions of the *Rāmāyaṇa, Mahābhārata,* and the *purāṇas*. The bow singers are only semiprofessionals who depend on income earned outside their singing. Some work as agricultural laborers; a few own small plots of land (or hold it on rent) with an areca nut or coconut grove, or even a small paddy field; others are small traders. Thus, even the singers from castes higher in status than the Nadar (the Piḷḷai, for example) are at the lower end of the economic ladder.

Still, the money earned from singing is not insignificant. Between January and May, an average group performs perhaps fifteen times in Nāñcil Nāṭu, and then a few more times in neighboring Tinnevelly where the season extends into August. During 1977 through 1979, a reasonably good group received approximately three hundred rupees for a standard three-day festival, and this is augmented by individual donations made during the actual performances; meals and lodging are also provided for the singers.[5] After subtracting their travel expenses, the group divides its income by a share system in which the lead (sometimes the aṇṇāvi) gets two shares—one and a half for singing, one-half for owning the bow and bells—and the others get one share each. In a five-person group (with six shares), the lead singer can earn about one hundred rupees per festival; multiplied by fifteen or more times a year, this becomes a vital source of ready cash.[6]

There is, then, a certain financial incentive to become a bow singer; indeed, almost anyone (except women as noted above) can learn to play the instruments and sing in the chorus because the skills are not highly specialized. Only the lead singer receives any formal training, and even that is not essential. Asked why they began to sing, most lead singers gave an answer like: "I heard the songs, liked them, and wanted to sing them myself." This passive, aural contact with the tradition is the key not only to the bow singer's initial interest, but to the entire development of a bow singer. Since most temples in a village present fifteen to twenty hours of song at their annual festival, a young boy or girl (with a little interest) could easily hear a hundred or more hours of singing in a year, and over a five- or ten-year period could gain a passive knowledge of bow songs. Later on the potential singer might study texts and music more consciously, but in this initial stage of exposure will internalize the basic patterns of performance, including the patterns of interaction between performers.

Stories and singing are learned during the second stage of a bow singer's development, but here too, the emphasis is on transmission by imitation. More than half the lead singers I met said they had received some regular instruction from an older, more accomplished singer, who often became their aṇṇāvi. Learners study with the senior singer from two to six months, visiting his home once or twice a week for several hours. The apprenticeship begins by learning a praise-song to Gaṇeśa, the remover of obstacles, and then centers on the Śāstā story (see Chapter 4), which is learned by echoing the aṇṇāvi line-for-line. The aṇṇāvi may also dictate his text for the student to write down, or he may lend his own handwritten copy, which is more valuable since it contains performance cues. Singing lessons are infrequent, and certainly less important than the transmission of texts. When the student can sing the whole Śāstā story without the aṇṇāvi's help, the training is complete. This transfer of tradition is then formally marked by a small rite in which the aṇṇāvi places the wooden sticks (vīcukōl) in the student's hands. The transfer is also remembered in the introductory sections to many performances, when the lead sings: "I will never forget my aṇṇāvi who put the vīcukōl in my hands."

Formal instruction from an aṇṇāvi, however, is not a necessary rite of passage for a bow singer, and many claimed they had received no coaching at all. Still, most of these singers had learned through an informal attachment to an older singer. After carefully studying a senior singer in performance after performance, the learner might be accepted and then guided by advice but not actual lessons; in time, the young singer might join the older singer's group to play the wooden blocks or hand cymbals. Other singers had apparently learned to sing without even this informal attachment, preferring to study many different singers in performance. No matter what the form of training, whether channelled through a particular aṇṇāvi or not, the singers learned chiefly by observation and imitation.

Some kind of a relationship with an aṇṇāvi, however, is advantageous and therefore more common. Having become attached to an active and accomplished singer, the initiate gains immediate access to a network of patrons after the senior singer dies. Apprenticeship also provides access to the aṇṇāvi's story repertoire, which the senior singer shares with the understudy as long as their bond continues.

The third stage in a singer's development commences with the first-time performance, a debut often arranged by the aṇṇāvi who allows the young performer to sing one song (usually the Śāstā story) with his group. From this point onward, and throughout his or her career, the singer perfects skills through their active use in performance and continues to study the teacher and others in performance to pick up new techniques, jokes, or even to add episodes to a known story. The singer also continues to acquire new texts (in handwritten copies), to study, and then to perform them by application of the basic skills he or she now controls.

This developmental process for a bow singer is similar to that described for oral bards in another region of Tamil Nadu (Beck 1982, 83–85); both these schema, in turn, recall that described for the Yugoslav *guslar* by Lord (1960, 21–26). Particularly striking similarities are the role of observation and imitation in the second stage, and the transition to the third stage as marked by the ability to sing one song completely through. Singers in all three traditions appear to learn primarily by direct observation, supplemented by active practice.[7] However, in contrast to the stress on individual creativity in the other traditions, a bow singer's training is fundamentally a process of exposure, absorption, and imitation of patterns presented by a senior singer. Handing over the vīcukōl signifies not so much the mastery of special skills as the successful transmission of the bow singer's role.

Delivery Styles

Much of the singer's role concerns the use of delivery styles; four styles are used but the two basic styles are *pāṭṭu* and *vacaṉam*. *Pāṭṭu* accurately translates as "song"; it is formed from the root "to sing" and carries most of the connotations of the English word. *Vacaṉam,* however, is more elusive; it is "speech" in the sense of a formal declaration, but also includes "talk" or "speaking." This combination of speech and song styles, common to many oral traditions, is usually described as "verse" and "prose," but this is misleading for oral performance. Verse and prose are defined by textual features of language, whereas "song" and "speech" in the bow song are distinguished by features of articulation. Song and speech are delivery styles, not literary styles.

Delivery styles are partially determined by the structure of the performing group described above and by certain ritual constraints to be discussed in the next chapter. However, and as a balance to the fixity in this tradition, they also allow for the display of individual talent. This relation between structure and talent is illustrated well in the song style. Essentially it is an antiphonal alternation of lead and choral singers. As is true for most antiphonal traditions, the lead dominates and the chorus only repeats. Nevertheless, the common pattern in which the lead sings a full line and the chorus repeats is rare in bow singing. Instead, the standard pattern is for the lead to repeat his own line or some portion of it, to play with it, echoing it back and forth before moving on to the next line; the echo effect may also be created by the aṇṇāvi selecting some portion of the line for repetition. Both of these methods are used in the following performance excerpt of a lead (L), aṇṇāvi (A), and chorus (C); note that the chorus only repeats the entire three-line segment at the end.[8]

L: The creeping *paṭalai,* the budding *mutalai,*
 tiṭulai flower, tiny *tuvarai* seed,
 grain and young fruits . . .

A: grain and young fruits . . .

L: The creeping *paṭalai,* the budding . . .

A: *mutalai* flower . . .

L: The creeping *paṭalai,* the budding *mutalai,*
 creeping *paṭalai,* budding *mutalai,*
 creeping *paṭalai,* budding *mutalai,*
 creeping *paṭalai,* budding *mutalai* . . . .

A: The *tiṭulai* flower, tiny *tuvarai* seed,
 grain and young flowers,
 grain and young flowers.

L: Milk, water, sugar,
 young mango and tender coconut.
 Milk, water, sugar,
 young mango and tender coconut,
 and areca nut flowers—
 Murukaṉ, I offer all these to you.

C: The creeping *paṭalai,* the budding *mutalai,*
 tiṭulai flower, tiny *tuvarai* seed,
 grain and young fruits,
 Milk, water, sugar,
 young mango and tender coconut,
 and areca nut flowers—
 Murukaṉ, I offer all these to you.

Although the song style is defined by these vocal patterns, it differs from the speech styles in certain features of language as well. In most songs, the local dialect is dropped in favor of standard educated Tamil; to this are added some poetic features, primarily rhyme. Bow songs follow traditional Tamil poetry in their use of initial rhyme, rather than end rhyme (which is very rare in any traditional Indian literature). The simplest compositions use an alliterative scheme known as *mōn̲ai* in which the initial sounds (= Tamil letters) of two halves of a line (or two successive full lines) are similar, though not necessarily identical. More complex songs use another rhyme, called *etukai,* in which the second sounds of successive lines are similar. A combination of mōn̲ai linking half-lines and etukai joining full lines is characteristic of the most sophisticated bow songs.[9] Each of these rhyme patterns and then their combination is illustrated in the examples below (one slash [/] indicates a half-line, two slashes [//] a full line). Note that the rhyming sounds are set off in boldface type.

Example A
Half-Line Rhyme (mōn̲ai)

(Describing how the Tampimār brothers in the "Death of the Tampimār" [Chap. 5] raised their sister.)

1. (To her) born after the younger brother/
   sister Koccumaṇi//
2. Sister Koccumaṇi/
   they gave the blessed name//
3. The rajas named her/
   and raised her proudly//
4. The brothers raised their sister/
   the sister with the shining forehead//

1. **Ku**ñcu tampikku pin̲ pir̲anta/
   Koccumaṇi taṅkai yen̲r̲u//
2. **Ko**ccumaṇi taṅkai yen̲r̲u/
   kūr̲uvārām tirunāmapēr//
3. **Pē**riṭṭu man̲n̲avārum/
   perumaiyuṭan̲ vaḷa(r)ttārē//
4. **Va**ḷa(r)ttārē tampimārum/
   vāṇutalāḷ taṅkaiyārum//

Example B

Full-Line Rhyme (etukai)

(Spoken by Viṣṇu to Śiva.)

1. Oh, brother-in-law, you may have years/
   but you've no brains.//
2. No matter how many go/
   aren't I alone enough?//
3. Don't you know my skill/
   which destroyed Tāṭakai?//
4. And that golden deer/
   did I let it escape alive?//
5. Didn't I destroy Śūrpaṇakā/
   who came to enjoy me?//
6. Didn't I kill twenty-armed Rāvaṇa/
   with only my two arms?//

1. Mai**tt**unārē uṉtamukku/
   vayaitiruntum putti illai//
2. E**tt**aṉaipēr pōṉālum/
   yāṉoruttaṉ pōrātō?//
3. Tā**ṭ**akaiyai kōppaḻittu/
   camarttaṟiya māttīrō?//
4. O**ṭ**ivanta poṉmāṉai/
   uyiroṭē viṭṭēṉō?//
5. Pa**r**akuvanta Cūrpaṇakai/
   paṇpukēṭṭum pōkillaiyō?//
6. I**r**upatukai Rāvaṇaṉai/
   irantukaiyāl koṉṟēṉō!//

Example C

Combination of Half- and Full-Line Rhyme (mōṉai and etukai)

(Spoken by a woman to a raja who has defeated her father in war.)

1. Although it's your land/
   although your law rules//
2. Of the noble Nadars' justice/
   you are ignorant!//

3. Coming here to rape me/
how honorable you are!//
4. You are nothing to me/
may you and your family be ruined!//

1. **Uṉ** cīmai āṉālum/
uṉatu caṭṭam naṭantālum//
2. **Vāṉ**cāṉṟōr nītikaḷum/
vakaiviparam nī aṟivāy//
3. **Kaṟ**pataṉai kulaikkaveṉṟu/
kaṉamāyai ceytāyō//
4. **Aṟ**pamallō nī eṉakku/
aḻintiṭuvāy kuṭimuṭivāy!//

Less regular patterns of repeated sounds, a scattering of assonance and consonance, also contribute to the overall poetic density of the song style. For example, in Example A the sound "p" recurs several times in the first line; "a" is repeated in line 4; and the sound "o" echoes throughout Example B. Other instances could be cited, but more important is the way these rhyme schemes determine the choice of vocal patterns. The half-line link in Example A, for instance, means that each line is best sung as an individual unit, with a choral repetition between lines. This allows each line to resonate within itself, since the alliteration (both regular and irregular) is contained within and not across lines. The same vocal pattern, however, would not work in Example B since the rhyme between full lines would not carry over a choral repetition between them. Instead, these lines are sung as a continuous string or run so that similar sounds at the front of the lines and the repeated "o" at the end can take effect. The lines in Example C were sung in a run pattern, with the half-line rhyme adding a resonating undercurrent.

A different kind of repetition, used for a different effect, is the *antāti* ("end-beginning"), a repetition of the last part of a line at the beginning of the next one. In some Indian poetry only the final syllable or word is carried over to the next line, but in the bow song tradition most of the half-line is normally repeated, as in Example A.[10] In that example the antāti creates a repetition that the full-line rhyme (etukai) cannot since the choral repetition between the lines places the potentially rhyming sounds too far apart in time. The antāti, in other words, does not repeat sounds as much as story content. It is a narrative bridge, but not a syntactic one because bow song lines tend to be complete thoughts, as the oral formulaic theory predicts.[11] What all this points out is that the antāti, or any other element of oral poetry, can only be understood as a part of the vocal pattern that employs it. The delivery styles of the bow song tradition are its oral poetics.

Bow singers also use a recitative, although they have no separate name for it, that makes the transition from speech to song. This chant-like style uses the same language as the song style, but a different delivery. With an aspirated voice and a stacatto pace that pushes out the words one by one at irregular intervals, the singer builds the tension in his voice until he finally releases it in full-fledged song. Skillfully handling the recitative to heighten performance at critical events in the narrative is the mark of a proficient singer.

Equally important as the song style are the three speech styles: formal, informal, and dialogue. All are lumped under the general term vacaṉam, but each has a different delivery and a different role in performance. The formal style is essentially informational and is the primary vehicle for narration. The lead singer, without any input from the other performers, uses this style to explain and comment on the sung lines, and then to add new material or advance the story. The language of formal speech is as educated as that of some songs, but less sophisticated than modern scholarly prose and closer to a high-quality newspaper or news broadcast. Formal speech varies from performer to performer, but each must use a language that gains the respect of his audience while staying within the range of effortless comprehension. If he wishes to "talk to" an audience as a tale-teller, the lead singer will switch to the informal speech style, which uses the local conversational idiom. Now he can digress from the main story, detail an event, or interject humor. In contrast to the strict monologue of formal speech, this informal style also includes other performers' comments on or responses to the lead's narrative.

A true exchange between performers, however, takes place only in the third speech style or dialogue. Using the same language as informal speech, the dialogue delivery is distinct in its vocal patterning. The two voices that are united in the song style and complementary in informal speech are placed in direct opposition in dialogue: one attacks with a question or riddle and the other jabs back. Jibes and insults are traded; jokes are cut at the other's expense. This repartee, like the antiphonal patterns of the song style, is partially determined by the structure of the performing group: it takes place primarily between the lead singer and the pot player, the leaders of the group's two divisions, who also hold the two ends of the bow.

Mixing these various delivery styles to their best effect is a skill that only

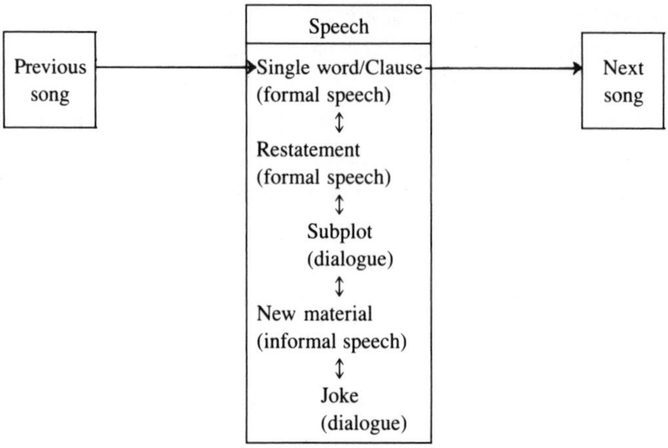

Figure 2. Basic Unit of Bow Song Composition

a few bow singers possess. Particularly difficult is carrying a narrative thread across the songs, which (because they are not always understood by the audience and often last for fifteen minutes or more) threaten to chop the story into fragments. In general, this is avoided by using the formal speech style as a compositional stitch: the singer hooks the previous song into the next speech segment, which in turn is hooked into the following song. At a minimum, this stitch is a single word question ("How?"), at most a clause ("If you want to know . . ."). Before this stitch, however, the speech segment usually restates the gist of the previous song (so that it may be understood) in formal speech style. After this restatement and before the final bridge, the singer may introduce narrative material, mostly in informal speech, and then present the song as a consequence of or reaction to it. At any point, the singer may switch to the dialogue style for digressions, jokes, and subplots. But no matter what pattern this speech segment takes, it must come back to its minimal form—the single word (or clause) bridge in formal speech—to lead into the next song segment. This chain from song to speech to song is the basic unit of composition in performance, as diagrammed in Figure 2.

Once stitched together, these basic units are combined into a larger narrative unit called a "section" (*kaṭṭam*). The narrative material contained in a section varies from a single detailed event to five or six events in broad outline; likewise, a section may take only five or ten minutes in performance, or cover an hour or more. Nevertheless, a section is easily identified because it closes with one of a select number of events, the major points of dramatic tension in bow song narratives: pregnancy, birth, sexual conflict, social conflict, marriage, and death. Some performing groups also announce the close of a section with a set of verbal and musical markers. After singing the first half of the final line, the lead singer suddenly pauses, slows the tempo, and drops his register; on this cue the instrumentalists stop, creating an interval of silence that serves to frame off the close of the section. Then, as the lead finishes the second half of the line, the other performers join in on the last sound, which they all hold for one musical measure. This extended sound, almost always, is the emphatic particle "ē" that is suffixed to the last word in the line. That last word, invariably, is a finite verb describing the definitive event of the section (death, birth, and so forth). Thus the entire section, which may last for an hour or more in performance, is condensed into its final word, which translates as "he was born" (*piṟantāṉē!*) or "he died" (*iṟantāṉē!*). For an example, see the birth of a raja's son in the Tampimār performance (p. 101).

Composition

These two building blocks of a bow song performance—the basic unit (song-speech-song) and the narrative section—raise the larger issue of composition. As noted earlier, the young apprentice learns the Śāstā story by repeating lines recited by his aṇṇāvi. Does this mean that he actually memorizes them? Does he learn the material presented in speech styles by the same method? And what about the other bow songs?

Ruth Finnegan (1977, 52–87) has shown that these questions are usually answered by reference to one of two models: prior composition or simultaneous composition. The first, in which material is composed by a poet and memorized for later performance, is characteristic of short (usually song) genres such as Somali or Eskimo oral poetry. In simultaneous composition (the oral formulaic) the material is composed as it is performed, a technique considered more natural for longer genres like the epic. Both models have advanced the study of oral tradition, but the distinction between them is sometimes overstated; in particular, the role of memorization in the longer performance genres has been, I believe, overlooked. Some oral epics in northwest India, for example, are at least partially memorized (Smith 1977; Kothari 1982), and the same can be said of the shorter bow songs.[12] My own field research with bow singers revealed two further facts: (1) that both prior and simultaneous composition are used, and (2) that a third method, prior preparation, is more common than either of them.

That different compositional processes operate in the bow song tradition is not unusual; most oral traditions probably fall somewhere between the oversimplified dichotomy of prior fixity on the one hand, and simultaneous improvisation on the other.[13] Generally stated, a text is "received" (brought under control by the singer by some method) and then recalled (and revised, to an extent) in performance. It is clear even from the information in *The Singer of Tales* that Yugoslav epics are not entirely composed during the performance event. One tends to remember the descriptions of the extraordinary improvisational powers of the *guslar*s (Lord 1960, 78–79), but in one experiment a singer produced two versions of a story seventeen years apart that were "remarkably close . . . but hardly word-for-word" (ibid., 28). Even if the second version was not a verbatim reproduction of the first, the near identity between them demonstrates a considerable degree of fixity. Indeed, fixity is implied by the very notion of the formula, the key to the theory of simultaneous composition. Formulas are almost as frequent in bow songs as in the south Slav epics. In the Tamil tradition, however, formulas are not used to compose songs in performance; they are, instead, a method for easy recall.[14]

Fixity and recall, then, are essential to a bow song performance. However, I found only two instances of actual prior composition, that is, composition and memorization by the performer himself.[15] In both instances, a family in which an unexpected and unexplained death had just occurred approached a singer, gave him the details of the event, and asked him to compose a story to be sung in a festival in honor of the now deified relative. According to their own explanations, the singers then created (*uṇṭākkatu*) the songs in their heads (no doubt from a pool of known songs or song lines), worked them out on their lips, and then memorized them. In one case, the initial performance of this composition was rejected by the family and temple patrons as inaccurate, forcing the singer to gather new information and revise it; two weeks later he sang the new version for the same audience and it was approved. He has now sung the "same story" (his words) in that festival for the past fifteen years.

Prior composition, however, is somewhat rare in the bow song tradition. The standard method for fixing a bow song before performance is what I term "prior preparation." Certainly this is a less demanding method than the others because in it a singer composes nothing new; he only memorizes what someone else has composed and then recalls it in performance. Prior preparation may proceed orally as in a young singer's training when he repeats the aṇṇāvi's words, or through written texts. As already described, the young singer receives handwritten texts from his teacher or writes them out from his teacher's copy. These texts he sets out to memorize by reading and reciting aloud to himself, a practice that is intensified as the performance date approaches (my conversations with singers were often curtailed by the necessity of this prior preparation of a story). Although this method is applied primarily to the sung lines, portions of the spoken material (vacaṉam), and even jokes, were also rehearsed and memorized. Memory, of course, is not perfect and the same line sung by the same singer on different occasions may show variation. But the practice and ideal for the bow singer remains memorization.[16]

Despite the predominance of this prior preparation, improvisation is by no means absent from bow song performance. Although it is sometimes difficult to know what is extemporaneous and what is fixed, the general areas of improvisation are clear. To begin with, singers often explained that they created a new line (or half-line) on the spot simply because they had forgotten the old one. In addition, although song texts are fixed, the sequencing of their individual lines is not. Moreover, even when all the sung lines are dictated from a manuscript (as in the translation in Chapter 5), they still must be fitted into the musical phrase, and that requires a degree of ad hoc manipulation. But composition during performance does not extend beyond this arrangement of lines to the creation of larger narrative units, and certainly not to new stories. Of course, if we wish to think of the composition process as stretching over hundreds of performances of the same story, each one reworking it a little more, then we could say that the stories are "composed in performance"; even then, however, the actual amount of improvisation in any single performance would be minor.

One performance that I witnessed did approach the model of simultaneous composition of an entire story. On this occasion, the lead singer did not know the story he was to perform (and had not prepared it beforehand because it was a last-minute request from a wealthy patron). A temple official gave him a very brief summary of the events (which I overheard); he began to sing ten minutes later and continued to sing for over three hours.[17] To be sure, the story's theme was not unfamiliar, but he had never sung this particular story before. In an interview the next day, the singer explained that he had taken known song lines and then strung them together with the compositional stitch described above. Thus, this is an example not of spontaneous composition, but of an equally exceptional ability to instantaneously recall known lines appropriate to the events in a story, and then to arrange them in a sustained narrative. In short, the bow singers' improvisational technique is not the opposite of memorization, but a select use of it.

Manuscripts and Bards

If bow singers only memorize and do not compose the songs they sing (and if we rule out communal recreation), we are faced with the question: Who does? Perhaps they were all originally composed by prior composition, as in the two cases cited earlier. Both those stories are still in oral form only and each is performed at a single temple. Over time, however, if the family moves or another temple of the deified relative is built, the story will spread, engage wider audiences, and be transformed by various singers in performances. At some later point, the story may be redacted into a written form that would standardize the various oral versions. Although I observed no concrete example of redaction, it seems very unlikely that a composition would go immediately into writing. Once created, the written text would become the basis for prior preparation by others and the story would enter the cycles of transmission (copying, memorizing, and performing) already discussed.

To the best of my knowledge, there is today no one who plays this crucial bardic role of giving written form to an oral bow song; the last bard, and the only one for many years, died in 1983. Many lead singers and aṇṇāvis are literate, but few are capable of redacting a story and none of inscribing it onto a palm-leaf manuscript. Such bards lived in the past, but little is known of them; aside from local oral history, the only evidence is found on the manuscripts they inscribed. The manuscripts extant in Nāñcil Nāṭu mention the name of the bard, his aṇṇāvi, his village, and the date of the composition. (Whether the extant manuscript is the first written record of a story or the last in a long chain is sometimes impossible to determine.)

Most of these bards were called *pulavar,* the term for scholar or learned man since the earliest Tamil literature; others used the title *perumāḷ* ("The Great One"), an epithet of Viṣṇu and a name normally forbidden to Nadars.[18] A third name was *paṇṭāram,* a class of priests among the Nadar, some of whom apparently were poets also. Nearly all the bards were Nadar (and a few Piḷḷai), all were male and all lived in the two villages of Akactīcuvaram and Itāmoḻi (see Map 2), which have remained major Nadar centers. The earliest dated manuscript is from the late seventeenth century; the most recent are those inscribed by the last bard, Āṟumukam Perumāḷ Nadar of Akactīcuvaram.[19] From one subgroup of the manuscripts, I reconstructed a chain of transmission from aṇṇāvi to aṇṇāvi that stretches across four generations and ends with Āṟumukam Pulavar of Akactīcuvaram who authored a manuscript of the Tōṭṭukkāri Ammaṉ story in 1776.

According to local oral history, Akactīcuvaram and Itāmoḻi were granted special favors by the Travancore maharaja in the seventeenth century. One family in each village was designated as *nāṭāṉ* ("ruler of the land"); the oldest man in each family was allowed to use the royal title *nākamaṇi mārttāṇṭa* (another name for Viṣṇu and thus forbidden to other Nadars), to keep one hundred men in arms, and to parade under bamboo parasols seven knotches high. With these privileges and resources, the two villages functioned as folk-level courts supporting the bow song tradition by patronizing its bards.[20]

This did not mean, however, that the bow song bards were accorded much respect in wider circles. After all, they were low-caste Nadars who composed songs only for village audiences. Like those who worked the trees and fields, they were barred from the Brahminical traditions of learning in the great temple centers at Cucīntiram and Kanya Kumari; and they were ignored by the Travancore maharajas who patronized music from all over India but never that on the bow, played literally outside their palace walls at Patmanāpapuram.[21] In these adverse conditions, the fact that the manuscripts maintained even a modest literary standard is a tribute to the Nadars and to the vitality of this folk tradition.

If not the bards, at least their manuscripts exist and continue to play a special role in the bow song tradition. They are made from the tough, fibrous, fan-shaped leaves of the female palmyra tree. When young and pliable, the leaves are stripped off, dried in the sun for a few days, and then trimmed with a knife to a size fourteen to eighteen inches long and one or one and one-half inches wide. Both surfaces are then prepared for inscribing by rubbing them back and forth against the bottom of the foot, and boring a tiny hole in the center of each leaf so that the entire stack may later be held together by a cord. To write on them, a pointed metal stylus (*eḻutāṇi* or "writing nail") is gripped in the right hand and guided from behind by the thumb of the left hand. When the manuscript is finished, the letters are blackened with charcoal paste or oil for easier reading. Mistakes can be simply corrected by rubbing off the surface with a knife and rewriting over it; spurious additions, however, are somewhat difficult since most words are linked through the rhyme schemes described earlier in this chapter.

Inscribing on palm-leaf remained the most common writing method in Nāñcil Nāṭu until the early decades of the twentieth century. A printing press was set up by missionaries in Nagercoil in 1820 and others followed, but these innovations had little impact on indigenous methods for a long time. Even as late as 1890, converts to Christianity continued to record biblical lectures on palm-leaf. Change came a few decades later as slate and chalk (and afterward pen and paper) became cheaper and more convenient than a stylus and palm-leaves. Today the old method has all but disappeared.[22]

Although no longer produced, the manuscripts retain a ritual role in the bow song tradition. A performance is thought to successfully summon deities only when their stories are accurately presented, and palm-leaf manuscripts are considered the most authentic form of a story. The demand for authenticity is such that in some temples the manuscript becomes a "script" for performance, read line-by-line to the lead singer who turns each line into song.[23] More commonly, however, the manuscript is only placed on the performers' platform as a legitimizing presence, and for reference if necessary.

Like ritual objects, these manuscripts are carefully controlled, either passed down within a family or horizontally disseminated by a performer to another man he has taught (as an aṇṇāvi) and over whom he has some control. Occasionally, a manuscript is lent out to be copied, but only under conditions that ensure a letter-for-letter reproduction: the new copy and the original must be presented to the owners for inspection before they will allow the new copy to be taken away. An exception occurs when a performer requests a manuscript from a temple where he has been contracted to sing; then he is permitted to take it home to study it (usually with someone's help) to build up his knowledge of the story he is to perform. Even in this situation, when no copying takes place, formal permission from the temple officials is required.

The traditional palm-leaf manuscript has been partially replaced by two newer forms: the handwritten text and the printed pamphlet. These two forms, however, are very dissimilar. Today most stories circulate as texts written in ink in notebooks (like those used by school children). Despite the use of new materials (pen and paper), these handwritten texts are similar to the old manuscripts in that they are manually inscribed. This means that, like the manuscripts, they are produced in limited numbers and that their distribution can be controlled. In fact, they circulate along the same channels as the palm-leaves do. As a result, they are accorded a measure of legitimacy and sometimes accepted as a temple's official text, but never as a "script" for performance.

None of this can be said of the printed pamphlet, which is mass produced (about five hundred per printing) by machine and impersonally sold on the street.[24] Although these pamphlets are also copies of palm-leaf manuscripts, they are considered of dubious ritual efficacy and never accepted as the official text at a temple.[25] Performers, however, do buy and consult them to improve their control over the stories they must sing. Moreover, these bow song pamphlets are less commercial than their counterparts in the rest of Tamil Nadu and India. Not at all intended for the general public or for entertainment, they are printed in close type, without pictures, and in the same language as the manuscripts upon which they are based. This last fact underscores an important point: a printed pamphlet may contain exactly the same words as a palm-leaf manuscript, but its mode of production and distribution puts it in a different category of ritual use.[26] The crucial distinction, then, is not between oral and written, but between oral or written forms and printed forms.

More generally, these differences between palm-leaf, handwritten, and pamphlet texts of the bow songs indicate that writing is not more homogeneous than speaking; it, too, has a variety of forms, uses, and contexts and requires its own ethnography.[27] In the bow song tradition, written and oral media are complementary, even supplementary as when the palm-leaf manuscript functions as a script for oral performance. In its reliance on written forms, this Tamil tradition is not unique; the idea that oral tradition is independent of writing (= education) is partly romantic, and partly ethnocentric.

The bow song's use of written forms is only one aspect of the fixity that dominates the tradition. A singer's training is largely imitation; composition is prior preparation; transmission is copying texts. Under this weight, improvisation must play a secondary role; a good example is the antiphonal singing style that does display individual talent, but only within a form determined by the structure of the performing group. The most influential constraint, however, is the demand for textual authenticity that produces the "scripted" performances. And these performances exemplify the convergence of narrative with ritual, to be explored in the next chapter.

Plate 1. A typical bow song temple (center, rear) with associated icons.

Plate 2. Two pītams (the distinctive bow song icon).

Plate 3. A Piḷḷai priest performing pūjā to a bow song god.

Plate 4. A pītam dressed in flower garlands during a festival.

Plate 5. Clay icons of Icakki Ammaṉ in her two roles (left, maternal; right, destructive [eating a child]).

Plate 6. Close-up of Icakki Ammaṉ in her destructive role.

Plate 7. A male bow song deity, flanked by his large wooden clubs.

Plate 8. Bow song group in action (the woman to the left is the lead singer).

Plate 9. Singing the Muttuppaṭṭaṉ story (see Chapter 6).

Plate 10. The audience (mostly female) during a daytime performance.

Plate 11. The lead singer leans in to hear lines read from a palm-leaf manuscript during a "scripted performance."

Plate 12. Possessed dancer (right) stands while monitor asks for knife to open coconut requested by the dancer.

Plate 13. Possessed dancers carrying swords and staffs as emblems of their possessing hero-god.

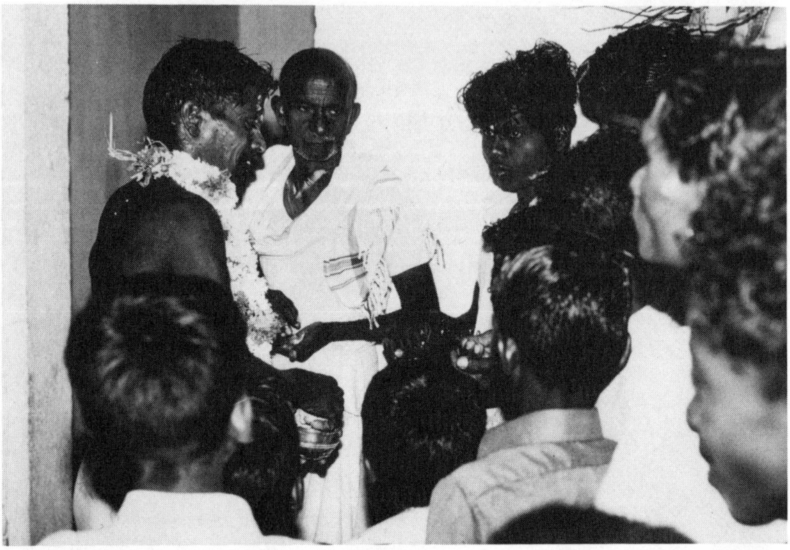

Plate 14. Possessed medium (left) distributes sacred ash and speaks kuṟi in response to questions.

3

Narrative and Ritual in Performance

> Without the bow there is no festival.

Although they merge in performance, narrative and ritual belong to different realms of the bow song tradition. The narrative realm is organized by a central contrast between birth stories and death stories that projects a local culture's understanding of the world. The ritual realm sets forth a desired rearrangement of that narrative contrast. Bow song performance is thus more than a conjunction of story and setting; it places a carefully constructed world view within a highly charged pattern of enactment. Victor Turner (1982, 91) once remarked that the word "performance" comes from the Old French *par fournir,* which means "to furnish completely." Singing on the bow is a performance in this sense, too, for it arranges the bow song narrative world within a ritual setting.[1]

A description of that arrangement is the goal toward which this chapter moves. First, the narrative world is explained in its own right, and then the ritual world of the festival. Finally, we will see that a correlation between these two, between narrative type (birth or death story) and level of ritual intensity, defines the structure of bow song performance. Throughout this interaction, it will be noted that the narrative world, although reorganized in a ritual pattern, remains the base of the bow song tradition.

The Narrative World

Local terminology divides bow songs into two categories: birth stories and death stories. Birth stories narrate the history of gods and goddesses grouped under the term *teyva piṟavi* ("divine birth") or *teyva vamcam* ("divine descent"); death stories tell the histories of *iṟantuppaṭṭa vātai* ("spirits who were killed") or *veṭṭuppaṭṭa vātai* ("spirits who were cut up"). Local people, particularly singers, use these labels to identify a specific story by saying, for instance, "Oh, that's a story about 'divine descent.'" The same distinction between birth and death is also made in the texts themselves, by self-referential tags. After the invocation, the singer identifies the story as a "story of X's birth" (X *piṟanta katai*) or a "story of X's death" (X *iṟanta katai*).[2] This division between birth and death stories is key to the entire bow song tradition, to its narrative world, and to its performance structure. What one needs to remember is that death stories are local histories, stories about people who lived and died (and then became gods); birth stories, on the other hand, are mythic histories of gods and goddesses of divine origin who are not less real than the death story heroes, but who are not men and women either.[3]

Birth stories and death stories follow different patterns, set in contrasting worlds (see Fig. 3), but they open similarly with an invocation or *kāppu* (lit. "protection," "support") in which the singer calls on various deities to aid him. He may also include the traditional disclaimer or *avai aṭakkam* ("humility [before] the assembly [of poets, kings]"), in which the lead singer compares his attempt to render the story to a woodcock's imitation of a swan's grace. On special occasions, the lead singer also pays tribute to his

Figure 3. Narrative Patterns of Birth Stories and Death Stories

Event	Birth story	Death story
Invocation *(kāppu)*	summon deity of story and allied deities	
Narrative *(varalāṟu)*		
Setting	distant, Kailāsa	proximate, earth
Birth	painless, divine	human, painful
Conflict	supernatural; deity vs. demon/spirit conjuror; sexual themes	sociological; human vs. human, leads to death; sexual themes
Death	none for deity	violent, murder/suicide; go to Kailāsa, receive boons from Śiva
Ending	deity descends, cult established; temple built, festival held to placate deity	

aṇṇāvi, his parents, the temple patrons, and goes on to explain how he was invited to sing in the festival and so forth.

Immediately following the invocatory verses, the performance moves into the narrative (*varalāṟu,* lit. "history") with formulaic descriptions of the setting. At this point, the story patterns begin to separate, and these differences in setting are crucial to the larger contrast between them. Birth stories are set in Kailāsa, the heavenly realm of Śiva and Pārvati, where countless sages, gods, and other celestials are entertained by musicians and dancers in awesome splendor and eternal light. In this mythic paradise, the birth of the main character can only be supernatural. The most important birth deities (Śāstā, Kāḷi Ammaṉ, Muttār Ammaṉ) emerge directly from Śiva's or Pārvati's eye, throat, or sweat, while lesser ones are cooked up in a huge sacrificial fire that the gods keep ablaze. Even when the birth is slightly anthropomorphized, as when Śāstā is born from Śiva's seed or when Vallarakkaṉ's mother is impregnated by Viṣṇu's discus (see Chapter 4), it is still magical and painless.

The setting for death stories is similarly idealized, but it is earthly and the birth is therefore human and painful. The local landscape is described in a formulaic set of lines (*nāṭṭiṉ ciṟappu* or "glory of the land") as fertile, cool, and peaceful; then, the singer telescopes to a more specific site, a village or town somewhere in the bow song region, and finally to a particular caste and family. Here the human frailty of the death stories appears—almost invariably in the form of childlessness.[4] The barren wife goes on pilgrimage to many temples, repeatedly performs acts of religious austerity (*tapas*) and charity until she wins a boon from a god and becomes pregnant. Month by month her body changes and then, in the last hours, when the pain is acute, the midwife is summoned. But now the tension builds for as the pain increases, the midwife delays: she cannot leave immediately; she must feed her infirm husband; she must care for her children; and she is in no hurry anyway because the last time she was underpaid.[5] Finally she reaches the woman, who is screaming in pain and swearing off both husband and child, and swiftly delivers the child. The tension is then relieved by a lullaby.

After their respective birth events, the two story patterns separate further into their narrative worlds. The newly arrived deity in birth stories completes a series of tasks, wins boons from Śiva, and descends to earth; there the god uses his boons to display his power, usually to wreak havoc among humans and win worship from them. The central conflict, however, is not with those frail humans, but with some other supernatural power—a god, a spirit (*vātai* or *pēy*), or a spirit conjuror (*mantravāti*). In the end, whatever the variation in details, the god or goddess from Kailāsa triumphs and remains immortal.

In death stories, by contrast, the defining event is the violent end of the main character; but death approaches only gradually. First, the hero is trained in martial arts and sometimes marries. Eventually, however, the protagonist is caught in a conflict over land rights or sexual rights, or both, that leads to his violent death. Heroes, like Nāṭāṉ Cāmi (Chapter 1), are often cut up with a machete-like knife (*arivāḷ*), hence the term "cut up" spirit for the deified humans of death stories. But murder takes other forms, too: a woman's head is crushed by a rock; a man is speared through the back or mounted on a pointed stake; heroines elect suicide (to avoid sexual violence and murder) by using the arivāḷ, pulling out their tongues, or jumping into a fire or pool (like Tōṭṭukkāri Ammaṉ in Chapter 1). After death, Śiva takes the victim to Kailāsa, gives him boons, and sends him back to earth where the boons are utilized to gain revenge on those responsible for his death. The central conflict in these death stories is thus the polar opposite of that in birth stories. In the latter, the conflict is between supernatural powers and ends with the god's triumph; in death stories, the issue is sociological and leads to the human hero's death.

Following the resolution of the central conflict, the story in either pattern is more or less complete. Just as the patterns have a similar beginning (the invocation), they move quickly toward the same closing: the birth or death deity wins worship from humans and a cult is established. Death deities attack those responsible for their deaths, and birth deities strike people who refuse them worship. Unable to explain these events, local people consult a diviner/astrologer (*cōciyaṉ*) who identifies the deity causing the trouble, and advises them to build a temple and celebrate a festival in its honor. When this is done and the deity enjoys *pūjā* (worship) in the festival, the story comes to a close.

Contrasts between birth and death stories will become sharper after reading the translations of "The Birth of Śāstā" and "The Death of the Little Brothers" (Chapters 4 and 5). For the present, we may illustrate them with the synopses of two other exemplary stories.

The story of Muttār Ammaṉ, the most popular goddess in the tradition, is an important birth story that contains no fewer than twelve different births, in seven separate scenes.[6] The narrative opens when Śiva and Pārvati watch a snake crawl out from a pot in which it was born; soon, seven *rākṣasa* ("demon") women are born in the same pot. Śiva sends a sage who cooks stones in a fire, gives them to the women, and they conceive. But after the immediate and painless birth of their three sons, the women flee. Meanwhile, the heat from another sacrificial fire causes Pārvati to sweat directly into the flames, from which arises Muttār Amman̲, Goddess of Smallpox.[7] She is then dispatched to mother the abandoned children, and together they build a fort. From this point, including several more magical births and celestial machinations, the bow song follows the classical Hindu myth of the destruction of the Triple City. In the final scene, after Śiva has demolished the demons' fort by a laugh and a clap of his hands, Muttār Amman̲ is sent down to earth in a chariot and enjoys a festival held in her honor.

Contrast this story of snakes, sages, and sacrificial fires with the following death story of Pūlaṅkoṇṭāḷ, a young Nadar woman. Born in a poor family in a small village, she spends her time playing with her brothers and spinning cotton. One day she asks them to go to market and buy her a special loom for weaving. During the brothers' long walk to market, they talk proudly of the sister's beauty and are overheard by another group of Nadar men traveling to the same place. The second group befriends the brothers, takes them to their house and treats them to a meal, all the time questioning them about their village and family. The following day, the second group arrives unexpectedly at the brothers' house, carrying baskets of gifts as part of a marriage proposal. Pūlaṅkoṇṭāḷ hurries inside, and the brothers angrily reject the proposal, scattering the baskets on the ground (since the suitors are of a slightly inferior lineage). Smarting under these insults, the suitors leave but vow to abduct the sister in seven days. Late on the seventh night, the suitors put the brothers to sleep with magic powder and steal away with Pūlaṅkoṇṭāḷ. But she fights back and the captors, unable to subdue her, throw her down an abandoned well, killing her. Transformed into a goddess, Pūlaṅkoṇṭāḷ then takes revenge on her murderers, their families, and others (Piḷḷais and Brahmins) who lent them assistance. The confused villagers decide to construct a temple and worship her in a festival.

The contrast between the birth story of Muttār Amman̲ and the death story of Pūlaṅkoṇṭāḷ is central to the organization of the narrative world in the bow song tradition. As these two stories illustrate, the contrast turns on differences in origins (earthly, human, and painful versus divine, mythic, and painless) that lead to differences in outcomes (a violent death versus the triumph of the gods). Although the final conclusion—the establishment of a cult—is similar in both story patterns, these differences in origins and outcomes predetermine different paths to that conclusion. In the birth story, Muttār Amman̲ descends from heaven (Śiva's Kailāsa) to earth; in the death story, Pūlaṅkoṇṭāḷ rises to heaven through deification.

These two movements, the essential patterns in birth and death stories, describe the primary interactions between gods and humans in Hinduism. The descent of the god in birth stories is part of the *avatāra* ("descent") process described in classical Hindu texts by which pan-Indian gods (usually Viṣṇu) take earthly forms and work in the world of men. The ascent of the human in death stories, by contrast, represents the deification of the hero common in folk Hinduism. These movements, however, are kept separate in classical literature; in the *purāṇa*s, in particular, human ambition to become gods is fraught with danger and meets formidable celestial resistance.[8]

In the bow song tradition, on the other hand, deification (death story) and avatāra (birth story) are related parts of a narrative system (see Fig. 4).[9] They are the complementary halves of a circular and symmetrical world view in which there is continual flow between Kailāsa and earth: humans go up (death and deification) and gods come down (avatāra). Birth stories and death stories are thus more than a series of narrative events. They are the two halves of a cultural construction of reality and their different patterns inscribe the important paths of interaction between gods and humans.

The *Koṭai* Festival

Bow song performance brings this narrative world into the ritual world of a festival called the *koṭai* ("offering"). The koṭai is a distinctive institution of the bow song tradition, for it is the only context in which bow songs are

Figure 4. Birth Stories and Death Stories as World View

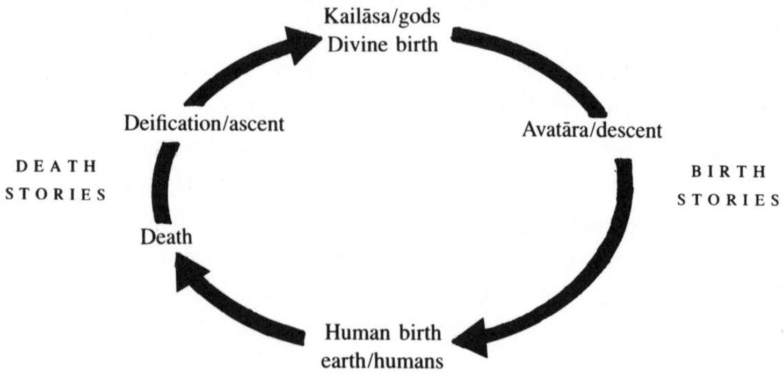

performed and it is held only in temples of bow song deities.[10] We approach the conjunction between narrative and ritual in the koṭai, the end point of this chapter, by looking first at the temples in which that festival is set.

Although denoted by the single term *kōyil* ("temple," lit. "house of the king"), bow song temples are architecturally diverse. The minimum requirement for a temple is a place where the chief deity resides during the festival: a building; a spot on the ground marked by lime paste; a painting or mixture of turmeric powder and oil on a wall; a tree; or a freestanding stone. The deities of birth stories, due to their high status through an association with Śiva or the goddess, tend to have structural temples:[11] a building with four walls and a central door, or a smaller shrine covered with a roof supported by stone pillars. The icon in these temples is often a somewhat expensive sculpted image (*cilai*) of stone or bronze. For the more local death deities, the "temple" is often the icon itself. The commonest icon for death deities is a *pītam,* an obelisk-like statue of clay or brick, covered with lime paste, that stands about three to five feet tall on a rectangular base of the same materials (see Plates 1–4).[12] Unlike the cilai, the pītam is not anthropomorphic, save during festivals when facial features of low-grade silver are added and a cluster of areca nut flowers is placed on top for hair.

Despite these material differences, the physical plan of all bow song temples is essentially the same.[13] The icon (whether a cilai or a pītam) of the chief deity is surrounded by icons of allied gods and goddesses, who are characters in the story of the chief deity. In larger temples, this group of a central icon and its satellites is joined by several similar configurations, each of which represents another story sung in that temple. In this way, by their cast of characters, the narratives prefigure the specific layout of icons in the temples in which they are sung. This is but one example of how the narrative world influences the ritual world in the song tradition. Another instance was noted earlier in this chapter during the discussion of the two story patterns. Both patterns, it will be remembered, lead to the building of a temple and the establishment of a cult, so that these narratives contain and give rise to the ritual realm. Bow songs are not just stories about hero-gods; they also explain the tradition to those who sing and hear them. Narratives and select narrative events also play a major ritual role in performance, as we will see shortly.

The koṭai is the most important ceremony held in a bow song temple, if only because it is the only one to which the entire temple community contributes financially. Contributions, or "shares" (*paṅku*), are made by "shareholders" (*paṅkāḷi*), who are usually defined as each household (or sometimes as each adult male) in the kin group that controls the temple. Each shareholder gives one share, but the amount of the share fluctuates from year to year, and from temple to temple. In 1978, for example, 120 Nadar families (almost an entire village population) contributed fourteen rupees each, or a total of 1,680 rupees for a three-day festival at the village-supported temple. That same year in a nearby village, a small but prosperous Nadar lineage collected 2,300 rupees, or more than 100 from each of its twenty-two male shareholders, to finance the festival at their lineage-controlled temple.[14] Most of the money is collected well before the festival to make the necessary cash advance to the bow singers, food suppliers, and other contracted labor.

First, however, the dates for the festival must be fixed. The possible choices in the season from January to May (with a preference for March–April, the Tamil month of *paṅkuṉi*) are considerably reduced by a convention that assigns Tuesday to goddesses and Friday to gods.[15] Centering the three-day festival on this special day means that those at goddess temples begin on a Monday and end on a Wednesday, and those for a god commence on a Thursday and finish on a Saturday. At the height of the season, when several temples in the same village hold festivals one after the other, this arrangement leaves only one day for the villagers to take a rest from the festivities that continue day and night for the other six days of the week. Sometimes, when resources permit and the festivals are stretched from three to eight days, one hardly knows when one begins and the next ends.[16]

But there is little activity and usually silence in a bow song temple before the festival actually arrives. Then, early on the first day, final preparations are made: ritual accessories are checked, clay icons (pītam) remolded or made anew, wood gathered, and food prepared. A most important event, requiring a specialist, is the construction of the *pantal,* a temporary thatch roof that stretches between the main deity and the performers' platform to shield everyone from the sun. Covered with embroidered cloth, festooned with clusters of flowers, supported by banana tree stalks, and strung with lights, it transforms a few mud pītams into a site for the gods (see p. 209).

The koṭai then unfolds in a fixed sequence of three slots, one on each of the three days of the festival. Each slot is a cluster of three separate but related ritual activities: a special form of worship called *tīpārātaṉai,* spirit possession and dance, and bow song performance.

The conscious purpose of the koṭai festival is to win the favor of the gods and goddesses resident in the temple, to enlist their powers to produce or continue desired states and prevent or remove undesired ones. The primary method for achieving these ends is worship (pūjā) either through the agency of a temple priest (of the same caste as that of the temple community), or directly by oneself or in a group. Every deity in a temple (there may be as many as twenty or more) receives a standard form of pūjā from a temple priest: the deity is decorated, covered with flower garlands, offered rice, bananas, betel leaves and nut, and coconuts, amid waving lamps and burning incense. Even the small mounds of raised earth are decorated, fed, and invoked sometime during the three-day festival.[17]

Only three deities, however, are honored with a special form of worship, the tīpāratanai ("lamp worship"). Śāstā is worshiped on the initial day with a tīpārātanai known as *makā/mulu kāppu* ("great/full invocation [protection]") to ensure the success of the entire festival; on the second day the chief deity of the temple is honored with a tīpārātanai known as koṭai (which gives the festival its name); and on the third day another deity is honored with a tīpārātanai called the *maṅkalam* (roughly, "blessing"). These rituals are very much like the pūjā to lesser gods in that they are also conducted by priests and utilize the same materials. What distinguishes the tīpārātanai is that everything is more elaborate: the food offerings are larger, the decorations are more grand, and more people and time are involved.

The timing of the tīpārātanai is also definitive. They occur at *ucci nēram* ("high time"), either twelve noon or twelve midnight, when the power of the gods is thought to be at its zenith.[18] Over the three days of the festival, these major rituals are conducted at midnight on the first day, at either noon or midnight of the second day, and at noon of the last day. Even when the festival expands to eight days or contracts to one, the number of tīpārātanai remains three and only their placement is adjusted to available "high times." The tīpārātanai are also marked by a number of other rites that cluster around them. Of particular importance are the mēḷam and the *kuravai.*[19] The mēḷam is an instrumental ensemble whose music is considered auspicious, and is played outside the festival at marriages and other temple ceremonies. The *kuravai,* which is also heard in other ritual contexts, is a high-pitched cry given out by the crowd of worshipers.

As the ritual center of the festival, the tīpārātanai to the temple's chief deity on the second day attracts several other rites, some of major importance. One that sometimes rivals the tīpārātanai itself is a special form of pūjā in which sweet cooked rice (*poṅkal*) is offered to the goddess. The rice is brought by families who place a portion in front of the goddess and keep the remainder for their own consumption at home. At times, the cumulative mass of poṅkal, decorated by adding sweets, fruits, and eggs, reaches five or six feet high. Another offering to the goddess made by family units is the "flour-lamp" (*māviḷakku*), rice flour shaped into a lamp with a burning wick and carried on a plate in a large procession of girls and women.

The most interesting ceremony of the bow song festival, again occurring during the center tīpārātaṉai to a goddess, is the *vaḻipāṭu nōṉpu* ("worship fast"). In this rite, perhaps unique to the bow song region, young children (aged 5 to 10 years) observe some minimal deprivations (one pure vegetarian meal a day) for eight days before the festival. On the second day, before the tīpārātaṉai, they walk in procession to the temple; the girls carry a flour-lamp, the boys hold upright a knife stuck through a lemon. The unusual feature of the procession is that a thin bamboo reed is inserted through the fleshy part of each child's waist so that it circles around the back and returns to the front. When the lamps and lemons have been presented to the goddess, the reeds are removed.

A more individual form of ritual offering in the center slot of all festivals is the *nērccai* ("vow"). The nērccai is both the making of a vow to reward a diety for help in solving a problem (usually illness, marital trouble, or barrenness) and the fulfillment of that vow by presenting a gift. The nērccai gift is similar to the pūjā offering, except that items of clothing may also be given: a silk sari for a goddess or a silk *vēṭṭi* (man's lower wrap) to a god. (Sometimes a vow is made to sponsor an entire festival in a god's honor [see p. 51].) During the course of the festival, small groups, families, or new couples, walk in procession from their house to the temple bearing the gifts, but on the second day, as the tīpārātaṉai approaches, there is a steady stream that competes with the priestly rites.

Finally, a sacrifice (*pali*) is closely connected with the center slot tīpārātaṉai. It is conducted shortly after the major pūjā, at some remove from the temple area. Although banned by law and increasingly replaced by vegetable (e.g., pumpkin) substitutes, animal victims are still very common; male goats are preferred, but chickens will suffice. After the animal's head has been hacked off with an arivāḷ (by a man of no special office), its blood is taken and consecrated to the four cardinal directions, beginning with the west.

Not all these rites are found in every festival, nor are they necessarily directly related to the tīpārātaṉai in the three slots of the ritual pattern. However, the convergence of several of them at the time of the tīpārātaṉai creates a dense ritual cluster in each slot. Spirit possession and bow song performance are also a part of that cluster, but are more complex.

Spirit possession is in fact the culmination of the tīpārātaṉai.[20] During the early stages of the tīpārātaṉai, which may extend for one or two hours, only the priests are seen near the icon, decorating and dressing it. Later, as these preparations draw near completion and the god is almost ready to receive his human worshipers, a large crowd gathers; at times, hundreds of people may push together to gain a glimpse of the god when he is finally activated by invocations, ringing bells, and waving lamps. Soon, as the priests step aside to reveal the deity, the mēḷam begins to play and the kuravai is heard. Only then does the crowd turn its attention to a man (whom an outsider might not have noticed before) who begins to shake and then dance, possessed by the god.

This possession dance is called, quite literally, "god dance" (*cāmi āṭṭam*), and the dancer is called a "god dancer" (*cāmi āṭi*).[21] Each major deity at a temple has a designated medium whom it possesses. These designated mediums are all men who come from the same socioeconomic level and castes as the bow singers and the rest of the temple community; their ritual status is not much higher either. Gods possess them, they do not become gods; when they dance, it is not they but the god who is worshiped. Unlike bow singing, the role of cāmi āṭi is properly transferred hereditarily, if not from father to son (or uncle to nephew) at least among male kin. If a good candidate is not available within the kin group, the office may be offered to someone outside; but given that the temple communities are normally mono-caste, the new dancer is rarely from a new caste. The transfer, called "giving the dance" (*āṭṭam koṭukka*), occurs during a festival when a possessed dancer takes a garland, some sacred ash, or flower and places it in the hand of the new man, screaming "Let him dance! Let him dance!"[22]

The dancer is both a kinetic icon of the possessing god and a medium for communication between that god and people in the audience. When the dance wanes, a crowd will gather and ask questions of the possessing god: Will I get pregnant? Will my wife recover? Will my son pass his exams? Speaking through the voice of his human medium, the deity answers in a speech known as *kuṟi* ("mark," "sign") because it has the force of prophecy (see Plate 14). This verbal level of possession, however, is still dependent on the kinetic; the dance must precede the speech in order to establish its veracity.[23]

To restate the discussion thus far, the ritual sequence of a bow song festival consists of three slots, in which the tīpārātaṉai (and their allied rites) coincide with a possession dance. Before adding the third element of the ritual pattern, the bow song performances, it is necessary to understand that the "ritual depth" of each slot in the pattern is variable. Ritual depth refers to ritual intensity. It is an analytic, not a native concept and derives from the attempts of other scholars to describe the affective quality of ritual experiences.[24] In the Indian context, ritual depth shares the many meanings of *śakti* ("power") and follows its fluctuations. Śakti, however, refers to the condition of the objects of worship, whereas ritual depth indicates that of the worshipers.[25] If "height" (as in the bow song term "high time," ucci nēram) is appropriate for the first, "depth" is more descriptive of the second.

Necessarily subjective, ritual depth does show certain visible, even measurable manifestations, the most dramatic being the possession dance. Few persons become possessed during a festival, but their dance is a register of the intensity of the atmosphere and of the audience's experiences, which vary considerably across the three days. In the first slot, during the tīpārātaṉai to Śāstā, the dance is relatively weak. Amid waving lights and ringing bells, his forehead covered with ash, the dancer stands before the god and soon begins to shake; this movement, sufficient to indicate possession, is sometimes all that occurs. At other times, the medium will shuffle a little in one spot while his dangling body trembles; if he does "dance," the steps are limited. After approximately fifteen minutes, the dancer (as deity) speaks kuṟi for another quarter of an hour, and the possession is over. Possession is similarly mild in the last slot, and sometimes is omitted altogether.

Possession in the center slot, as part of the worship of the chief deity, is entirely different. Like the other dances, it begins with the end of the tīpārātaṉai, but it continues for two or three hours as an event in its own right.[26] After the initial shaking, the dancer moves in circles, vigorously pumps his arms and legs, and, at the most intense moments, totally abandons his body to crawl or roll on the ground. The dancer is also more elaborately costumed than at other times; on his chest hang heavy flower garlands, from his waist a silk sari (if a goddess dancer) or an expensive vēṭṭi (if a god dancer). Dancers possessed by the hero of a death story will run over to the god's icon, grab the weapon leaning there—the sword, knife, staff, or arivāḷ (machete) with which he fought and died in the story—and brandish it wildly in the air. Dancers for birth deities carry in their arms burning torches or *pantams* (tightly packed cones of kerosene-soaked cloth) as an emblem of the sacrificial fire from which they emerged in Kailāsa.

The extreme ritual depth in the center slot is also indicated by the way these dance props are handled. Dancers hold the burning torches close to their chest and face; others strike their heads, foreheads, or back with the flat edge of the weapons they carry. In some festivals, dancers may walk over a bed (about 30 feet long) of burning coals, or scoop them up and cradle them in their bare hands. The parts of the dancer's body exposed to the heat are treated with a mixture of sandalwood paste and oil (in case the possessing deity should suddenly leave), but the potential for danger is real and a group of men is assigned to monitor these dances. If a dancer lingers too long on the coals, carries the torch too close to his body, or strikes himself too savagely with a weapon, the monitors step forward and apply more of the sandalwood and oil mixture to cool him down. But if the danger continues, they will stop the dance altogether.

The extreme ritual depth of the dance in the center slot affects more than the designated medium. It also becomes the focus of attention for the large festival crowd that gathers in a circle around the dance area. From the crowd come mediums for other gods in the temple or other nearby temples. These designated dancers are also sometimes joined by ordinary individuals in the festival crowd. But even this latter kind of possession is not spontaneous because most of the individuals will have danced this way before or have been possessed outside the temple context. Many of these unofficial dancers are women, who dance very differently from the designated, male dancers. The women loosen their long, black hair, bend at the waist, and slowly sway in small circles. If the atmosphere is particularly charged, the total number of dancers may reach eight or ten, each careening around, waving their weapons and burning torches, while others sway in the crowd and urge them on with cries of the kuravai.[27]

As indexed by these several features of the possession dance, the three slots of the festival sequence display greater or lesser ritual depth. In the first slot ritual intensity is weak, it increases in the center slot, and it falls away in the final slot. Into this ritual pattern of the festival, we must now place the performances on the bow, without which, as the epigraph to this chapter reminds us, there can be no festival at all.

The stories of many (but not all) deities in a temple are sung during its three-day festival. Most performances are rather short—from a few minutes (enough time to sing an invocatory verse and ask for blessings) to perhaps an hour. Three stories, however, are given a major performance that will last from four to six hours, or longer. These are the stories of the deities honored with a tīpārātaṉai. Thus, Śāstā's story is sung in a major performance in the first slot, the story of the main god or goddess is sung in the important central slot, and the story of another deity is sung in a major performance in the final slot.

These three major performances begin long before the tīpārātaṉai, during a lull in ritual activity. Each major performance is, in fact, a separate ritual arena and must be bracketed off by a series of rites. As the singers arrange themselves on the platform of wooden benches, the aṇṇāvi takes the strung bow before the presiding deity of the temple and asks that it be blessed, an event known as *vil vaṇaṅkuvatu* ("honoring the bow"). Later, after the bow has been set up on the platform, a singer arranges bananas, a split coconut, burning incense, flowers, and a brass vessel full of paddy, and quietly prays to Gaṇeśa for a successful performance. Finally, sacred ash is brought from the temple, sprinkled on each instrument (to ensure flawless playing) and then rubbed lightly on the singers' foreheads.

The singing begins, as we have noted, with the kāppu, a series of invocatory verses meant to summon the god whose story is being sung, as well as other *kāval* ("protective") deities, to the festival. By the time these verses are completed, and the main story (varalāṟu) commences, the early stages of the tīpārātaṉai will have begun also. From this point forward, the bow song performance is closely linked to the ceremonies of the festival. Narrative has become ritual.

Performances of birth stories are ritually focused on the birth of the god in the narrative (for an alternative focus on marriage, see Chapter 6). The singing is carefully measured to reach that narrative event at the exact moment that the tīpārātaṉai culminates in the manifestation of the god in the possession dance. Thus, the deity appears in narrative and ritual worlds simultaneously. At this point, the singing stops but the possession dance continues, extending the deity's presence for some time more.

Performances of death stories are more ritually developed. Not only the births of the heroes or heroines (and sometimes their mother's conception), but their marriage, sexual or land conflicts, and other events that raise dramatic tension are all ritually marked by the playing of the mēḷam and the shouting of the kuravai. In this way, the singing builds to its finale in the death of the hero or heroine. Like the birth event in birth stories, the death scene in death stories is sung at the exact moment that the tīpārātaṉai culminates in the possession dance. When the hero is killed in the story, he appears in the form of his dance-medium. And, again, at this point the singers stop; having induced possession, the bow song performance has fulfilled its ritual role.

There is also a careful correlation between narrative and ritual on the level of the koṭai festival. In observing more than fifty festivals during field work, I noticed that the ritual pattern has a definite narrative dimension in that only certain types of stories are performed in each slot. In the first slot, a birth story is sung; in fact, only one birth story, the Śāstā (or Vallarakkaṉ) story, is sung in every festival. This is the prototypical birth story (as the translation in the following chapter will make clear) describing the origin of one god from two others. The final slot is likewise always filled with a performance of a birth story, but a wide variety of birth stories are sung in this slot. Often the story is of a birth goddess who is important in the temple but not its central deity, or of Cuṭalai Māṭaṉ, a widely worshiped god whose name ("Māṭaṉ of the Flames") is emblematic of a class of birth gods who emerge from the flames of a fire in Kailāsa. Because the ritual depth of this final slot is very weak, stories of figures who are not worshiped in a particular temple are also sometimes sung at the close of its festival. The story of Rāma and Sītā's marriage and a variant of the Muttuppaṭṭaṉ story (see Chapter 6), both of which conclude with a wedding scene instead of a god's birth, are popular examples.

Performances in the center slot, on the other hand, are dominated by death stories. Although death stories are not always sung because center-slot performances must present the story of the temple's central deity whoever it might be, there is a decided preference for them. Death stories, in fact, are sung only in this center slot. Moreover, a death story is very often performed in this slot even when the chief deity is a birth god (his story is shifted out of the center slot to the last slot). Performances of death stories in the center slot are also more ritually elaborated than the performances of birth stories in the same slot; they are considerably longer and are marked by the intense possession dances described earlier.

The narrative sequence of performances in the festival, then, is this: birth story-death story-birth story. When this narrative pattern is superimposed on the ritual pattern (see Fig. 5), a correlation becomes evident. We see that birth stories in the first and final slots are accompanied by weak ritual depth, and that the death story in the center slot is associated with extreme ritual depth. This correlation between narrative type and ritual depth tightly binds

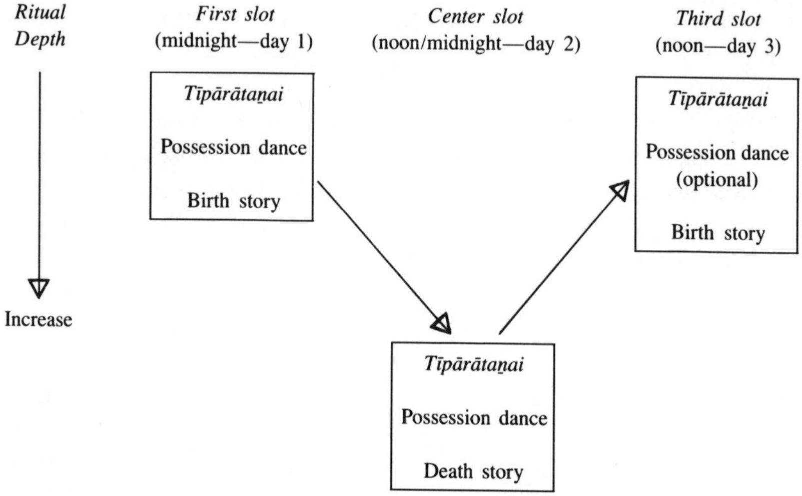

Figure 5. Pattern of Narrative and Ritual in the *Koṭai* Festival

the stories sung on the bow into the ceremonial worship of the festival. As the rearrangement of the bow song's narrative world (birth stories vs. death stories) within its ritual world, this correlation defines the fundamental structure of the entire bow song tradition.

The tripartite nature of this structure invites an immediate comparison with van Gennep's classic schema for the rites of passage.[28] The series of bow song performances, however, does not effect a passage or produce a new social state. The movement in the festival is cyclical and repetitive, not linear and progressive. That cycle, moreover, has a center, defined by the factor of ritual depth, in the middle slot where a death story leads to a ritually deep possession dance. In this way, the ritual rearrangement of the bow song narrative world in performance changes a simple diachronic sequence into a synchronic paradigm.

It is a paradigm of enclosure. Death stories with extreme ritual depth are boxed in between birth stories with weak ritual depth; violence, sexual conflict, and painful death are set within the boundaries of a supernatural world of auspicious births and marriage. In terms of the stories translated in this book, the death of the Tampimār brothers is encased between the birth of Śāsta and the marriage of Muttuppaṭṭaṉ. But I do not interpret this enclosure as an attempt to ritually cushion death within the protective borders of births and marriage; on the contrary, I believe it is designed to provide access to the power of death. However, before discussing this point further (it is taken up in the final chapter), it is necessary to leave these formal descriptions and enter into actual performances. The following three chapters, therefore, present translations of performances in the standard sequence of a bow song festival.

4

The Birth of Śāstā

When Yaśodā looked inside Kṛṣṇa's mouth,
she saw the whole world,
but first she saw the bow.

Introduction

Death stories are the ritual center but not the whole of bow song performance. Their significance, as noted at the close of the previous chapter, is dependent on a contrast with the other type of bow song, the birth stories. Built around auspicious births and marriage, the birth stories create a very different kind of narrative world in which singers and audiences enjoy humor, especially sexual comedy, social satire, fantasy, and beauty. Nowhere is this world more successfully created than in the story of Śāstā's birth, or the Vallarakkan̲ story, translated in this chapter. This is the quintessential birth story, performed in the initial slot of every koṭai festival in order to set up the contrast with the death story sung on the following day (and translated in the next chapter).[1]

The Birth of Śāstā combines two separate stories known throughout India in variant forms in both classical and folk traditions. The first of these describes the birth of a god from the seed of Śiva when he sees Viṣṇu in his form of the beautiful woman Mōhin̲i; in most variants, this god is Harihara-putra ("Son of Viṣṇu-Śiva"), identified in South Indian texts as Śāstā (or Aiyan̲ār or Ayyappan̲). He descends to earth, captains a raja's army, and eventually retreats to a shrine in the mountains. The second story, found in classical sources but more commonly told in folk traditions, concerns a demon who threatens Kailāsa with a boon received from Śiva; Śiva then enlists the aid of Viṣṇu who takes his Mōhin̲i form and destroys the demon.[2]

In the bow song tradition, the second story about the demon (Vallarakkan̲) is a prelude to the first about the birth of Śāstā. The link between them is Mōhin̲i, who first disposes of the demon and then excites Śiva to spill his seed so that Śāstā is born. (The motif of the seed is omitted from the performance translated here because it is "dirty" [*acinkam*], as the singers explained.)[3] In written texts, the first part about the demon occupies less than one-third of the narrative, whereas the second part about Śāstā's birth and exploits fills the remaining two-thirds. In performance, however, the demon's story is expanded to comprise nearly the entire narrative, while Śāstā's birth, the event with which most South Indian texts begin, forms the conclusion. Thus, most of Śāstā's story—his descent to earth, his warring, and retreat to the hills—is never sung on the bow.

In effect, the bow song tradition has taken these two stories, expanded one, truncated the other, and fashioned a performance with a narrative focus on the demon but a ritual focus on the birth of Śāstā. The reasons for these alterations lie in the structure of bow song performance: songs sung in the first (and last) slot should conclude with an auspicious event that, in association with the tīpārātaṉai, induces possession in a mild form. That event occurs when Śiva and Viṣṇu, the great gods of Hindu mythology, combine to produce Śāstā; at his birth, the singing stops, but the worshiping and dancing continue.

But the long prelude to Śāstā's birth, the story of the demon Vallarakkaṉ, is equally important in the creation of the narrative world of birth stories. It sets the action within the frame of classical Hindu mythology, in Śiva's Kailāsa, and then introduces the myth of "The Churning of the Ocean," making Vallarakkaṉ's conflict with Śiva a multiform of the archetypal struggle between demons and gods. Vallarakkaṉ's own magical birth (from a woman impregnated by Viṣṇu's discus) belongs to that mythic world and sets up a sharp contrast to the protracted, painful deliveries in death stories. Most performances, including that given below, also incorporate episodes from the life of young Kṛṣṇa, whose play and mischief are at home in the world of birth stories. Some singers give a revealing twist to the incident in which Kṛṣṇa's foster mother looks inside his mouth to determine if he has eaten dirt: ". . . and when she looked inside," the bow singers comment, "she saw the whole world, but first . . . first she saw the bow!"

Within this mythic world, performances of the Vallarakkaṉ story are generally lighthearted. Except for the invocation and the final five minutes when Śāstā is born, there is little that one could call pious or devotional. Much of the humor arises from the central character of Vallarakkaṉ, the "Mighty Demon." Vallarakkaṉ is the epitome of the ambiguous Hindu demon, the "demon devotee" (O'Flaherty 1976), who is also a comic demon—heroic, but foolish. He is the good boy who obeys his mother, studies well, marries, and is finally crowned raja of Pātāḷam (the demon underworld). Power, however, goes to his head and the dutiful son becomes a ruthless tyrant overtaxing his subjects; yet he is not sinister either because Vallarakkaṉ is a devotee of Śiva. When his tributaries turn against him, Vallarakkaṉ, alone and defenseless, turns to Śiva. His motive—to keep the kingdom he has disgraced by his injustices—may be questioned, but no one in the audience can doubt his sincerity when they hear the demon singing the names of Śiva while hanging upside down for twelve years from the tip of a gleaming sword.

Eventually the demon wins an unusual boon from Śiva—to destroy anyone by pointing his thumb at him—but is then undone by his own foolishness. With the boon, Vallarakkaṉ marches toward Pātāḷam when he is stopped by the sage Nārada, who convinces him that Śiva has given him a false boon. Either way, the demon has been fooled: by Śiva, if the boon is false; or by Nārada, if it is genuine. Vallarakkaṉ is duped once more in the final scene when he is tricked into destroying himself with the (not so false) boon. In Vallarakkaṉ, the bow song has its antihero, a demon who is more comic than wicked.

Lord Śiva is no less foolish and humorous than the demon with whom he is paired. When he gives away the boon that could bring his own destruction, or stumbles over the other gods fleeing Kailāsa, or crawls out from a garden to ask Viṣṇu for help, he is hardly awesome. Even the serious description of Gaṇeśa in the second verse of the invocation is parodied later on (pp. 67–68) when the portly god has difficulty moving to avoid danger. Comedy reaches a high point in the exchange (pp. 83ff.) between Mōhiṉi and the eager demon. Here, and at many other points in this performance, the lead singer and the pot player produce a repartee that more than anything else reflects the light atmosphere of the birth stories in performance. The song texts are fixed, but in the extended speech segments the singers enjoy the latitude to entertain.

Yet, behind all the laughter there is sometimes heard another voice. The description of Vallarakkaṉ's unjust taxes (on home, animals, trees) and the famine they produce are spoken and sung in a tight, harsh tone that sets out each detail like a black and white photograph. Later, when Vallarakkaṉ travels to Yama's hells, the sins listed are instructive: cheating when selling grain, underpaying washermen, midwives, and healers (nowhere is caste purity an issue); and when these examples of economic exploitation were listed, one singer turned to another and said (inaudibly to the audience), "Yeah, and they get so little anyway." Such statements are enough to remind us that the birth stories with their mythic-comic tone are nevertheless part of a folk tradition whose singers and audiences are not unfamiliar with poverty and hardship.

The particular performance translated here was sung in February 1978, in the village of Kuṇṭal only three miles from Kanya Kumari (see Map 2). The main, "village" temple is dedicated to the birth goddess Muttār Ammaṉ, but this performance was sung in a festival held at a smaller temple to the deified heroes, the Palavēcam Brothers (see Appendix). Inside the Brothers' temple, are three pītam icons: one for each of the brothers, and one for their mother who died with them. Outside, to the right, are nine slightly raised dirt mounds (about four inches high) marked with white lime powder as the sites where minor deities are fed pūjā. To the left of the entrance stands a temporary shrine (like a tower) made of banana fronds as a resting place for Viṣṇu (Perumāḷ) during the festival. Next to this is another temporary shrine to Śāstā.

The festival itself differed from others in that it was not a three-day annual koṭai, but a one-day *ciṟappu* ("special") financed by a single family in fulfillment of a vow. For this reason, the ceremonies began early in the morning, about seven o'clock, when a local priest (a Nadar), conducted pūjā to each of the many deities, first in the large Muttār Ammaṉ temple and then at the smaller Brothers' temple. At ten o'clock the scene shifted to the patron's house where the same priest blessed the house and family, the swords of the Brothers, and finally the two goats to be sacrificed late that night. During these rituals, the Brothers' mediums went into mild possession and began to dance and, still dancing, led the group back along the one-mile walk to the temple.

The first public ritual at the Brothers' temple was the performance of the Vallarakkaṉ story. By noon the performers, who participated in none of the preceding rites, had assembled on the wooden benches covered with cloth that functioned as their performing stage. The group, all local Nadars, was led by Pūṅkāṉi, one of the most talented singers in Nāñcil Nāṭu, assisted by her aṇṇāvi (her husband) and the standard set of instrumentalists. In particular, she is one of the few singers to master the recitative style: beginning in formal speech, she would slowly raise her pitch and then, as the instrumentation grew louder, shift to a deep-throated, aspirated voice, pulling out the phrases one-by-one before finally breaking into full song.

The audience of about one hundred villagers sat, like all bow song audiences, on the ground in front of the performers' platform. Men and women were present in equal numbers, and in all ages; most were Nadars, a few Untouchables stood at the back. Outside the immediate temple area, more people milled around the temporary stalls that sell tea, coffee, and sweets, while small knots of men gambled with cards. On the stage, the performers were ready. The bow had been blessed; the short ritual to Gaṇeśa had ended. First the drummer played the traditional solo to draw attention to the stage, and then the lead, in her slow and deliberate voice, intoned the invocation.

Performance Translation

Vināyaka! I honor you,
hold you in my heart.
God of elephant face and single tusk,
broad chest and round stomach,
small eyes and sacred thread,
at your feet I worship.
Come to me, Gaṇapati,
come rest upon my tongue!

Blessed by the five-handed god,
the god with six faces,
the god of six letters,
who fills the eight directions,[4]
I place upon my head
the feet of my kind parents.

Come circling, come dancing![5]
come Bhadrakāḷi and Durga,
come Māri, Cauntri, Gauri,
Come stand as guardians of the north.
Come Icakki,
come Ayyaṉ of the mountain,
come with your armies,
Come stand as guardians of the south.

Come Vaṉṉiyaṉ, come Tampi,
come Vairavaṉ and Yama,
come now Cuṭalai Māṭaṉ.
Come stand as guardians of the east.

Come sky-borne vātai,
come vātai who pierce the chest
and rip out the heart.
Come stand as guardians of the west.
And let Kantaṉ at Tiruccentūr
be our refuge!
Protect me, Gaṇapati,
protect as I sing
this story of Ayyaṉ's birth.

Gaṇapati, older brother to Centi,
protect me as I sing
in correct Tamil
this story of great Śāstā,
son of Hari and Hara.

Protect me as I sing
of the demon
who won a boon from Lord Śiva;
Of Śiva,
who ran from his own boon,
and begged Māyaṉ for help;
And of Māyaṉ
who became Mōhiṉi
to destroy the demon.
Protect me, Gaṇapati,
as I sing of Ayyaṉ's birth.

In golden, imperishable Kailāsa
sages and saints sang to Śiva.
Nandi played drums, Nārada the vina,
oil lamps burned brightly
as sweet incense filled the air.
Gaṇeśa blew the conch,
Murukaṉ played the cymbals,
singing of Vaḷḷi and Teyvayāṉai.
Showered with flower blossoms,
praised in song
by gods and saints,
Śiva sat in state.

The Omnipotent, the All-Being, the Eminent Teacher, the Omniscient, the Imperishable, the Eternal, Mahādeva, Lord Śiva and the Goddess Pārvati . . .[6]

– Well . . . what about them?

They were ruling in Mt. Kailāsa, surrounded by the 33,000 gods and sages. And . . .

With Śiva and Pārvati in Kailāsa,
the gods and demons
churned the milky ocean.
They churned and churned together
'til the ambrosia flew up
and the demons stole it away!

Using the ocean as a huge vat, Mt. Mahendra as the staff, the snake Vāsuki as a rope, and the moon as a pillar, the gods and the demons churned the ocean. The gods took one end of the rope and the demons the other, and they pulled it back and forth. But when the ambrosia came up, those devilish demons ran away with it all!

- Wait a minute! They churned together, right? Then how come the demons got the ambrosia? What happened to the gods?
- Well, the gods didn't get it, that's all.
- You see, the demons had grabbed the head of the snake; that's why they got it.
- Right. And who grabbed the tail end? The gods. They're gentle folks . . . like us.

But the gods wanted to get the ambrosia back, so they went to Kaṇṇaṉ [Viṣṇu] and pleaded their case:

"Oh, Great-Soul! Endless One! World Savior! Lord of Vaikuṇṭa! Great God who took pity on the Pāṇḍavas, divided the land, and gave it to them—we ask that you get back the ambrosia the demons stole and divide it among us!"

Kaṇṇaṉ acceded to their request, and he took a special form,

Becoming lovely Mōhiṉi,
  Kaṇṇaṉ hurried to the demons,
Bewitched them with his beauty
  and won the ambrosia back.
The demons stood and watched,
  as he gave it to the gods.
And when the demons attacked,
  Kaṇṇaṉ let fly his arrows,
Driving them back
  back to their world of Pātāḷam!

Taking pity on the gods, Kaṇṇaṉ became that lovely Mōhiṉi and went to the demons; he looked first at them and then at the gods and said,

"Tell me, what's the cause of this conflict?"

"Well, it's really nothing at all . . . we just had a little disagreement. We both churned the ocean for ambrosia. When it came up, the gods said it was theirs, and we said it was ours. And we took it. That's all."

"In that case, demons, give that ambrosia to *me!*"

Receiving the ambrosia, Kaṇṇaṉ said,

"Demons, you sit in a line over there, and gods, you sit in a line right here."

"All right, we'll do as you say."

Kaṇṇaṉ sat them down and then served the ambrosia. He went down the gods' line first, and when their line was finished, so was the ambrosia! Suddenly that half-real Mōhiṉi herself had vanished! The demons looked at themselves and said,

> "Tricked again! That woman came, took the ambrosia right out of our hands, and gave it to the gods!"

In retaliation the demons turned against Kaṇṇaṉ, but the god took out his powerful discus and flung it on them all. Wham! Some demons died, some lost a limb, and the rest were driven back into Pātāḷam. And then . . .

> Driven by Kaṇṇaṉ's dark discus,
> the demons lay defeated in Pātāḷam
> Until one of their women gave birth
> to the heroic Vallarakkaṉ!

After the demons were driven back to Pātāḷam, something important happened.

– What's that?

A demon named Cakaṭaṉ married a woman Cātmiki; she was childless for a long time, but did tapas to Brahmā and gave birth to a beautiful boy.

– Just look at that! Do tapas [bodily austerities] and you get a child!
– That's what everyone says.

They cut the umbilical cord and shouted the kuravai, and then the mother named her son. He was born with great strength, so she named him Vallarakkaṉ, the "Mighty Demon." Placing him in a golden cradle, she sang a lullaby,

> Oh, my jewel,
> jewel of my eye!
> My sweet Kaṇṇaṉ, oh . . .
> close your eyes, my little one.
> Oh, my jewel,
> my precious one!
> My little son, oh . . .
> close your eyes, my little one.

Vallarakkaṉ's mother sang to him and pampered him in every way so that, day by day, month by month, he grew bigger and bigger. Until . . .

– What?

Until he reached the age of five years, when his mother looked at him and said,

> "Go to school,
> study, well, my son.

You'll find all types there,
so don't make enemies!
Learn horsemanship, elephant riding,
mathematics and the arts,
Study well, my son,
and come back to me."

Obeying his mother's words, Vallarakkaṉ went off to school, setting out early in the morning, just as his mother had asked.

"Now listen here, son! You're a full five years. Go and study well and get an education. Off with you now."

"You mean 'school,' Mom? No problem. You send me and I'll do it."

– And what did he learn?

The three ancient books,[7] the four Vedas, the six *śāstras*, eighteen *purānas*, thirty-two *dharmas*, sixty-six literatures, ninety-six philosophies, and the eighteen languages in Manu's treatise. He learned all this.

– Wow! He's some kid!

He learned horsemanship, elephant riding, swordsmanship and archery, right hand, left hand . . .

– Right hand? Left hand? What's that?
– That's the art of wrestling.
– Oh, you mean he learned to "box."

He learned all the arts and then returned to Pātāḷam a famous man. But when the local rajas saw this, they got together and said to themselves,

"Vallarakkaṉ is more educated than us—this could be a problem."

"Yeah, he's even got a bunch of degrees."

"Well, I guess we should make him king."

"True. What else did we suffer this long for, if not for this guy who's going to be a good-for-nothing anyway?"

"Might as well get *something* for it."

When the rajas crowned Vallarakkaṉ king of Pātāḷam, he turned immediately to his parents and said,

"Mom?"

"Yes."

"I want to get married."

"Sure thing. Marriage is one thing you can't do without. Besides, you can't be the raja unless you're married."

Vallarakkaṉ's parents married him to a girl named Nēcamuṟṟāḷ, and then he was the ruler of Pātāḷam, but he was a particular kind of raja . . .

Over this wide world
  girdled by the sea,
Vallarakkaṉ ruled without *dharma*
  without justice at his hand.
Listen, friends,
  to this raja's ways.
Turning his back on charity
  providing no patronage,
He ruled this land
  in a reign of pride.

That's the sort of raja Vallarakkaṉ turned out to be; he put the fifty-six lands under his thumb and ran the whole world.[8]

– Fifty-six lands? What lands?

Aṅka and Araṇa, Avanti and Avatīram, Naṭai and Yavaṇa, Oṭṭi and Kar-aku, Kāliṅga and Kaṇṇaḍa, Kāci and Kāshmir, Ghandāra and Kuruhukhū-chira, Cāhum and Cāhavira, Cadama and Cindhi, Cōḻa and Viḷi, Iṭara and Ēvala, Macha and Malayalam—the demon ruled over all of them, and with an iron hand.

– Really? Every one of them, huh?

Not only that. He was cruel.

– How?

Taxes on your house,
  taxes on your labor,
Taxes on cattle,
  taxes on goats.
He levied taxes everywhere,
  plundered day and night,
Made alliance with the wicked
  and spent the treasury on himself.

And then the rains failed, and famine stalked the land. Even then that cruel-hearted Vallarakkaṉ . . .

– What did he do?

Although there was no rain for twelve years, he squeezed blood from the people.

– Terrible! What happened?

Do you know what happens when there's no rain for twelve full years?

– Horrible hunger, I guess . . .

A famine that breaks your plates
and takes away your wife,
A famine that empties your bowls
and takes away your children,
A famine that smashes your cups
and takes away your husband.

That's what that cruel Vallarakkaṉ did when he was raja.

– A truly outstanding citizen!

He taxed your house, and he taxed you if you worked.

– What else?

He taxed your cattle and your goats . . .

– He can go to hell!

And that's not all!

– What else?

The heinous crimes of lying, stealing, murder, drinking liquor, and abusing one's guru—he didn't punish any of them! But, instead, he tried to take the women of his underling rajas.

– Oh, a womanizer!

– Then he'll get his! Shouldn't go after another man's wife.

Now when the local rajas realized this, they vowed to kill him. They raised an army against him and marched on the palace; Vallarakkaṉ saw them coming and was gripped by fear . . .

All the fears he dared not fear
filled his mind.
"I'm alone
there's no one;
No older brother,
no younger brother,
No friends,
no one by my side.
No one to help me!"

All alone and afraid, the demon raja thought,

"Those rajas are coming for me, and there's no one to support me! If I fight them, who will help?"

– There's no one; you're all by yourself, Raja.

"If I fight them, I won't come out alive . . ."

In the midst of his fear, the demon suddenly got an idea,

– What was that?

He remembered him whose generosity supports the whole world—Lord Śiva.

"If I do tapas to Śiva, then . . . maybe I can handle these rajas."

– Right. That's his only way out now. Otherwise, he's through!

And so Vallarakkaṉ, with Śiva on his mind, left Pātāḷam and went to the wilderness, a place unseen by man, and there he began his tapas.

The demon began his tapas
  to win a boon from Śiva.
He cleared the ground,
  and planted a pole
  sixty feet tall.
He prepared for a tapas so fierce,
  even the *ṛṣis* would shake!
To gain a boon,
  he worshiped the Great Lord Śiva.

First he made a mud altar with six corners, and on top of that,

– What?

He set up a tall pole,

– And on top of that?

He balanced a pot,

– And on the pot?

He put a coconut,

– And on that?

He placed a cool lemon,

– And on the lemon?

He put jasmine flowers,

– And on the jasmine?

On top of the jasmine, flashing like lightning . . .

– Yes . . .

With all that brilliance . . .

Fixing a long needle,
  sharp as a lightning bolt,
He kindled a sacrificial fire,
  flaming high like a mountain!
He worshiped Śiva for a boon
  to conquer the enemy rajas.
To rule the world again,
  he built a fire
  flaming high like a mountain!

The demon Vallarakkaṉ put a needle on top of everything, inhaled the five-letter *mantra* inside himself, and blocked any outflow of breath. On top of the needle, he put his gleaming, sharp sword, and with fire raging around him, he sat on the sword and did his tapas. Then, surpassing even the tapas of Arjuna, who won a magical weapon from Śiva in the *Mahābhārata,* this demon hung upside down and sang the names of Śiva!

Śambō! Śaṅkarā!
  Gaṇa Nāthā!
  Śambō! Sadāśivā!
    Kailāsa Nāthā!
King of heaven, king of earth!
  Lord of Umā!
  Śambō! Sadāśivā!
  Lord of Kailāsa!
Aruṇā! Ātipūrṇā!
  Śambō! Śaṇkarā!

"Oh, Śiva! Śaṅkarā! Śambō! Taṇḍavā! Mahādevā! Lord of Kailāsa! Bearer of the axe and deer! Parā! Śekarā! Harā! Nirmalā! Kaṟaikaṇṭaṉ! Lord of the 33,000 *ṛṣi*s! Śiva, give me a boon so I can conquer my enemies."

– What a tapas! Śiva will have to give him a boon for sure!

– Right! That demon turned himself upside down, a very difficult tapas!

And who felt the hot fire of his tapas? None other than that Lord of Kailāsa, Śiva himself. When the heat became intense, he turned to his minister Nandi and said,

"Down in the forest
  in fiery tapas sits a demon
  who may turn against us.
Go, Nandi,
  go quickly,
  bring the ascetic demon here."
Loyal Nandi rose to leave,
  but stood at Kailāsa's gate,
  his mind troubled with doubts.

"Now listen, Nandi. There's a devotee down there who's begun a difficult tapas in my name. But the fire from his tapas is more than I can bear. I can't stand it any longer."

"What do you mean? What can I do?"

"Go and bring him here."

At Śiva's command, Nandi the bull, prepared to go, but stopped:

"If I go down there like this, it could be a problem. Those humans won't know who I am; they'll probably think I'm just an old bullock and throw stones at me."

"That's the least of it! I'll probably meet lots of sages on the way, and they'll want to talk my ear off. I'll never get on with Śiva's business. I've got to change this bullock-face of mine."

With just a little magic
  Nandi changed
  from a bullock into an ascetic.
Blowing a conch,
  beads around his neck,
  Nandi traveled as a mendicant.

Changing his bullock-face and dressing like a perfect *sādhu,* Nandi crossed over forests and rivers and came to the isolated spot where Vallarakkaṉ was in tapas. The demon was lost in meditation on top of his platform, but Nandi called up to him.

"O Pious One, the seven worlds have yet to see such a tapas as yours! In appreciation the Lord of Kailāsa has sent for you. Please come with me; climb down from your pole."

"Who are you? Making a lot of noise and telling me to stop my tapas! Some kind of ascetic are you, huh? Or are you some god of this forest? Or maybe some ghost? Or worse! Identify yourself!"

"I'm from Kailāsa."

"From Kailāsa?"

"Yes, and my name is Nandi."

"Now how can I believe that?"

– Yeah, Nandi has a bullock-face, but you don't!

"All right, demon! Take a look now!"

Then in a flash, Nandi changed back to his old form with a bullock-face, and Vallarakkaṉ was repentant:

"Swami, forgive my indiscretion. Let's go to Kailāsa."

Off to Mt. Kailāsa,
  the demon rode on Nandi's back.
Over mountains and forests,
  they traveled far away,
Crossing a river of fire
  and on to the other side,
They entered the worlds of the gods,
  the fabulous lands,
Where the demon saw Brahmā's world,
  and his body trembled with awe.

As Nandi and Vallarakkan̲ rode toward Kailāsa, they came to an unusual bridge, suspended by human hair over a river of fire; and no one from the human world could cross over it. But because of his devotion and because Śiva's messenger, Nandi, was with him, Vallarakkan̲ crossed it! They entered Brahmā's world, and then Yama's realm where they saw the strangest things:

On all four sides
  flames rose up like mountains,
In the middle
  on a tall, tall pole,
On top of a high platform
  sat Yama Raja.
Over his head,
  suspended by hair,
  a giant mountain hung.

What a scene they saw in Yama's realm—in the middle of the huge fire was a steel pole supporting a platform, and sitting on top of it all was Yama Raja, Lord of the Dead!

– What's this mountain tied up by hair above his head?

Well, you see, Yama is also known as Caman̲, the "Even One." Long ago he was given a curse that if he did not rule justly, the mountain would fall on his head and drive him into the fire pit. That's why he's sitting there with a mountain over him.

– Well said!

Of course, Yama had all the dead people from earth up there, too.

– What did he do with them?

Those who cheated when selling grain
  hung from sharp hooks in their legs,
Those who adulterated rice paddy
  lay crushed under huge rocks,
Those who abused their parents
  crawled in a deep black pit.

That's what happens if you don't give enough wages to teachers, to healers, to midwives, or to washermen . . .

– And they get *so* little anyway!

People who had cheated them hung from hooks and were left to swing like monkeys; those who had mixed good rice paddy with rotten paddy were put under heavy rocks; and those who had committed sins against their parents or against women were put in a dark hole.

– What Yama did for those crimes is fine . . . but what about someone who says he will come and then doesn't show up?[9]

– Oh them! They'll get theirs in the end.

Having seen all this in Yama's realm, Vallarakkaṉ continued on toward Kailāsa.

On to Mt. Kailāsa
to Lord Śiva,
bearing the axe and deer.
As Nandi hurried along,
the demon looked up
at the splendor of the Lord.

When Nandi and Vallarakkaṉ crossed all that difficult terrain and reached Kailāsa, the demon finally got a good look. And he was stunned,

"How beautiful! It's incredible!"

– Blinding, isn't it?

Of course, no one can ever describe the beauty of Kailāsa, but do you know what it looks like?

– No, what?

A vast palace ceiling
covered with gold paintings,
stretching out of sight.
On a jeweled ceiling
parrots and peacocks drink honey
and play under a lustrous moon.
Halls sculpted in marble and gold,
fashioned by hand,
the hand of Lord Brahmā.
Kailāsa was golden and jeweled,
dizzying to the eye
and dazzling to the mind.

Mt. Kailāsa was just like that—gold and silver towers ringed the outside, and inside the gods and goddesses played. There was Nārada the sage, powerful

Brahmā, Sarasvati, Bhumi Dēvi, Vināyaka, Āṟumukam, Devendiraṉ, and all the goddesses . . .

– What were they doing?

They played little drums
  and chimed brass cymbals,
While long flutes sang,
  and young women danced.
Garlands and incense
  filled every room,
And led to the royal chambers,
  where Lord Śiva sat in state.

All the instruments were playing—the small waist drum, the barrel drum, flutes, the *kiṭupiṭi* . . .

– *Kiṭupiṭi?* What's that?

– That's a type of mēḷam.

– A mēḷam, is it? Anything else playing up there?

– Well . . . there was another type of mēḷam. You know, the one that plays with us sometimes . . .

– Oh, that one . . . the "mess-up mēḷam"?

All those thirty-two instruments were making music in Kailāsa . . .

– Gosh, and all we've got is this little bitty mēḷam.

– Yeah, it just makes a lot of noise . . .[10]

In that shining palace in Kailāsa, Śiva sat majestically on his golden throne, his body radiant, his chest covered with *rudrakṣa* beads. Then . . .

Entering the palace,
  Vallarakkaṉ went to the feet of Śiva,
  consort of Umā.
As if melted by fire,
  his heart began to soften
  his body lost its strength.
He bowed to Śiva
  and laid flowers at his feet,
  devotion flooding his heart.
Lord Śiva looked down,
  saw the demon,
  and spoke.

When, finally, that demon saw Śiva in Kailāsa, he was overwhelmed. He danced, he sang, and he held his hands above his head in deference to the god. Then Śiva said to him,

"Devotee! Come here. Tell me. Why have you undertaken this difficult tapas?"

"Well . . . that's just it, Śiva. I really concentrated on my meditation in Pātāḷam."

"But what for?"

"It's like this . . . I was minding my own business when, out of jealousy, the fifty-six rajas took up an army against me. So, I decided to do this tapas in your name, in the hope that you might offer me a small boon. Just a little tiny boon."

"And what boon is that?"

"I want a boon so I can destroy anyone by pointing my thumb at them. That boon."

"You want *that* boon? What about something else?"

"No. Only that. Listen, Śiva, I want it *now*—a boon so that I can point my thumb at someone and knock their head off."

"Well . . . alright. But listen carefully: 'In the wide world known as earth, let your body be reduced to ashes.' That's it. You've got the boon you asked for."

"Really? How?"

"You asked for it, and now I've given it."

"But how? How did you give it to me?"

"Just like that. You ask and I give. Now beat it!"

When Śiva said he had given the boon, the demon simply accepted his word. But one doubt remained:

"Śiva, this boon you've given me. Will it really work?"

"Of course."

"Alright, I'll return to earth now."

"Good. But there's one final thing I want to say to you. Don't act like such a despot anymore. Be fair, because only then will the boon work."

"I'll be very careful, Śiva."

And so the demon took his boon, left Kailāsa, and headed toward earth. On his journey he met Nārada, who came up to him and spoke:

"Tell me, demon, where are you coming from?"

"I'm glad someone asked me that. I'm coming from Kailāsa."

"From Kailāsa? What for?"

"I did this fantastic tapas and then got a nice boon from Śiva up there."

"A boon? From Śiva? Well, well, let's have a look at this boon of yours."

"What do you mean? 'See the boon?' I've got the boon, that's all."

"Sure, sure, demon. But *where* is it?"

"Well . . . Śiva gave it to me. I heard him say so."

"That's *all* he did?"

"Well, he did say some funny-sounding words, but at the end, he said he gave it to me. Then I left."

"Poor fool! You believed that?"

"Why not? Hey, are you saying Śiva lied to me?"

"Well, you know the saying: 'Does a gourd drawn on palm-leaf make a curry?' Well, does it?" [11]

"No."

"It's the same thing with your boon. If he only *said* he gave it, then it's in his mouth, that's all."

"In his mouth? You're telling me my boon is in Śiva's mouth?"

"Right. He didn't put it in your hand, did he?"

"Gee, maybe you're right. It's true he didn't give me anything. He just said he gave it, and I left. He didn't put anything in my hand, or in my lap, or on my legs, or on my head. Not a thing! Hmmmm . . . now suppose I go to Pātāḷam and test out the boon and it doesn't work? What then?"

– You can always make it into chutney! [12]

"Nārada, are you saying that Lord Śiva gave me a false boon?"

"That's what I'm saying."

"No fooling?"

"No fooling. He gave you a false boon."

When the meaning of Nārada's words sunk in, the demon let out an angry yell:

"Giver of false boons!
  that rotten Paramaśiva!
I'll chase that wily god
  and drive him from Kailāsa
  drive him off that mountain,
He'll not sit there anymore."

"I'll find him somehow, that Śiva. Gave me a false boon, did he!"

As Vallarakkaṉ ran back to Kailāsa, he had all sorts of thoughts:

"If I can kill Śiva,
  if I get rid of that god,
  Kailāsa will be all mine!

If I can slay Śiva,
  if I can make him flee,
  I'll rule the whole world!
If I can kill Śiva,
  and chase him away,
  Pārvati will be mine!
And the Primordial One,
  the first son Gaṇeśa,
  will call me father
As the illustrious gods
  gather together
  to worship at my feet!"

But all this is nothing . . .

– Nothing?

Well, you see . . .

"He who rests on the vast ocean,
  the Dark One,
Viṣṇu will be my brother-in-law!"

With these thoughts running through his mind, Vallarakkaṉ raced toward Kailāsa to try out his boon on Śiva. He began to plan his strategy:

"Since he gave me the boon, I'll try it on him first. I'll point my thumb at him, and if his head doesn't fall off, I'll . . . I'll kill him somehow and rule Kailāsa myself."

– Good, that's the first thing to do.

"Now if the boon *does* work, and his head falls off . . . well, then Śiva can't do a thing to me."

– Right. We'll try it first. And if his head doesn't fall, we'll gobble him up anyway.

After listening to Nārada's clever words, Vallarakkaṉ sped toward Mt. Kailāsa . . .

– Where else could he go after what Nārada had said?

Listen everyone!
  Listen to what the demon did.
He ran after Lord Śiva
  to kill him with his boon,
Like a pet animal
  turning on its master.[13]

It was just like that. Suppose you had raised a goat with a lot of love, and then it suddenly turns and attacks you—that was like the demon going after Śiva.

Now when he got to Kailāsa, it was total chaos . . .

– What happened?

Everyone fled in confusion. The 33,000 gods, the *ṛṣi*s, Śiva and his family—they all started running at once. And since they didn't know where they were going, they fell on top of each other!

– What about Śiva's sons?
– You mean Murukaṉ. He's got that peacock for a mount and just flew off!
– And his older brother, Gaṇapati?
– Ah, him. He's got a problem.
– How's that?
– Well, have you seen his feet?
– They're club feet.
– And his stomach?
– Looks like a huge vat!
– His head?
– It's an elephant's head.
– What about his ears?
– They're like winnowing baskets.
– And what kind of a mount does he have?
– I don't know.
– It's just like the saying, "She married someone even worse than herself." [14] That is, what's the biggest rat among the rats?
– A mouse!
– No, stupid. A bandicoot! His mount is a bandicoot, and it can't go very far.
– It stops every five seconds to eat.

When Vallarakkaṉ got to the top of Mt. Kailāsa, everyone had run off. Since no one was in sight, he called out:

"Śiva!
  What kind of god are you?
You give me a false boon
  and then desert Kailāsa.
Śiva!
  What kind of god are you?
Run where you want,
  hide where you may,
  you'll not escape from me!"

Off ran the demon,
chasing Śiva through Kailāsa
like rabbits through a field.
They ran around,
one following the other
like bullocks around a grinding stone.

Vallarakkaṉ chased after Śiva, yelling at him,

"You *are* something! You give me a false boon, and now you flee your home! Run and run, but I'll get you in the end . . . Listen Śiva, as soon as I get my hands on you, I'll break you into little pieces. If you try to escape and change into fire or something, I'll follow as fire. Or if you change into wind, I will too and follow behind you."

With the demon chasing him, Śiva ran here and there looking for a place to hide. Suddenly he came to Nandavaṉam, and jumped in.

– What kind of a Nandavaṉam was it?

A garden
dense with flowers and trees,
buds, blossoms, and vines.
In the mornings the women came
and picked fresh flowers
for the gods.
They wove long, long garlands
and placed them in worship
at Lord Śiva's feet.

With Śiva hidden away in the garden, Vallarakkaṉ stopped. He was confused and a little sad and began to cry,

"Where have you gone, Śiva?
Where are you now?
Why have you left me
all by myself?
Did I do tapas
did I sing your names
Just to come here
and find you gone?
Where have you gone, Śiva?
Where are you now?"

With Śiva hiding under the flowers, Vallarakkaṉ searched frantically and cried even more painfully.

"Oh Śiva!
I am your slave!

For twelve long years
  I did tapas in your name.
Humbly I begged for a boon,
  yet you deceived me,
  and now you are gone!
Oh Śiva!
  Will I ever see you again?"

As Vallarakkaṉ wailed and wailed in misery, Śiva lay under the flowers. He was safe but trapped. But then came a thought:

Of Kaṇṇaṉ,
  who gobbled butter
  and dragged a mortar.
Of Achuytaṉ,
  who stole saris,
  and hid in a tree.
Of Gōpālaṉ,
  who danced with the Gōpis,
  and gave them love.[15]

Lord Śiva, the god whose mount is the bull, thought of his brother-in-law Kaṇṇaṉ.[16]

"In order to get rid of this demon, we need Kaṇṇaṉ. But where is he?"

– Good question. *Where* is he?

As the eighth incarnation of Viṣṇu, Kaṇṇaṉ was born to Devaki to kill wicked Kaṃsa and grew up . . .

In the fertile land of Ayarpāti
  in the house of Yaśodā,
  in the home of Nandakōṉār,
Kaṇṇaṉ grew as a young boy.

As he was growing up in the house of Yaśodā and Nandakōṉār, Kaṇṇaṉ was a real nuisance—he caused no end of trouble to the women in Ayarpāṭi. They churned milk, buttermilk, butter, and curds and put it aside. But he came and stole it all, grabbed it and gulped it down.

These women
  made milk and butter,
  buttermilk and curds.
But Kṛṣṇa
  made it disappear,
  stealing and swallowing it all!
That Kaṇṇaṉ took young girls,
  led them by the hand
  to play with him in the street.

Kṛṣṇa took everything that the women made—he drank the milk and buttermilk, and ate the curds and butter. His mischief didn't stop at that either!

– Yeah! His pranks were too much!

He played tricks on all the young women, and eventually they began to complain.

"Listen Yaśodā
to the tricks of your Gōpālaṉ,
born in our cowherd caste.
He's a rascal, that one;
comes and teases
and deceives us with his lies!
Acts like he's our own,
demands we give him butter,
and pulls our saris, too."

"Listen Yaśodā, your Kaṇṇaṉ is a real brat. He comes to our houses and steals everything we have—milk, curd, butter—everything."

"My son?"

"That's right! And what's more he won't let our girls alone. He grabs them in the street and wants to play with them!"

"What exactly does he do?"

"He grabs their saris and pulls, that's what."

"Now why would he do that?"

– Maybe he thought there was money tied up in the sari.

– Yeah, maybe he wanted to buy an ice cream.

"Listen Yaśodā, this has got to stop. We won't have it."

"What do you mean?"

"Your son comes and steals everything we have."

"Gōpis, I don't believe a word you say. Let's call Kaṇṇaṉ and see."

So Yaśodā called Kaṇṇaṉ and asked him, and he replied,

"They're no-good Gōpis, Mom,
they'll tell you anything.
Anyway,
even on tiptoe,
could I reach a milk pot?
They're no-good Gōpis,
they'll tell you anything.
don't believe them, Mom,
they're always slandering me.

Think about it—
in the dark,
could I find their butter?
They're no-good Gōpis, Mother!
they'll tell you anything.
Suppose I could,
suppose I found their milk,
why would I take it?
They're no-good Gōpis, Mom,
they'll tell you anything."

"Mother, don't listen to them, those stupid girls. You know me, Mom. I didn't do a thing. Really!"

"Yes, you are a good son, Kaṇṇaṉ. You don't take things from here, so why would you take from others?"

"Mom, do they say I steal in the night or in the day?"

"At night."

"But Mom, at night how could I possibly know where the milk or the curds or the butter is?"

"That's right. You wouldn't go there; you're my son, a good boy."

After this conversation with her son, Yaśodā turned on the Gōpis angrily,

"Women with no sons!
Mothers with your daughters!
Stop your jealous talk!
If Kaṇṇaṉ steals from you,
catch him by the hand,
and bring him here to me.
I'll tie him to a mortar
so he won't move again."

"You're all women without sons, aren't you? You have only daughters . . . But my child is a boy, so you're just jealous. Besides, most of you aren't even married, are you? You aren't supposed to see men during the day, yet you say that Kaṇṇaṉ comes at night. Just what are you doing at night?"

"We aren't doing anything except staying home."

"Well, I should hope so!"

"You want us to catch that Kṛṣṇa red-handed, is that it? Only if we bring him to you with the milk on him, you'll believe us?"

So the Gōpis went to their houses and stood guard through the night. Now when Kaṇṇaṉ went to steal, he was selective, and always went to his aunt Lakṣmi's house first.

– He goes there for a reason, too.

– Right . . . if he gets caught there, he has an excuse—he can just say, "Auntie, I came because your son asked me to play."

But his aunt Lakṣmi stayed awake all night and sure enough, she grabbed that Kaṇṇaṉ in the act. She held his hand firmly and dragged him to Yaśoda, who was furious and tied him to a heavy stone mortar with a rope. But Kaṇṇaṉ, dragging the mortar and killing off a couple of demons on the way, crawled over to his mother and said sulkily,

"Listen, Mom, you don't have to punish me anymore. I'm not going to let those Gōpis laugh at me like this; I'm leaving and going off to be a cowherd. Just give me a little food. I'm off."

Then Kaṇṇaṉ left Ayarpāṭi and went to graze cows,

He gathered up some cows,
  to make his own herd,
Took them over the river
  and grazed them on grass.
Herding them with a staff
  when the day is done,
Even if a tiger appears,
  Kaṇṇaṉ doesn't worry—
Relaxing on the grass,
  he plays his magic flute.

Kaṇṇaṉ became a cowherd, sitting all day under a tree and playing his flute. The music traveled through the air, and who do you think heard it?

– Probably Śiva, who had run from the demon and was hiding in Nandavaṉam. Probably he heard it.

Right, Śiva heard the sound of the flute and thought,

"Who could be playing that flute? I know who—only one person ever plays like that—Kaṇṇaṉ, my brother-in-law!"

Hearing the sound of the flute,
  Śiva came out of hiding.
His matted hair in tangles,
  staggering on a staff,
He stumbled up to Kaṇṇaṉ.

When Śiva heard the music and crawled out of his hiding place in Nandavaṉam, his hair was a mess, his whole body a fright! But he made his way toward Kṛṣṇa.

– Right. Wherever the sound of that flute is heard, there's always a crowd of odd-balls that goes after it.

Seeing Śiva in that state, Kaṇṇaṉ was confused; he couldn't understand what could have happened to his brother-in-law. Concerned, Kaṇṇaṉ took Śiva by the hand, sat him down and asked,

"Brother-in-law, Śiva!
  Why this frightful sight?
Your strong arms are limp,
  your perfect body dirty
  your holy brow bathed in sweat!
Brother-in-law, Śiva!
  Why this frightful sight?
Haven't you, great Śiva,
  been through this before?
Didn't you carry mud
  and then a beggar's bowl
  when you wandered alone?
Didn't your oldest son,
  didn't Gaṇeśa,
  ask to marry his mother?
And didn't the other one,
  didn't Vēlavar,
  take a Kuṟavar bride?" [17]

"Brother-in-law, you're a mess! Your body is streaked with sweat. What has happened? Where is Pārvati? You didn't leave Kailāsa alone, did you?"

"If you only knew the trouble I'm in you wouldn't pester me with those old stories about me being a beggar and my sons' escapades. You've got to help!"

"What's the problem?"

"Someone's after me."

"Who?"

"A demon came and asked me for a boon so that he could kill just by pointing his thumb at someone. Well, I gave him the boon, and now he's coming after *me!*"

"The same old story, huh, Śiva? You give boons to everyone, whatever they want. And then I have to come and save you. Well, I'm tired of this game. It's got to stop!"

Still, Kaṇṇaṉ felt sorry for his brother-in-law and once again agreed to help.

"Śiva, I am your servant. Tell me what has caused your distress, and I will remove it."

"How can I tell you, Kaṇṇaṉ?
even my tongue feels shy!

After twelve years of tapas,
  a demon asked for a boon,
The boon of the thumb,
  and I gave it away!"

"Kaṇṇaṉ, I've done it again! I've given another boon to one of my devotees. A demon proved himself through arduous tapas and asked for the special boon—the boon of destroying by pointing his thumb. And I gave it to him."

"Oh, you stick your thumb out at someone and then their head falls off? That boon?"

"Yes."

"Who asked for it?"

"A demon named Vallarakkaṉ."

"And then you gave it?"

"Yes. He asked and I gave it. But then . . ."

"Like a burst of thunder
  the demon came for me!
Threatening to test the boon,
  he charged Mt. Kailāsa.
The gods shook with fear,
  and ran to save their lives.
Everyone ran away,
  and left me all alone."

"Brother-in-law, it was terrible! That demon, I gave him the boon, and then he came to try it out on me . . ."

"What! The demon came after you?"

"Yes."

"So? Why did you run?"

"What are you saying? How could I stay there?"

"No one around to help, huh?"

"Yes . . . everyone had run off. Even your sister, my wife, Pārvati . . she left without even telling me! Vallarakkaṉ chased me out and finally I managed to jump into that flower garden over there. But now you must go after him and kill him."

"Why should I? This has happened so many times in the past—someone asks you for a crazy boon, you give it of course, and then in the end you ask me for help. This time I refuse!"

"But brother-in-law . . . please . . ."

"Go now, as Mōhiṉi,
go destroy that demon,
before he destroys me.
If you should refuse,
Pārvati will no longer
sit in Mt. Kailāsa;
You will not see me;
I'll run away
and never, never return."

"Kaṇṇaṉ! Please do this for me! Kill that demon! I just lost all my senses when he came after me."

"How come?"

"Fear. I was afraid. Now you've got to kill him; otherwise I can't stay in Kailāsa with your sister Pārvati any longer. I'll run away."

– Run off somewhere? Well, we can't let our poor brother-in-law do something like that. Even if a relative comes in the middle of the night, you've got to help.

Of course, secretly Kaṇṇaṉ was pleased at Śiva's troubles. He remembered a time when Śiva was sitting happily with Pārvati and made fun of him:

[In a coarse accent] "You know Pārvati, that brother of yours, Kaṇṇaṉ, he's something! Grazes cows and drinks that smelly gruel!"

Remembering this, Kaṇṇaṉ said to himself,

"When Pārvati came and told me what Śiva had said, I knew that, although I might have to wait, someday I would get even with him. And now, we've got him! Śiva's in trouble."

– Yeah, now we've got that Śiva right where we want him.

When Kaṇṇaṉ reminded him of his past insults, Śiva, too, remembered a conversation when Kaṇṇaṉ had insulted him. Trying to keep things even, he spoke to Kaṇṇaṉ,

"Kaṇṇaṉ, remember when you made fun of me just because I went around as a beggar and ate handouts? Anyway, why bring all that up now? Especially when I've got this serious problem."

"Alright. We'll let that be. However, there is one thing you must do for me if I am to go after the demon."

"What's that?"

"Will you tend my cows,
will you graze my herd?
If you do,
I'll destroy the demon.

If not, Śiva,
  I will not go."

"Śiva, you've got to do this for me. If you want me to take care of the demon, then you have to graze these cows."

"Graze cows? But I don't know how . . ."

"It's easy."

"What if I just let them wander around by themselves? Look, Kaṇṇaṉ. If I become a cowherd, what do you think they'll say about me in Kailāsa? They'll think I'm a nobody and laugh at me."

"Maybe. But then I don't go after the demon."

"Hmmm . . . that would be a problem."

"You've got to graze these cows, otherwise no deal."

"You're sure about that?"

"Definite!"

"You win, Kṛṣṇa. I'll look after your cows. Now you go kill that demon."

"Fine. But listen, brother-in-law, you can't graze cows dressed like that!"

"No? Then tell me what to do."

– Well, to be a really good cowherd, all you have to do is go off in the woods and play around.

– Right. That's all those kids ever do.

"In order to graze the cows . . .

You must dress like me
  like a cowherd boy,
Cut off your long hair
  shave off that beard!
Remove your mustache, Śiva,
  and your sacred thread!
Put down your royal umbrella
  wipe off your sacred ash!
Throw away your garlands
  and your fancy jewels!
Dress like me, Śiva,
  like a cowherd boy,
Then that demon
  won't even know you!"

"Śiva, you have to become a cowherd like me."

"I'm ready. But first call a good doctor."

"What for?"

"If I have to take off my skull, I'll need some help. Probably have to break it first."

"Not your *head,* stupid. It's your *hair* that has to be cut."

"Oh, a haircut! No problem."

– That's funny—I thought he was keeping all that hair to burn at his father's funeral, and that's why he never cut it.[18]

"Listen Śiva. There's more than just cutting off your hair."

"What else?"

"Shave your beard."

"Done. What else?"

"Remove your mustache."

"OK. What else?"

"Hide your royal umbrella."

"Hide it? Alright. What next?"

"Throw your beggar's bag into the river."

"My beggar's bag in the river? Nothing doing. I'll put it somewhere else."

So Kaṇṇaṉ changed Śiva into a cowherd by making him throw away all his high-class things; when Śiva had done all this, Kaṇṇaṉ looked at him and said,

"Good! You're a perfect cowherd now. You look after these cows, and I'll take care of that demon. I won't be long."

With these words, Kaṇṇaṉ left. In order to kill Vallarakkaṉ,

Primordial Viṣṇu,
  the Dark One,
Took his Mōhiṉi form
  as a lovely woman.

Kaṇṇaṉ walked a little distance from Śiva and then changed himself into that beautiful Mōhiṉi.

That cloud-colored god,
  the son of Kausalyā,
  changed his bodily form.
The Imperishable One
  astonished even the gods
  as mysterious Mōhiṉi.

When Kaṇṇaṉ changed to a woman so he could kill the demon, he looked lovely. He had hair like dark clouds, a head shining like a mirror, a forehead like a three-day moon, eyes like the *keṇṭai* fish, a nose like a young flower, a mouth like a night flower, a row of teeth like newly budded jasmine, a face like the moon, a neck like an areca nut tree, shoulders like bamboo, elbows like a lute, nails like a parrot's beak . . .

– Nails like a parrot's beak?

– That's right.

– Good god!

. . . breasts like lotuses, a waist that you could hold in your hand, a navel like the center of a whirlpool, thighs like banana sheaths, legs like prawns, and feet like a turtle's shell. Kaṇṇaṉ changed into a woman with all these thirty-two marks of beauty.[19]

– Without them, how could he overcome the demon?

And that's not all. Listen to the ornaments he put on . . .

Anklets and toe rings
  and bells on her feet,
Necklaces and pendants
  and rings on her hands;
    to see
    her ornaments of gold
    one needs a thousand eyes!
Seeing her walk,
  one stood still and stared;
Hearing her step
  one grew faint at heart;
    to see
    her ornaments of gold,
    one needs a thousand eyes!
Silk saris from Kāsi
  bordered with golden threads,
Coral beads and gold chains,
  jewel bracelets on her arms.
Diamond rings on her hands,
  a fan-shaped pin in her nose,
Gold pins and emerald rings
  flashed upon her nose!
In her hands
  she held a fan;
She was Sītā and Lakṣmi,
  Rādhā and Rukmiṇi!
She sang as she walked
  and swung her arms,
She held her head up high
  and looked from side to side.

Do you know the ornaments she wore? Jewel-encased rings on her toes, necklaces, *kaṭṭuvam, pīli, mayalaṭi, muntāṅki.*

- Why did she wear a *kuṭṭuvam* (pestle)?[20]
- It's the same one your mother wears!
- But why did she wear it?
- Wear what?
- The pestle.
- Stupid! It's a necklace (*kaṭṭuvam*), not a pestle (*kuṭṭuvam*)!
- Oh, an ornament! I thought she hung a pestle on her ear.

She wore anklets, toe rings, and a beautiful golden belt . . .

- Oh, a golden belt to keep that expensive sari from falling off.
- No, no. Not for that. She wore the belt to shrink her waist so it looks like an hour-glass drum.
- Then when the demon sees her, he'll fall flat on his face.
- Right. When a man sees a woman, he gets confused, you know.
- I see. When the demon sees her, he'll lose his senses.

Then, in her nose, on one side she had a tiny nose pin and in the other a fan-shaped pin, and in the center she wore one of those big nose pins they used to wear, a *pulākku.*

- A *pulākku?* I thought she would have worn a money pin.
- A money pin? You know how it would be to speak with that? The coins would come out with your words . . .
- Sounds like you've got ideas! What else did she put on?

Around her neck a necklace, a pendant on her forehead . . .

- Now why did she wrap a necklace around the pendant on her forehead?
- No, silly! The necklace and a forehead pendant are two *separate* things.
- Oh, that makes more sense.

Kaṇṇaṉ also wore a pearl necklace, a flower necklace, a "thunderbolt" necklace, a *mōkaram* necklace, a *tirukaṇṭa* necklace . . .

- *Tirukaṇṭa* necklace? What's that?
- A necklace worn by the gods, and seen only by the gods.
- I "see." You mean that we mortals can't "see" it, huh?

A moon necklace, a *talvaṭum,* a *nūvaram,* and *urkaṭṭu.* And there's one more important ornament that Kaṇṇaṉ wore . . .

A golden marriage *tāli*
  dangled from a chain.
A *poṭṭu* lit her forehead
  above her moon smooth face.
Dark lines marked her eyes,
  powders scented her hair.
Covered with garlands and jewels
  that sparkled as she walked,
Her anklets with nine gems
  jingled as she walked.

That special ornament she wore was a finely made gold *tāli,* a marriage pendant . . .

- You know why Kaṇṇaṉ wore it?
- Why?
- Well, if a woman goes without a *tāli,* no man will speak directly to her. But if she wears one, then everyone will say, "Morning, ma'am, how are you." That's why she wore a *tāli.*

As Mōhiṉi, Kaṇṇaṉ looked devastating! He put a shining *poṭṭu* on his forehead, powdered his hair, put strong-smelling jasmine in his hair. Then he rubbed his body with scents and oils, and off he went . . .

As beautiful Mōhiṉi
  Kaṇṇaṉ went to kill the demon,
Strutting through the trees
  freely swinging her arms,
While sages and gods looked on,
  dazzled by her beauty
  and overcome with desire.

When she was walking alone like that in the forest, swinging her arms, the gods looked at her and said,

"Wow! Is she Urvaśi? Meṉaki? Dēvarambai? She is lovely!"

- Or maybe she's a *picācu?*
- *Picācu?* But then her feet wouldn't touch the ground.
- Well, that's what they say, but who knows?

She walked there, thinking to seduce the demon who had chased Śiva into the forest. As she walked briskly, her anklets resounding in the air, who do you think heard the sound?

- Must have been the demon who chased Śiva. He was waiting for something to happen!

– Sure. When Mōhiṉi lifted her feet and placed them on the ground, and the bells rang, I'll bet the demon heard the noise.

And what did he do when he heard it?

Like a thief
 after a treasure of gold,
He leapt over tree and bush
 and flew straight toward her.

He ran in the direction of the sound and looked. From a distance, he saw her . . .

Walking alone,
 confidently,
 like a woman without her man,
Lovely Mōhiṉi
 strolled along the river bank
 and stood under a banyan tree.

When the demon saw Mōhiṉi, she was walking like a woman who had fought with her husband.

– Oh, she was angry, huh?

She looked like she might even kill herself. With her hair disheveled, she came to the river bank and stood under the vines of a banyan tree. When the demon saw her, he thought,

"Is she a woman or a pēy? Well, whatever she is, let's go have a closer look. Even if it's only the vines, so what? After all, this is a forest!"

From a distance
 you might compare her to the sun,
 but even the sun is eclipsed.
Or you might think
 she looks like the moon,
 but it has dark spots too.
Pick up a perfect pearl,
 study it in your hand,
 you'll see a blemish or two.
A pomegranate
 is a beautiful fruit,
 but inside its seeds are dark.
Even a lime
 may have a flaw
 inside its cool green skin.
Though running water
 is often clear,
 it has at least one dirty drop.

The dancing snake
  is magnificent,
  but its underbelly is black.
Yet she,
  like a form
  molded in the blacksmith's forge
  or fired in the potter's kiln,
Like pure gold
  melted in the goldsmith's fire,
She is perfection itself!

Vallarakkaṉ looked at Mōhiṉi with amazement,

"Wow! Her beauty makes your eyes pop out! But she seems a little angry. Maybe she's had a fight with her husband or maybe she just doesn't like men. Anyway, we can at least say 'hello.' What's the harm in that?"

– Right. We'll just saunter over and be friendly.

– Because if we aren't polite, she might knock out our teeth!

– So, at first we'll do it slowly and carefully.

– Exactly, when a man talks to a woman, you do need a little propriety.

A little afraid, and very interested, Vallarakkaṉ walked over to Mōhiṉi and began talking,

"Excuse me, miss . . . but . . ."
Tell me, miss,
  where are you from?
  what is your name?
Please tell me
  who is your father?
  what's your mother's name?
And in this dark forest,
  why do you walk alone?
Please tell me, miss,
  are you married?
  or are you not?"

"Miss, tell me, if you would, what you are doing all alone in this place. There are lions, tigers, and bears here. It's dangerous."

"So what?"

"You're a woman, so why are you alone? In any case, tell me where you're from."

"I'm from Ayarpāṭi."

"What's your father's name?"

"Nandakōṉār."

"Mother's name?"

"What's it to you?"

"Nothing. Just tell me this one thing, and I'll go."

"My mother's name is Yaśodā."

"What's your name?"

"I've got to tell you *my* name? All right. I'm Krishnamati."

"Krishnamati . . . a good name."

"Are you married?"

"Something wrong with your eyes?"

"Oh, yes. You're wearing a marriage *tāli*. Now what's your husband's name?"

"Stupid! Who ever says her husband's name?"[21]

"Well, the two of us are alone in this forest . . ."

"So what?"

"Just say his name."

"And if I don't?"

"Well. . ."

"Alright. Shall I tell you one letter?"

"Tell me just one."

"Va."

"Probably Vandakōṉār."

"No, his name is Varamakōṉār."

"A fine name! But why are you off alone in this forest? Let's see, how old is your husband?"

"Don't ask me that. Fate played a trick on me. He's ninety-seven."

"Ninety-seven? Hmmm . . . and how old are you?"

"I'm almost sixteen."

"Sixteen! That's the right age for sure. So, then, why are you here?"

"My mother-in-law is terrible! Day and night she's bitching at me. I can't take it anymore, and I'm going to my mother's place."

"I see. You fought with your husband, and so now you're going to your mother's. Wait a minute. He's ninety-seven and you're sixteen. What kind of marriage was that? Must have been arranged."

"What do you mean 'arranged'? You think an old man would say no if he got a young girl like me?"

– Right, and even if the old goat can't do anything else, he'll grab her hand and drag her off.

"So you're going off . . .?"

"In the mornings
I fight with my husband,
At noon
with my father-in-law,
In the evenings
it's my mother-in-law."

"It's awful! In the early morning I fight with my husband . . ."

"What about at noon?"

"Then it's my father-in-law."

"And in the evening?"

"That's my mother-in-law's turn."

"Tell me, why do you cause all these fights?"

– Sounds to me like all of them are a little crazy.

"With all that fighting, I decided I can no longer live in this illusory, impermanent, material world, so I came to this forest."

When Vallarakkaṉ heard this, he said,

"You came to this forest because of a fight? Then can I ask you something?"

"Sure, go ahead."

"Miss, if you come away with me . . ."

– Who *is* this guy?

". . . I'll marry you."

"You got a big house?"

"Oh, yes."

"How many rooms?"

"Seven rooms."

Suddenly Mōhiṉi stopped all this and said indignantly,

"Out of my way, demon! You are asking me to go off with you, but I'm on my way to my mother's house. Step aside! Wait a minute, demon. You're asking me to go off with you, but what about you? Are you married?"

"Yes, I'm married."

"What's her name?"

"Nēcamuṟṟāḷ."

"What a disgrace! You've already got a woman at home and you ask another to live with you! If I listen to you and go there, what'll she say?"

"What can she say?"

"She'll say, 'Do this, do that . . .'"

"So? What can I do about that?"

"You must take a vow that you will never talk to her and only talk to me."

"Fine. But how do we take this vow?"

"Shall we take a vow
  in the name of Śiva,
  who sits in Mt. Kailāsa?
Or make a vow
  in the name of Viṣṇu,
  who sleeps on the watery ocean?"

"Mōhiṉi, how shall we do this vow? We could do it in the name of Mahādeva, who supports all life on this earth, or . . ."

"No. That vow wouldn't work."

"Well, how about a vow to Vināyaka?"

"That won't work either. He's always off somewhere eating."

"What about a vow to Murukaṉ?"

"Never. He's got two wives himself, and this is a problem between two wives."

"So how are we going to do this vow?"

"We can do it right here ourselves. No need to go anywhere else,

To make this vow
  we won't move an inch,
Just point your thumb
  carefully at your head,
And when you touch your head,
  the vow will be made."
Confused by desires,
  forgetting his own boon,
  trusting the words of a woman,
In front of Mōhiṉi,
  the demon pointed his thumb
  directly at his head.
When he touched his head,
  it exploded
  and rolled into the sea!

And then . . .

The head of the wicked demon
  crashed into the sea.
As the serpent Śeṣa
  and the wind god Vāyu
  watched from a watery perch,
Vallarakkaṉ's body
  fell into the sea
  with a thunderous roar!
As if the world was ending
  the eight directions shook,
As all the fourteen worlds
  shattered and split,
Lord Viṣṇu stood above
  shooting a shower of arrows.

In the temple at Chidambaram,
  Kaṇṇaṉ changed his form
  to remove the demon's death.
Śiva cast off his disguise,
  put the moon into his hair
  and ash upon his forehead.
Kaṇṇaṉ went before Lord Śiva,
  held his hands in worship
  and stood in adoration.
And Śiva,
  with snakes in his hair,
  spoke these words to him,
"In what manner, Kaṇṇaṉ,
  did you kill the demon?"
Then Kaṇṇaṉ,
  the butter thief,
  spoke softly in reply,
"I destroyed the demon
  as you requested, Śiva,
  and now I have returned."
"Reveal to me," said Śiva,
  "that form in which you killed."

As Umā and the sages watched
  and goddesses gave the kuravai,
Under an auspicious asterism
  on the fourth day of Ciṅkam
  in the favorable week of Caṉi
  on the seventeenth day of Paṅkuṉi,

To rule this earth
  and its oceans,
  the powerful Aiyaṉār,
The great god Śāstā
  was born!

(Singing stops; tīpārātaṉai and possession dance continue.)

5

The Death of the Little Brothers

These are songs of sorrow,
songs stained with blood.[1]

Introduction

The story of the Tampimār ("Little Brothers") differs from the story of Vallarakkaṉ and Śāstā in every possible respect. It is local history, not mythology; its theme is deceit and human death, not the auspicious birth of a god. And it is a death story, performed in the center slot of a festival, at the ritual heart of the bow song tradition.

The narrative itself is based on historical events from eighteenth century Travancore, the kingdom of which Nāñcil Nāṭu was a part. When the Maharaja Rāma Varma died in 1729, he named his sister's son, Mārttāṇṭa Varma, and not his own sons, the Tampimār, to succeed him. Although the Tampimār received land and tax rights, they demanded the throne and laid claim to it on the basis of patrilineal succession; this was rejected by the authorities at the Patmanāpacuvāmi temple in the capital, since matrilineal succession was the tradition in Travancore, and Mārttāṇṭa Varma was crowned as the new raja. Soon the Tampimār found support for their cause among the peasants of Nāñcil Nāṭu, particularly among the Nadars, who had long suffered excessive taxation; and, as Tamils, the Nadars respected patrilineal inheritance, which was the basis of the Tampimār's challenge. With their material and moral support, and irregular reinforcements from disgruntled Nāyar chiefs, the Tampimār raised an army and fought with the raja's soldiers.[2] After initial victories, the rebellion was defeated and the Tampimār executed in 1731.

This is the story recorded in standard historical sources: the Tampimār, in short, were rebels put to the sword.[3] From the perspective of the low castes who preserve the story in the bow song tradition, however, the Tampimār played a different role. They were champions of justice, heroes who were treacherously murdered and are now worshiped as gods; they also were seen, in the story translated here, in positive domestic roles as obedient sons and protective brothers.

As brothers, the personalities of the Tampimār have been given a particular mold by folk tradition. Conforming to a pattern that appears to be widespread in Indian folklore, a patient, controlled older brother (Valiya Tampi) is paired with a headstrong, rash younger brother (Kuñcu Tampi).[4] Consistent also with this pattern, the trusting older brother Valiya Tampi often proves foolish as when he hands over his sword to Mārttāṇṭa Varma in an act that ensures his own death. By the same logic, the impetuosity of the younger brother impels him to take the necessary, dangerous actions as when Kuñcu Tampi actually confronts the raja (as Valiya Tampi rarely does), nearly kills him in battle, chops up his ancestral bed, and attacks him in the palace in the final scene. Certainly this pairing of personalities is not uniquely Indian or folk, and the valorizing of the younger brother is a worldwide motif, but the particular associations with the brothers in heroic narrative has a special prominence in Indian folklore.[5]

The portrait of the Raja Mārttāṇṭa Varma, the most celebrated figure in Kerala's modern history, has also been shaped by folk tradition. From the glorious, if somewhat nondescript raja of the official sources, he becomes a power-hungry man, driven by sexual desires, a coward who runs in battle and survives by deceit. Not only does he trick the Tampimār into a death trap in the final scene, he also takes a false oath before Śiva in the palace temple. As part of a peace pact, Mārttāṇṭa Varma is forced to vow that he will not harm the Tampimār as long as "this life (*ī uyir*) continues"; however, because the phrase *ī uyir* can also mean "fly-life," the raja frees himself from the vow by crushing to death a fly held in his hand.[6]

An even more revealing transformation of history by the folk tradition is the reworking of Koccumaṇi, the Tampimār's sister. She plays no role at all and is often left out of the historical accounts, but in the bow song story she is a pivotal (if silent) figure whose presence redefines the conflict that leads to her brothers' deaths. In the historical accounts, as stated earlier, the conflict concerns succession to the throne in which the usual practice of matrilineal transmission favored Mārttāṇṭa Varma over the Tampimār. In the bow song story, this issue arises only indirectly, and much later, as part of a new conflict over the marriage of Koccumaṇi. When the old raja (Rāma Varma) dies, no one contests Mārttāṇṭa Varma's coronation, and the Tampimār serve him loyally as the new ruler. Conflict develops only when Mārttāṇṭa Varma himself asks the Tampimār for permission to marry their sister; citing the custom of not marrying into a "distant house" (*turuvam*), here the Āṟṟiṅkal family of Mārttāṇṭa, the Tampimār refuse his request. This reverses the role of the Tampimār from challengers of tradition (matrilineal succession) in historical sources to defenders of it in the folk story.

When the Tampimār refuse his request, Mārttāṇṭa Varma is enraged and demands their sister in marriage. Knowing that such a marriage into the matrilineal line of Travancore would mean that neither they nor their sister's future sons would have any status, the Tampimār continue to resist. They finally agree to the proposed marriage on the condition that their sister's future son be named the raja's heir. Not wanting to undermine his own family, Mārttāṇṭa Varma rejects this offer, curses the Tampimār, and orders them to leave the palace. When the new raja takes away the Tampimār's rights to land and taxes, they go to war.

This tension over land and political power, intensified by a sexual or marital issue, is common in death stories. When, as in the case of the Tampimār or Nāṭāṉ Cāmi (see pp. 6–7), the protagonists are men, the stories lead to the emergence of gods. Just as often, however, the main actor is a woman; again there is violence and death, but now deification produces a goddess. Some of these goddess stories center on problems of land and inheritance, as does the story of Āṉantāci.

A barren Brahmin, Āṉantāci performs religious austerities at several temples, and becomes pregnant. But when her baby girl is born, the astrologer predicts "snake danger" (*cārpa tōṣam*); to avert this fate, she and her husband keep a mongoose, the archenemy of snakes, in the house as a guardian for the child. One day Āṉantāci sees the pet mongoose dripping with blood and, thinking it had killed the baby, kills the animal. Only later does she realize that the mongoose had killed a snake to protect the child, who lies safe in a corner of the house.[7] To counteract this evil act, her husband goes off on a pilgrimage to Pāpanācam, but the snake danger is not removed; the dead snake returns in another skin, bites and kills the husband. Widowed without any sons, Āṉantāci is ordered out of the village; she turns to her senior male kin, an uncle, who goes to the village headman from whom he accepts money and remains silent. With no recourse, Āṉantāci leaves the village, first cursing all her relatives to die, and climbs to the top of a mountain. Taking her daughter in her arms, she leaps into a pool, which suddenly swells into a flood that crashes down the mountain and washes away her relatives who have gathered for a marriage. Śiva lifts Āṉantāci and her child from the water, takes them to Kailāsa, gives them new names, and sends them back to earth as goddesses.[8]

The emergence of a goddess in death stories just as often results from physical violence (often sexually motivated) to a woman. The story of Pūlaṅkoṇṭāḷ, carried off and thrown down a well by suitors, was mentioned in Chapter 3, but a more detailed (and gruesome) example is the tale of Icakki Ammaṉ (known as Nīli in other parts of Tamil Nadu).[9] The story begins as a Brahmin takes a temple dancer (*dāsi*) for his lover and squanders the temple treasury on her whims. When he has no more gifts to offer, the dancer's mother turns him out and he leaves the village in anger; but the dancer follows and pleads with him to return. He agrees, they make love, and fall asleep under a tree; but the Brahmin is only feigning sleep. He opens his eyes, takes back the dancer's jewelry and kills her, but in escaping is bitten by a snake, falls down a well and dies.

The dancer's violent death transforms her into Icakki Ammaṉ, one of the most powerful death story goddesses in the bow song tradition. She tracks down her Brahmin murderer, reborn as a merchant, finding him in a deserted wasteland. He runs in fright to a nearby village and asks for protection against the fierce Icakki; but when the goddess enters the village, she is carrying a child and tells the villagers that the merchant is her husband who has abandoned her. Confused, yet believing that Icakki is a woman and not a goddess, the villagers decide to put the couple in a temple for the night, and consider the matter in the morning. Inside the locked temple, Icakki first sings a lullaby to calm any remaining doubts of her identity, but then turns on the man, rips out his heart, and drives a stake through his chest.

Violated woman transformed to violent goddess, Icakki Ammaṉ illustrates the bow song version of the split-image of the Hindu goddess: benevolent and malevolent, mother and murderer.[10] Other examples from the bow song tradition are numerous. Kāḷi Ammaṉ, for instance, mothers a child in one scene and then destoys a demon in the next; and Mōhiṉi, as already remarked, brings first death to Vallarakkaṉ and then birth to Śāstā. These goddesses of birth stories may well have inherited their double identity from classical Hindu mythology, to which they are linked by their births in Kailāsa. Even in the local death stories, however, the split-image of the goddess divides the narrative in half, on either side of the death scene: the faithful, maternal woman in the first half becomes the dangerous, aggressive goddess in the second. The dual image thus cuts deeply into the Tamil folk tradition, often into its iconography. Village icons of Icakki Amman̲, for example, present figures of two sisters: the older cuddles a child in her arms, while the younger crunches several children with her large teeth (see Plate 5).

Since death stories are the ritual center of a bow song festival, it is important to realize that the Tampimār story, with its male conflict and hero-gods, is but one major type. Equally representative of death stories are the histories of violated women—Icakki, Ā̲nantāci, and Pūlaṅkoṇṭāḷ—who become powerful goddesses.[11] What these stories of both gods and goddesses share is the pattern of violation and violence that leads to death and deification.[12] These events, believed to be the true history of men and women who lived in some village in the bow song region, generate the ritually deep possession dances that mark the performance of a death story in the center slot.

The performance of the Tampimār story translated here is no exception. It was sung in 1978 in the large Nadar village of Ammāṇṭiviḷai (see Map 2), near the old Travancore capital of Patmanāpapuram where the events took place two hundred and fifty years before. Although the Tampimār and Mārttāṇṭa Varma are well-known figures in Kerala history, the bow song story is sung only here, the center of the Tampimār cult, and in four other villages in the vicinity.[13]

At Ammāṇṭiviḷai, performances of the Tampimār story are always read from an official temple manuscript (see Plate 11). The text is read line-by-line to the lead singer who must turn each line immediately into song; as one line is being repeated by the chorus, there is just enough time for the next to be read (shouted over the music) to the lead. Unlike the Vallarakkan̲ performance, then, the entire performance of four and one-half hours is filled with song only—no dialogue, no commentary, no comedy. Variation is provided only by quickening or slowing the pace, and by closing each section (kaṭṭam) with the emphatic "ē" and other vocal effects.

However, even in this kind of scripted performance, not uncommon in the bow song tradition, the sung lines do not all correspond to those in the text. First, the manuscript is selectively performed; all lines sung come from the text, but not all lines in the text are sung. Of the 1,875 lines in the manuscript, thirty-seven were left out of the performance translated in this chapter. Most of the omitted lines were lists of place names where the Tampimār traveled, but in one case the omission was significant. The text describes the heroes' raid on twelve villages in Nāñcil Nāṭu, whereas the performance included only two (p. 129); both of these are villages of Piḷḷais (enemies of the Tampimār) and the ten omitted villages are settlements of Nadars (supporters of the Tampimār and patrons of their cult). It is also true that since the singing ended with the culmination of possession (described below), the final 250 lines of the manuscript were not sung.

A second difference between text and performance is that some lines were altered. Most changes were accidental, due to the lead singer's inability to hear clearly the lines over the loud music and chorus. Most were also semantically trivial, on the order of changing "having said" to "he said," a shift from participial phrase to finite verb that avoids enjambement and conforms to the oral formulaic model.[14] The actual sense of a line was changed occasionally ("the raja having risen" became "the great army of the raja," for example), but not in any way that affected the narrative. The only constraint was timing, fitting each phrase within the limits of the musical measure. Twice, however, the lead singer deliberately changed the line read to him to maintain narrative coherence. The brothers are born two years apart, but the text is inconsistent when giving their ages: in one line they are said to be "three and seven" and in another "three and eight." When both these lines were read to the lead singer, he simply sang them as "three and five."

Certainly these are minor alterations in a performance that lasted for more than four hours. The text is fixed in writing and to a certain extent memorized by the lead singer, who has sung this story many times; more than once in the present performance the singer was able to fill in the next line even though the reader could not be heard or had lost his place. This fixity was made clear in one particular place when, due to an outside disturbance, the reader totally lost his place. Quickly the singer turned and glared at him, for even the briefest pause would break the pace of the singing, which was moving at the rate of one line (song and chorus) every eight seconds. But before the reader could locate the next line or the singer remember or extemporize it, it was shouted out by a man in the audience. Without even looking up, the reader nodded in assent, the lead sang the line, and the two swung back into their normal pattern.[15]

This and other scripted performances demonstrate the interdependence of text and performance, a concept fundamental to this book. By closing the temporal and physical gaps that normally separate text from performance, the scripted performance exposes their complementarity. A written text is required to ensure accuracy, but that text must also be sung in order to bring possession. Fixed text and oral performance, far from being at odds in the bow song tradition, actually enhance each other in reaching a common ritual goal.

In the performance translated below, the ritual goal of possession began about midway through the night, when the conflict between the Tampimār and Mārttāṇṭa Varma became irreconcilable. After the brothers refused the raja's request to marry their sister and he ordered his soldiers to seize a bed belonging to the royal family, the performance became highly charged. Then Kuñcu Tampi defied the raja's order and destroyed the bed himself, and the raja revoked the Tampimār's rights. As the singers were describing these events, they broke off suddenly and sang a devotional song to Perumāḷ (Viṣṇu), who then possessed his medium (the father of the Tampimār's dancer).[16] After ten minutes of dancing, this possession ended as abruptly as it had begun and the singers returned to the main story, singing at a rapid pace until the Tampimār gods possessed their medium. Trembling for a few minutes before the icons, the young man then began to move and, as the singing continued, he danced with more and more intensity while the crowd responded with the kuravai cry and the mēḷam played.

For ninety minutes the medium danced, moving from the singers' platform to the crowd and back to the gods' icons, all the time waving two sharp, steel swords. Periodically he would stop and plant his legs apart; jackknifing up and down, he would beat the swords across his shoulders and down his back, alternating them in a crisscross motion. When the dancer seemed close to self-injury, the monitors stepped forward and emptied bottles of scented water on his head to "cool" him down and bring him back to his normal motions of swinging the swords in the air. But this was only temporary, and again he would begin to whip the swords across his shoulders and back, and again the monitors cooled him. The dance wore on and on, until all the bottles of water were exhausted and the monitors had to use another cooling solution of sandalwood paste and oil. When the sword-beating reached a danger point, they would throw handfuls of the mixture on the dancer's back and suddenly he would freeze, like a marionette whose strings had been pulled taut.

After many repetitions of this cycle of dancing, beating, and cooling, the man's father and others in the crowd grew fearful that he had lost control and might seriously injure himself. They asked the festival officials to halt the singing, since the dance would stop only if the music did; but others in the crowd demanded that the music continue, saying the dancer still had control. As this discussion was held, the dancer almost collapsed with exhaustion. Quickly the monitors stepped up and poured a full bucket of the sandalwood mixture on his head. He fell unconscious on the temple's tile floor and the performance came to a premature close. By this time, the singers had reached the event of the brothers' deaths and, as is usual, they stopped.

The following performance was sung by five Nadar men, led by Krishna Nadar. As noted above, there is no dialogue; the continuous singing is punctuated only by vocal and musical patterns. The dominant pattern is that which marks an episodic section (kaṭṭam) of the story (see pp. 22–23): the harsh voice and loud music would slowly rise in tempo and then break in a crescendo at a dramatic event (indicated in the translation by three asterisks); falling away, the voice and music would then begin to build, culminate, fall away, and begin again. The large crowd was quiet and intent as Krishna Nadar sang the invocation.

Performance Translation

Kantaṉ of the Red City!
   Protect me as I sing
   this story of the Tampimār.
Cruelly killed
   on this earth
   by a great hate,
They now rest
   at Śiva's feet
      in Kailāsa.
I sing of the Tampimār,
   sons of golden Kiṭṭiṇāttāḷ,[17]
   blessed by Vināyaka,
      son of Śiva and Umā.
I sing of the Tampimār,
   murdered by the raja.
May their story be known!

In the best of lands
   in the good southern land,
In the best of countries
   in the Travancore country,
In Trivandrum
   in the outlying palaces,
In Tiruvañcikara, in Paracāla
   in the Patmanāpapuram palace,
Surrounded by countless lords
   and ministers at court,
The Raja Rāma Varma
   ruled this wide earth.

Taking one-sixth in tax
  driving off his enemies,
Reigning over this land,
  the bell of injustice never rang.[18]
Ceremonies filled the temples,
  and the festival banners flew.
Then in the month of Mārkaḻi
  when the proper time had come,
He ordered the banner raised,
  for the festival at Cucīntiram.
With his great army
  the raja came,
And raised the banner
  at the Cucīntiram temple.

* * *

Meanwhile in the north country
  in the good town of Ayodhyā,
In a cowherder family
  lived the fair Apirāmi
  and her brother Krishna.
Serving at Mahādeva's temple
  they somehow survived,
Until a famine struck
  and ruined that great land.
Looking at each other,
  brother and sister spoke:
"If we remain,
  surely we will die!
We must go south
  and try to live."
Leaving their family and goods
  they walked from Ayodhyā.
South past Kaṅkakoṇṭāṉ,[19]
  past Kayattāṟu, past Kaṭampūr,
Traveling by day
  and sleeping at night.
In every town and village
  Apirāmi looked for help;
But there was none,
  no refuge anywhere.
When they came to Cucīntiram
  and saw the festival there,
Apirāmi went to the temple
  and raised her hands in prayer.

"Where can we go?
  Who will help us?"
Apirāmi prayed to Tāṇuliṅgam,
  the god who was three gods.[20]
From the outer entrance
  she walked toward Tāṇuḷiṅgam,
Wearing gold
  and a *poṭṭu* shining like gold.
Covering herself with scents
  and a soft silk sari,
Quickly through the crowd,
  followed by her brother,
She walked to the god
  and worshiped at his feet.
She stood there,
  still and lovely,
  looking at the face of the god.
And then the raja saw her,
  looked into her face
  and spoke,
"From where have you come?
  What is your name?
And tell me:
  Why are you alone?"
Hearing the raja's words,
  gentle Apirāmi touched his feet,
Folded her hands in respect
  and spoke,
"I am from the north,
  from the town of Ayodhyā.
My name is Apirāmi
  my brother is Krishna.
We served Mahādeva's temple
  and managed to survive.
Then the rains failed,
  a famine hit the land.
With nothing to give
  and nothing to receive,
We left
  and journeyed here."
Hearing these words,
  the raja was moved,
Looked at her great beauty
  and wanted her for himself,

To offer the marriage cloth[21]
   and his bed.
He spoke to his ministers
   and they nodded.
The festival came to an end;
   the god's great chariot
   was pulled around the temple,
The sacrifices performed,
   and Rāma Varma worshiped Tāṇuliṅgam.
In ceremonial procession
   he then prepared to leave.
Surrounded by silver-speared men
   men who quickly kill,
Surrounded by powerful bowmen
   and an entourage of guards,
Surrounded by his great army,
   the raja left Cucīntiram.
They passed through Accirāmam
   and over the Elephant Bridge,
To the Vaṭivīcuvaram temple
   and worshiped Śiva there.
Standing with his hands in worship,
   the raja pledged gifts of gold.
Passing through Nagercoil,
   the procession reached Kōṭṭār,
And there in the palace
   the raja sat in state.

* * *

Inside his royal residence
   the raja made up his mind;
Summoning his ministers,
   he made a formal announcement
To offer the marriage cloth
   to gentle Apirāmi.
Beckoning his ministers,
   he made his statement brief,
      and he was happy.
He waited for her consent
   and for a proper day,
      and then the ceremony began.
The marriage cloth was brought,
   and handed to the raja
      who called to Apirāmi.

He presented her the cloth
  and her brother Krishna
    with a silken shawl.
The gifts were given,
  the kuravai was heard
    and music filled the air.
The *nāgasvaram* played,
  white yak tails waved in the air,
    and the raja rose to leave.

* * *

Raja Rāma Varma
  left the Kōṭṭār palace,
Riding in royal procession
  inside a palanquin.
Apirāmi rode beside him
  inside her palanquin,
And behind on horseback,
  her brother Krishna rode.
They moved through Nagercoil
  past Veṭṭuruṇi,
Past the grove at Pañcavarṇakāṭu,
  where the Five Brothers lived.[22]
Past Pārvatipuram
  Kaḻḻiyāṅkāṭu and Kaṉṉiyaṅkuḷam,
Past Cuṅkāṅkaṭai and the Turatti temple
  Akkiṉikulam and the fort at Ciṅkanallūr.
Past Aṭṭaṅkarai and over the river
  to the Vēmpaṭivāḷ palace,
Where the procession stopped,
  and the raja spoke,
"Apirāmi will have a new name;
  what shall it be?"
They called her Kiṭṭiṇāttāḷ,
  Kiṭṭiṇāttāḷ Tampurāṉ Ammai,
And they named her brother
  Kocumara Piḷḷai.
Then the raja and Kiṭṭiṇāttāḷ
  retired to the bedroom,
Rested on soft couches
  and enjoyed themselves that night.
They lived heart in heart
  in total happiness.
But there was no child
  for gold-braceleted Kiṭṭiṇāttāḷ.

Rāma Varma hoped and hoped
  but they knew only sadness.
Kiṭṭiṇāttāḷ fasted and prayed
  until by a boon from Śiva,
And by the mercy of Māyaṉ
  she finally conceived.
Time wore on
  and in the tenth month,
When the pain was terrible
  the midwife quickly came,
And firmly held Apirāmi
  as she brought forth a child.
Conch and discus in his right hand,[23]
  his body a tender mango leaf,
To rule this world
  to make it prosper,
Her son was born!

* * *

When his son was born,
  Rāma Varma smiled.
To determine his future,
  he summoned a cōciyan diviner,
"Please look carefully,
  what is this boy's fate?"
The cōciyaṉ smoothed out the earth,
  placed a lamp to one side,
Arranged his fifty-eight items
  and scratched a design in dirt.
He rolled his divination stones
  picked them up,
Washed them in milk
  and placed them on a board.
Looking at a manuscript
  he calculated the nine planets,
And then spoke to the raja:
  "Listen to your child's future.
Born in the moon of Uttiram,
  this boy has good luck.
Look at his planets and his moons,
  nowhere is there a flaw!
But there's another horoscope
  and it is crystal clear."
"Whose horoscope?
  Tell me," commanded Rāma Varma.

"Kiṭṭināttāḷ will have more children,
  first another son
  and then a girl.
After the girl is born,
  her brothers will be killed."
"How?" asked the raja,
  "How will they die?"
"A raja will rule this world,
  and demand the girl in marriage.
He will offer the wedding cloth
  to take her to his bed.
The raja will order the marriage,
  but her brothers will refuse.
They will say 'no,'
  and they will stand firm,
And then they will die
  at the hands of the raja."
Hearing these words of death,
  Rāma Varma grew pale,
Gave gifts to the cōciyaṉ,
  and sent him away.
Then he called a goldsmith
  and gave him coins of gold.
The goldsmith heated the metal,
  fashioned fine ornaments
Ornaments of many shapes,
  and brought them all to court,
Where the raja took them
  and placed them on his son;
On his twenty-eighth day
  the boy wore twenty-eight jewels.
Then came the naming ceremony
  and the raja said,
"What name shall we have?
  Speak your mind."
Then he announced the name,
  "Let it be Valiya Tampi."

* * *

When the boy was named,
  the women sang a lullaby.
Holding Valiya Tampi on their laps,
  they softly hummed the tune,
  ohhh . . . ohhh . . . ohhh,
    Shining like gold,

you have come
to rule this earth.
Valiya Tampi, golden one,
born to light this world,
my son, ohhh . . . ohhh . . .
Born of Kiṭṭiṇāttāḷ,
my sweet, soft child,
ohhh . . . ohhh . . .
To command elephants and horses,
and the rajas of this world,
my son, ohhh . . . ohhh . . .
To raise an endless army,
to rule this earth
you have come.
Like a royal monarch
you have appeared,
my son Valiya Tampi, ohhh . . .

When Valiya Tampi was one,
he was beautiful.
When he was two,
he began to walk.
When he was three,
dark-haired Kiṭṭiṇāttāḷ,
By the grace of Māyaṉ,
again conceived a child.
Ten months passed
and a second boy was born.
At the naming ceremony
it was decided,
"This brother of Valiya Tampi
will be named Kuñcu Tampi."[24]
Together they grew up,
Valiya Tampi the older
Kuñcu Tampi the younger,
And no one in this world
could equal the Tampimār.
When Valiya Tampi was five
and Kuñcu Tampi three,
Again their mother gave birth,
to a little baby girl.
At the birth of her daughter
Kiṭṭiṇāttāḷ rejoiced.
Summoning the cōciyaṉ,
again the raja said,

"Tell us in detail
  the future of this child."

* * *

The cōciyan̲ cleared the ground
  drew his lines in dirt,
Arranged the fifty-eight items,
  rolled his divination stones,
Washed them in milk
  and placed them on a board.
Looking at the formation of planets,
  he spoke out forcefully,
"Listen now, Raja.
  I tell this child's fate.
Death will come to the Tampimār
  who know nothing of defeat.
At the hands of another raja
  they will be cruelly killed."
Shocked and angry
  the raja cried aloud,
"What death and why?
  Speak without fear."
"Listen, Raja,
  listen to their future.
Valiya Tampi will be twenty-one
  Kuñcu Tampi nineteen,
And sister Koccumaṇi
  will be sixteen years.
Two brothers and their sister
  will grow up happily,
Until the first of Tai
  when you leave the palace,
And travel to Vāliyān̲pār̲ai
  to take the ceremonial bath.[25]
You will reach Vāliyān̲pār̲ai
  but on your return,
The great goddess Ulakāṇṭāḷ
  will appear on her chariot,
The goddess Ulakāṇṭāḷ
  will spread pox in her path.
Pox will fall on you, Raja,
  and you will grow weak.
Losing your life and kingdom
  a young heir will come to rule.
Wearing the crown of victory
  a new raja will reign.

He will befriend the Tampimār
  ask to marry their sister,
Order the wedding cloth be given
  and that she visit his bed.
The raja will insist,
  but the Tampimār will refuse.
They will stand against him
  and firmly tell him 'no.'
The raja will take their rights
  and take away their lands,
Then they will quarrel
  and become bitter enemies.
Going to a foreign land,
  the Tampimār will raise an army,
They will defeat the raja
  and take all his forts.
The raja will raise an army
  and battle the Tampimār,
But again
  the Tampimār will win.
Finally the young raja
  will deceive the Tampimār;
In a wicked, backhanded plan
  he will call them to Nagercoil,
And murder them
  as they stand before him.
This, oh Raja,
  is your daughter's horoscope."
Rāma Varma heard this prophecy
  and slowly spoke these words:
"Should parents ever abandon
  even an ill-fated child?"
He gave gifts to the cōciyan̲
  and sent him on his way.

* * *

When the cōciyan̲ had gone,
  women gathered near,
Sang the girl a lullaby
  bathed her in scents,
Painted a *poṭṭu* on her forehead
  and laid her in a bed.
Her hair was a beautiful black,
  her body a ripening fruit.
Her father called a goldsmith
  and gave him coins of gold

To mold fine ornaments,
  ornaments of every shape.
To the royal court
  the goldsmith brought the jewels
Where the raja took them
  and put them on his daughter.
On her twenty-eighth day,
  she wore twenty-eight jewels.
The naming ceremony came
  and the sister of the Tampimār,
Born after Kuñcu Tampi,
  was named Koccumaṇi.
Two brothers and their sister
  lived happily together
Under the word of the raja
  and the care of Kiṭṭiṇāttāḷ.
Soon Valiya Tampi was seven
  Kuñcu Tampi five
  and Koccumaṇi three,
Time for them to learn
  to write and to recite.

* * *

Before they studied the letters
  the Tampimār worshiped them.
They sat at the feet of a teacher
  who chanted effortlessly,
"Hari, Śrī, Gaṇapati,
  Hari, Om, Om!"
He put nuts into their hands
  and taught them how to count.
When the teacher sang out clearly—
  "Hari, nām, ō"—
  the Tampimār repeated perfectly.
He chanted each letter
  first the short sounds,
  and then the long.
And the Tampimār repeated,
  letter for letter,
  sound for sound.[26]
They learned from ten manuscripts,
  in short- and long-hand form,
Mathematics, the *Koṉṟaivēntaṉ,*[27]
  respect for their parents,
Single words and compounds,
  composition and multiplication,

Eight kinds of calculation,
  eight letters and literary styles,
Malayalam and Grantha scripts[28]
  and the language of rajas.
They learned to speak in English
  to read and write its letters,
To write to distant kings
  and read messages from them.
The teacher looked at the Tampimār
  and spoke with a smile,
"Nowhere in this world,
  have I seen such wisdom as yours!"
The raja took pieces of gold,
  1,008 coins of gold,
Tied them in a bundle,
  which he put in the teacher's hands.

* * *

When Valiya Tampi was seven
  and Kuñcu Tampi five,
The Tampimār were strong
  like fierce attacking tigers.
They wore silk clothing
  more valuable than gold,
Jewels and rings on their hands
  glistening belts on their waist.
When Valiya Tampi was nine
  and Kuñcu Tampi seven,
The raja called a teacher
  to teach the use of swords.
On the ground
  the teacher cleared a circle,
Set an image of Gaṇapati inside
  lit a lamp to the god,
And in the middle
  placed a special sword.
The teacher stood to the right
  the Tampimār to the left;
And when they began to fight,
  the noise reached the gods.
They battled and shouted
  like thunder crashing down,
The crowd yelled and screamed
  like mountains splitting apart.
A sword in his right hand
  and a shield in his left,

The teacher challenged the boys,
  "Come hard now and strike!
Swing your sword to the right,
  duck, rise, and strike!
Swing your sword to the left,
  come on, young Tampimār!
Swing like this, like that,
  swing and follow through!
Swing short and quick,
  cross swords and push away!
Crouch down and swing,
  jab for the stomach and spin!"
When the Tampimār mastered it all,
  the teacher said to them,
"There's still more,
  come on, boys, push hard.
Here comes the enemy army,
  elephants charging in front!"
Riding on an elephant
  the handsome Valiya Tampi,
Charged at elephants and horses,
  killing them right and left.
They learned to leap into battle
  like a flying *poṉṉuravi*.
They learned to hurl spears
  and how to grab them back.
"There's even more,
  come on, you Tampimār!"
They learned hand-to-hand combat
  and all the wrestling holds,
Arm-holds, lock-holds,
  leg-holds, and kicking,
Long blows and short blows
  and how to get up quickly.
On and on they fought
  until they wounded their teacher.
Then the raja,
  proud of his sons,
Put 1,008 pieces of gold
  into the teacher's hand,
Who bowed at the raja's feet
  and left.

* * *

When Valiya Tampi was nine
  they learned to use the sword;

When Valiya Tampi was ten,
  Kuñcu Tampi eight,
And Koccumaṇi six,
  the raja gave an order,
"In the tenth year
  they must learn to ride.
We need a horse that flies
  and an expert trainer."
When the trainer came,
  the raja spoke in a hurry,
"We need a long-legged horse,
  a horse that runs hard."
At the raja's command,
  the trainer went to the stables,
Selected a strong horse
  and led him to the river.
He bathed him and dried him
  sprinkled him with coconut water,
Dressed him in fine cloth,
  with a pendant on his forelock.
The saddle was made of silver,
  the undercloth of soft cotton,
The saddle was made of gold,
  the horseshoes were golden, too.
The bridle was made of gold,
  the reins were golden, too.
Gold covered the horse in front,
  gold covered him in back.
The trainer took the horse
  up to Valiya Tampi,
Bowed to the young prince
  and then stepped aside.
Valiya Tampi and Kuñcu Tampi
  climbed upon the horse,
They jumped on the magic horse
  and flew off at a gallop.
The brothers rode the horse
  the flying, dancing horse,
Away on the beautiful horse
  driving it on and on.

* * *

Around and around they rode
  pulling in the reins.
Bucking and kicking,
  the horse flew higher and higher,

Flew beyond the sky,
  till the Tampimār made him walk.
They walked him in four directions,
  as the crowd cried out,
"Look at the Tampimār!
  Look at their swinging swords!"
On horseback they sprang
  into a huge army,
Killing rajas and elephants
  as the horse flew through the sky.
Golden necklaces and jewels
  on the chests of the Tampimār,
And necklaces lay thick
  on the chests of fallen kings.
Without touching those bodies
  the Tampimār took the jewels,
Lifted them off
  with the tips of their spears,
  and wore them on their crowns.
The crowd saw the necklaces
  and cheered the Tampimār
Who took them from their crowns
  and wreathed them on their chests.
No one,
  no one in this world
  had ever seen such riding!
The Tampimār brought the horse
  down to the earth below,
  and bowed before the raja.

* * *

They rode and rode the horse,
  mastering the martial arts,
Rings on their hands
  glittering belts on their waist.
Gold, golden belts,
  and a fast flashing *poṭṭu*.
Gold, golden arrows,
  and sharp golden swords.
Gold, golden shields
  and gold-tipped arrows.
Gold, golden chains,
  and rings on their hands.
The prince Valiya Tampi
  stood on the raja's right,

The prince Kuñcu Tampi
  stood to his left.
The Raja Rāma Varma
  rested in his heart,
With the brave Tampimār
  standing by his side.

* * *

In the village of Vairavaṅkōṇam,
  the trusted Cekkāḷiyaṉ governed.
At the court Kuñcukāḷi Nāyar,
  Iravi Kāṅkayam and Kuṭṭi Maraikkāṉ,
  the Kurup tax collectors,
Poṉṉaṟavāḷ Pēy Kurup, Muṇṭa Kaṇṇu Piḷḷai,
  the Tampimār and Koccumara Piḷḷai
  stood beside the raja.
To the Tampimār and Koccumaṇi,
  the raja gave tax lands.
To Valiya Tampi
  the rights to Nālāl Mūṭṭu
  and the market taxes there.
To Kuñcu Tampi
  the rights to Tāḻakkuṭi
  and the market taxes there.
To Valiya Tampi
  house and tax rights in Kuṭippuli
  that Civaṉāṇṭi Nadar held.
To Kuñcu Tampi
  house and tax rights in Koṭuppaikuli
  that Kulacēkara Nadar held.
To Kuñcu Tampi
  house and tax rights in Ammāṇṭiviḷai[29]
  of Muttiruḷaṉ Nadar and Muṉṉāṭi Kāruppu Nadar.
To Valiya Tampi the teachers' street,
  to Kuñcu Tampi the stables.
The village of Vampumalaikōṇam
  belonged to Kuñcu Tampi,
The fields of Tāvukaṭai
  belonged to Koccumaṇi,
Near the fort at Ciṅkanallūr
  the taxes upon the land
  on palm trees and turmeric root
  all taxes were given to her.
The raja gave to Kiṭṭiṇāttāḷ
  the fertile lands of Kiḷḷiyūr,

the fields of Vittumūlai
which produced three tons of rice.
To the strong Tampimār
who ruled over these villages
Rāma Varma conferred rights
to the land and its produce.
They collected rent and taxes
and governed there in peace.
In the fort at Ciṅkanallūr
inside the Vēmpaṭivāḷ palace,
The Tampimār stood as servants
to the Raja Rāma Varma.

* * *

Daily in the Vēmpaṭivāḷ palace
the Tampimār served the raja,
They bowed at his feet,
and held their hands in worship.
Then came the month of Tai
and the raja's ceremonial bath.
The raja called his ministers
and announced the Tai *tīrttam*.
Thinking of the ritual bath,
the raja was pleased;
All the earlier rajas
all those who had worn the crown,
had performed the Tai *tīrttam*
at Vāliyāṉpāṟai rock.
The royal procession
formed in front of the raja,
the horsemen and elephant riders
rows of horses and foot soldiers.
Then he made the announcement:
"Begin the journey to Vāliyāṉpāṟai."
Messengers ran to the eight directions
ministers to the four directions,
And ordered the district chiefs
to assemble in procession.

* * *

At the head of the long procession
rode the Tampimār,
Ornaments of gold
gold chains upon their arms,

Rings on every finger
  necklaces on their chests,
Jeweled rings in their ears
  flashing belts around their waists,
They wore the finest cotton
  gold belts upon their hips.
Gold sheaths carried their swords,
  gold quivers their arrows.
Jewel necklaces lay on their chests,
  gold belts upon their waists,
Shining *poṭṭu*s on their foreheads,
  scented oils on their skin.
Valiya Tampi rode on a horse,
  Kuñcu Tampi in a palanquin.
Valiya Tampi on the raja's right,
  Kuñcu Tampi on his left.
The kettle drums banged
  and silver flutes sang,
The raja's army marched sharply
  and the kuravai was heard.
Conch shells blew
  flutes sung in a line,
Big drums boomed
  and the long horns played.
Temple girls danced
  and the women gave the kuravai.
On the backs of elephants
  the kettle drums rang out,
The *nāgasvaram* played
  and guns fired overhead.
As the raja's procession advanced
  larger and larger each mile,
To protect his royal body
  guards unsheathed sharp swords,
And held their weapons high
  circling around the raja.
Row after row of soldiers
  dressed in yellow and brown,
Pennants waved from elephants
  tall camels walked behind.
In the center came the horses
  rows and rows of horses,
And above the palanquins
  the big cannons boomed.

The long procession moved on
  pulled by ox-drawn carts,
Lines and lines of carts
  carrying the big cannons,
The big cannon balls
  and missiles that pierce the air.
Silver-speared soldiers
  guards that quickly kill,
Bowmen from the town of Kollam
  Nāyars from Kuñcukūṭṭam,
Officials and their assistants
  marched along in procession.
The Tampimār took the lead
  as the raja rode in state,
Umbrellas floating above him
  and horses swarming around him.
Leading the raja's procession
  The Tampimār left Ciṅkanallūr,
Down the Pan̲n̲ikōṭu road
  and past the eastern gate,
Quickly the procession moved on
  past Talakkuḷam and Accan̲pār̲ai,
Raja Rāma Varma rode in state
  with the Tampimār by his side.
Past Vaḷḷiyāpuram and Kaluṅkumuṭam
  past Periyakuḷam to El̲uttupār̲ai,
To the "letter-rock"
  where a *bhūtam* had written a message.
The Tampimār read the message
  and then they were pleased.[30]
Past Pēykkaṭukāy they marched
  past Periyamuṭam and Kūṭṭateṅku,
Valiya Tampi on his horse
  Kuñcu Tampi on a palanquin,
Valiya Tampi on the raja's right
  Kuñcu Tampi on his left.
On and on they rode
  past Pampattumūlam and Kun̲r̲umaṇal,
  Past Paṇṭaka Cālai
  where Muslim families live,
Toward Vāliyān̲pār̲ai
  toward its sacred waters,
Where the Raja Rāma Varma
  would take his ritual bath.

* * *

When they arrived
  the raja surveyed the waters
  at Vāliyāṉpāṟai rock.
"Is it here," he asked,
  "the rivers flow as one?"
His ministers and advisors
  bowed to his feet and spoke,
"Here they join together
  and flow out at Vāliyāṉpāṟai."
Surrounded by his ministers
  the raja entered the waters,
Returned to the bank
  and rubbed his body with scents.
While musicians played
  he scooped up coins of gold,
And distributed them
  as his *dharma* required.
When he gave away the gold
  and climbed into his palanquin,
The sea which circles the earth
  rose up in angry waves,
And rolled toward the raja
  who screamed, "It's the kali yuga!"
His body shook with fear
  as he held out his hand,
Slashed his little finger
  and pointed at the rushing waves
Which drew back into the sea
  as the crowd hailed their raja.
"From this blood," said the raja,
  "this place will be named
  'the cut-hand village.'"[31]

* * *

He gave the name
  and the procession moved on,
The raja sitting on an elephant
  umbrellas spread above him,
With the women
  crying the kuravai
And the Tampimār by the raja
  one on either side.
They left "the cut-hand village"
  past Paṇṭaka Cālai and Pampattumūlam

Past Kūṭṭateṅku and Periyakuḷam
past village after village,
Past Periyamuṭam and Pēykkaṭukāy
past Kaluṅkumuṭam and Kuṭṭikuḷam,
Past Vaḷḷiyāpuram and Tālakkulam
past the western gate at Ciṅkanallūr,
Onto the Paṉṉikōṭu road
past the Bhadrakāḷi temple,
Through the streets of the fort
where the raja dispensed gifts.
But Muttār Ulakāṇṭāḷ
brought her gifts too.
The beautiful goddess Ulakāṇṭāḷ
took seven bags of pox,
And flung her pearly pox
on the people of this world.
Riding upon her chariot
scattering pox upon the land,
She traveled through the south
and seeing the raja's procession,
Scooped up her pox,
and threw them in his face!
The raja's body went faint
attacked by a terrible fever,
Surrounded by his ministers
and his great army,
The raja entered the palace
into the royal bedchamber,
And lay on soft cushions
his body aching with fever.
On the fever's second day
they performed a curing ceremony.[32]
Bringing fire and earth
special vessels and cups,
They mixed bark and herbs
to fight the terrible pox,
Which attacks a budding lotus
and strikes inside the body.
The pox kills in eleven days
it kills in eighteen days,
The pox kills in twelve days
it kills in sixteen days.
For seven days it attacked,
the raja neither ate nor drank;

The raja who slept on soft cushions
was about to lie in the earth.
The Tampimār and Koccumaṇi
their mother and Koccumara Piḷḷai
Were worried and afraid
and all began to cry.
But the raja raised his hand
to calm the weeping ones.
"After today," he said,
"the cure cannot save me;
Soon the crown must be worn
by another on this earth.
Go now to Āṟṟiṅkal
to the young prince there,
Bring the prince Mārttāṇṭa Varma
show him honor and respect.
Bring him here!"
the raja commanded.

* * *

They readied horses and elephants
for the journey to Āṟṟiṅkal.
They went to the queen of Āṟṟiṅkal,
bowed at her feet and spoke,
"The raja lies ill in the palace,
and sent us here to you.
He asks that Mārttāṇṭa Varma,
your son return with us."
Hearing the raja's command
but speaking no reply,
She ordered Mārttāṇṭa Varma
to go with the ministers.
Not eating even a bite
they left Āṟṟiṅkal,
In a procession of elephants
they came to Trivandrum,
To the temple of Patmanāpa Perumāḷ
and gave gifts to the god.
Mārttāṇṭa Varma left Trivandrum
came to Ciṅkanallūr fort,
Entered the Vēmpaṭivāḷ palace
and went before the raja.
Seeing Rāma Varma ill
he broke down and cried,

But the raja took his hand
and spoke these words to him,
"Without error or disgrace
you must rule this wide earth."
The royal scepter and seal
he put into his hands,
Then took the Tampimār's hands
and joined them all together.
"Whatever they may do,"
he said to Mārttāṇṭa Varma,
"The Tampimār and Koccumaṇi,
Kiṭṭiṇāttāḷ and Koccumara Piḷḷai,
No matter what wrong they do,
treat them as your own."
The raja spoke these words,
and then his life was gone!
He left this world below
and entered Śiva's realm.
When the raja left this earth,
all ports and shops were watched;[33]
Sandalwood trees were cut
the wood stacked and lit.
On the sixteenth day after death
the ceremonies were performed.
And the world he left behind
a new raja ruled.
Reigning over the land
as others had reigned before,
He held the scepter upright
and maintained prosperity,
Taking one-sixth as tax
the bell of injustice never rang
Without fault or error
he ruled over our land.

* * *

Mārttāṇṭa Varma was raja
and the Tampimār his servants;
They stood beside the raja
as his bodyguards,
Valiya Tampi on the right
Kuñcu Tampi on the left,
Ministers all around him,
ready to do his will.

Surrounded by his entourage
  the raja ruled righteously,
He ruled from Keralapuram
  from Patmanapāpuram and Paracāla,
But the fort at Ciṅkanallūr
  where Rāma Varma once ruled,
And the Tampimār now lived
  was his only desire.
Mārttāṇṭa Varma gave the order
  and a great procession formed,
Dancers and temple musicians
  rows of servants and soldiers,
With the raja in the lead
  left Patmanāpapuram palace,
Through the western gate to Āḻvārkōvil
  to circumambulate the temple,
Where Mārttāṇṭa Varma gave gifts
  and received sandalwood paste.
Bearing the victory crown
  the raja came to Ciṅkanallūr,
And surveyed the Vēmpaṭivāḷ palace
  where Rāma Varma once ruled.
Joined by the Tampimār
  the procession marched on,
Through the streets of Ciṅkanallūr
  through the market at Iraṇiyal,
The Tampimār riding in front
  and Koccumaṇi among the women,
Circular umbrellas for the men
  white umbrellas for the women.
With gold-backed mirrors
  and sweetly scented powders,
The women took their baths
  in the Vaḷḷiyāṟ River.
Stepping onto the bank
  wrapping themselves in cloth,
Thin waists swayed
  gold bracelets glistened.
Their lips were shy
  their bodies beautiful,
Dancing before the raja,
  who looked at every one.
Seeing a honey-faced woman
  pale with soft powders,

"Who is she?" he asked.
  "Who is that woman there?"
"She is Koccumaṇi," they said,
  "sister of the Tampimār."
At these words
  the raja left the river,
Hurried through the Iraṇiyal market
  past Muḷakupeṭṭai and Tekkukōṭṭavācal,
On to Patmanāpapuram
  where the ruler of this earth
Entered the palace
  and sat in state.
Wearing the victory crown
  the raja paced his palace,
Lay down to rest
  and quickly rose again,
Love-struck by Koccumaṇi,
  sister of the Tampimār.

* * *

Early in the morning
  to his ministers he said,
"Call the Tampimār now,
  I wish a word with them."
Silver-speared soldiers sped
  from Patmanāpapuram to Ciṅkanallūr.
They hurried to Valiya Tampi
  strong as a strutting elephant,
And to Kuñcu Tampi
  proud as an attacking tiger.
Tampimār had strong men—
  Piccaikaippali Nāyar and Poṉṉaṟavāḷ Pēy Kurup,
Kuñcukāḷi Nāyar and Māṭaṉ Poṉṉaṟa Nāyar,
  soldiers with the flying *poṉṉuravi*.
Reaching the fort at Ciṅkanallūr,
  the raja's men said to the Tampimār,
"You have been summoned,
  leave immediately."
"Why? What is the reason?"
  the Tampimār cried.
"I don't know. Come quickly,"
  was their reply.
Hurrying to leave
  The Tampimār bathed in a well,[34]
Ate quickly
  and dressed for the journey.

They wore gold on their arms
  and rings on their hands,
Gold belts around their waists
  and rings in their ears,
Gold necklaces upon their chests
  and gold sheaths for their swords.
They went before their mother
  and waited for her to speak.
She gave her blessing
  and they left the palace,
But in the street saw an evil omen:
  a Brahmin with a shaven head
Counting *rudrakṣa* beads
  and carrying fire in his hands.
Though frightened
  the Tampimār were firm,
"What comes will come:
  who knows the laws of fate?"
The Tampimār went to the raja
  to the Patmanāpapuram palace,
Entered the inner courtyard
  where Mārttāṇṭa Varma sat,
And stood there,
  summoned by their king.

* * *

The Raja Mārttāṇṭa Varma
  looked at them and said,
"Welcome, my Tampimār,
  I wish a word with you.
In the fort at Ciṅkanallūr
  your sister Koccumaṇi lives.
I'll give her the wedding cloth
  if you will agree."
Holding their hands
  he spoke as a brother-in-law,
"As the daughter of Rāma Varma
  who once ruled this earth,
Is she not my cousin
  and a proper bride for me?[35]
I ask for your permission
  to marry Koccumaṇi."
Hearing this proposal,
  the Tampimār stood speechless.
Who in this world
  can defy the raja?

Yet the Tampimār did;
  "Raja, your request is improper.
There are two groups of kin,
  the 'house' and the 'distant house.'[36]
Can one marry his sister
  to a man from a 'distant house'?"
Seething in their chests,
  the Tampimār spoke again,
"Our good raja,
  please listen to these words.
Since you are thirty-two,
  if you marry our sister,
And she should bear a son
  before you pass away,
You must name her son
  to succeed you on the throne."
Hearing these words
  the raja boiled with anger,
Turned like a wild tiger,
  and cursed them with words of fire,
"What you ask is an outrage!
  You'll not last on this earth!
Refusing my order and giving your own—
  it's unbelievable!
Don't let me see you again!
  Leave this palace now!"
Raging and waving his hands
  the raja blasted his words,
But the Tampimār stood silent
  unmoving and unafraid.
Protected by high umbrellas
  surrounded by white yak tails,
Without waiting for permission,
  the Tampimār calmly left.

* * *

They hurried out of the palace
  and headed for Ciṅkanallūr,
Entered the Vēmpaṭivāḷ palace
  where their mother asked,
"What happened with the raja?
  Why this sudden return?"
To her questions,
  the Tampimār hung their heads.
But then,
  without eating or drinking,

They spoke in a rush of anger
  and told her of their journey.
They told her the raja's order
  to give Koccumaṇi in marriage,
To give the wedding cloth
  and have her for his bed.
They told her what they said
  and of the raja's curse.
When she heard their story,
  Kiṭṭiṇāttāḷ shouted in anger,
"No matter what is asked
  you cannot refuse the raja!
I told you this before
  but look what you have done!
You answer the raja's order
  with an order of your own!"
They quarreled for a day,
  then lived in peace at Ciṅkanallūr.
But in the palace at Patmanāpapuram
  Mārttāṇṭa Varma sat in state,
His heart burning with hate,
  split like a heated rock.[37]
"Those Tampimār brothers
  must not live in this land!
I'll drive them out,
  no matter what the means."
Summoning his ministers
  he issued this order:
"Bring me the bed and the cushions
  that belonged to my uncle.
Bring me the bed and the cushions
  now kept in Ciṅkanallūr."
The silver-speared soldiers
  and the guards who quickly kill
Hurriedly assembled in the palace
  and set out into the streets.
They ran to the fort at Ciṅkanallūr
  into the Vēmpaṭivāḷ palace,
Entered the Tampimār's room
  and grabbed the bed and cushions.
The palace guards called out,
  "Who are you?"
"We've come by royal order,
  nothing less than that," they said.
They grabbed the bed and cushions
  and rushed into the street,

But the guards ran to Kuñcu Tampi
  and shouted out to him,
"The raja's men have come
  to take your bed and cushions."
Kuñcu Tampi heard these words
  and became a ball of fire!
His eyes blazed with anger
  as he ran into the street,
Where he found the raja's men
  and spoke these words to them:
"This bed was my father's;
  he gave it to my mother.
I'll not let you take it;
  never! never! never!"
The soldiers shouted
  and Kuñcu Tampi shouted back,
Until he lost control
  and took out his knife,
Hacked the bed to pieces
  and threw them in the air,
Scattering the bed
  in the streets of Ciṅkanallūr.

* * *

The soldiers returned to Patmanāpapuram
  to the inner palace courtyard,
Where the raja sat
  wearing his heavy crown.
Bowing at his feet,
  they told him the story:
"We went and took the bed,
  but Kuñcu Tampi stopped us.
Raging like an animal,
  he shouted and grabbed his knife.
He cut the bed to pieces
  and flung them into the street!
Now the bed lies shattered,
  scattered in the street."
The raja fumed and raved
  and bellowed out his words:
"It was my uncle's bed
  that Kuñcu Tampi destroyed!
My army, my scepter,
  and my royal seal,
What use are all of these
  if I control only this umbrella?

The Tampimār's army
  is but one-fourth of mine,
But with popular support
  they are invincible.
I'll take back their lands,
  take back their tax rights,
I will take them all away
  and drive them from this land!"
The raja took from Valiya Tampi
  the rights his father gave.
And he took from Kuñcu Tampi
  the lands his father gave.
And he took from Koccumaṇi
  and from Kiṭṭiṇāttāḷ, too.
The Raja Mārttāṇṭa Varma
  left them nothing at all.
Stripped of lands and rights,
  the Tampimār said this:
"We vow our revenge
  on this robber raja!
In a foreign land
  we will raise an army,
And defeat that raja
  in every fort of his!
We'll win back
  the rights he stole from us.
We will rule this land
  it will be ours!
If not,
  we're not Rāma Varma's sons!"

* * *

The Tampimār spoke these words
  with anger and with pleasure,
And without anyone knowing
  quickly began to act.
They took bags of money
  brass and silver vessels,
They took the palace gold
  and all the palace vessels.
They made thirty bundles
  and put them on thirty heads.
Carefully in the middle watch
  in the very dead of night,
Valiya Tampi rode in a palanquin
  Kuñcu Tampi upon a horse

Koccumara Piḷḷai rode a colored horse
  Kiṭṭiṇāttāḷ and Koccumaṇi in a palanquin.
Traveling together at night
  they left the Vēmpaṭivāḷ palace,
Across the Vaḷḷiyār River
  past the market and Iruvaṉ Mūṭam.
They traveled along the highway
  past Vallaṅkaṭṭi and Kallaṅkāṭu,
Past Pañcavarṇakāṭu where the Five Brothers lived
  past Pārvatipuram and Kaṉṉiyaṅkuḷam
Rode through Nagercoil and Kōṭṭār,
  past the shops and soldiers' camp,
Across the Elephant Bridge to Accirāmam
  and on to Cucīntiram.
"Where can we sleep tonight?
  Where can we hide?" they worried.
To Ramakrishna Gurukkal Pandaram
  they went and asked for help,
"Let us stay in your house
  until tomorrow morning."
Their sister and all the gold
  they hid inside his house,
And then they slept the night.

* * *

There in Cucīntiram
  Valiya Tampi and Kuñcu Tampi
Gathered together their followers
  and announced their next move:
"We will leave here
  and travel north in secret
To the Nawab's country
  raise an army and return.
Attack the Patmanāpapuram fort,
  and burn it to the ground;
Within three days or less
  this land will be ours!"
They put their gold in a bag
  and fake gold in another,
Carefully tied them both
  and set off in procession.
Umbrellas above their heads
  white yak tails by their sides,
Māṭaṉ Poṉṉāṟa Nāyar and Piccaikaippali Nāyar
  and soldiers with the flying *poṉṉuravi*,

Valiya Tampi rode a colored horse
  Kuñcu Tampi followed behind.
Hiding their mother and sister
  in the fort at Kōṭṭār,
The Tampimār traveled north
  where local chiefs shouted in fright:
"They will bring war
  and destruction to our villages!"
They met with the Tampimār
  and told them of their fears,
"Why have you come?
  What do you want?"
And Valiya Tampi replied,
  "The rights our father gave us
The young raja has taken away
  and we have nothing left."
"You speak fine words, Tampimār,"
  the village chiefs remarked.
"But you'll bring rows of elephants
  and like mosquitos on their skin,
Our villages and our lands
  will all be destroyed."
Thinking of the revenue
  that they would lose,
The chiefs pleaded with the Tampimār
  not to ravage their lands.
Thinking of the money
  that they would gain,
The Tampimār countered,
  "We're not going to listen.
We are sticking to our plan,
  you can't stop us now."
They left the village chiefs
  and marched to the north.
Out of Cucīntiram, through Tērūr
  past Tirupaticāram and Cītāpālam,
Through Kaṭukarai and Koṟṟaṉpāṟai
  past Aṉantāpuram and Āṉaikkoppaṉ,
Past Pātipuḷimūṭam and Tirukaṇaṅkuṭi
  past Acuttirayacuraṉ and Piḷḷaimuṭam,
Past Māvaṭi, past Maittanvaṭali
  the Tampimār marched on,
Past Cālapuram and Tēvanallūr,
  past Ciṅkikuḷam and Ōmanallūr,

Past Oṭṭataruvai and Miṉṉipāḷayam
  to the Periyāṟ River,
Where they stopped for rest,
  chewed betel nut and talked.
"Now where do we go?
  Where can we raise an army?"
Confused and lost,
  they hailed some villagers,
And the Tampimār asked,
  "Who is the local chief?"
"Aḻakappaṉ Mutaliyār,
  he is our chief," they said.
"He has driven off the thieves
  and holds taxes on the land."
Taking their bags of gold
  they went to Aḻakappaṉ Mutaliyār,
And stood before him
  like proud, powerful tigers.
Aḻakappaṉ Mutaliyār rose and said,
  "Welcome, rajas from far away."
Bowing respectfully,
  the Tampimār spoke,
"We are not rajas now,
  we are the Tampimār."
Aḻakappaṉ Mutaliyār was relieved
  and he spoke again,
"Where have you come from?
  And why?"
He took them by the hand
  and sat them on soft cushions.
The Valiya Tampi explained,
  "In fertile Nāñcil Nāṭu,
In the fort at Ciṅkanallūr,
  in the Vēmpaṭivāḷ palace
We are the Tampimār,
  the sons of Rāma Varma."
As he spoke, he put the gold
  into Aḻakappaṉ Mutaliyār's hands,
"Go plunder Nāñcil Nāṭu;
  this is our permission."
Accepting the gold
  Aḻakappaṉ Mutaliyār smiled.
He bolstered the Tampimār's army
  with men of different castes.

With Kampaḷattār and Reṭṭiyar
  and fierce Muslim soldiers,
With Vaṉṉiyar and Ceṉṉiyar
  and the Tūtaṉ from the north.
He raised an army
  that filled the four directions.
Valiya Tampi rode in a palanquin
  Koccumara Piḷḷai rode a horse,
Aḻakappaṉ Mutaliyār a dancing horse,
  and Kuñcu Tampi led the attendants.
The army left the Tirunelveli fort
  and marched to Amarpēṭṭai,
Reached the Periyāṟ River,
  and crossed the deer *ghat*.
The army rumbled through Miṉṉipāḷayam,
  past Tiṭilūr and Ciṅkikuḷam,
Past Kaḷakāṭu and Cālapuram,
  past Māvaṭi and Maittanvaṭali.
In village after village
  people stood and shouted,
"It's the kali yuga!
  Look at this army,
The Mutaliyār and Tampimār's army
  marching to Nāñcil Nāṭu!"
The Tampimār led it southward
  past Uppukaṇṭaṉ and Tirukaṇaṅkuṭi,
Past Vēppalakātu to Kaṭukarai
  where they camped for the night.

* * *

That night as the army rested
  Aḻakappaṉ Mutaliyār spoke,
"Tomorrow we will break camp
  tomorrow we will attack!"
So the Tampimār gathered their men
  to ravage and pillage the land.
In the morning before the dawn,
  the men stood in lines;
In the village of Kaṭukarai
  they stood in silent rows.
Led by three commanders,
  they plundered and destroyed.
Into Kaṭukarai, into Kāṭu Puttūr
  the right division charged,

Into the fertile villages
  the left division charged.
Twelve districts of Nāñcil Nāṭu
  they looted and they burned.
The Tampimār and Aḻakappaṉ Mutaliyār
  led armies through Nāñcil Nāṭu,
Until they reached Vaṭacēri
  and there spent the night,
But rose early in the dawn
  to plunder town after town.

* * *

Then to Kōṭṭār the Tampimār went
  to see their mother and sister;
"No need to worry now,
  we'll conquer the Malayalam country
And drive Mārttāṇṭa Varma
  back into the mountains.
Within three days," they said,
  "Patmanāpapuram will be ours!"
Then Aḻakappaṉ Mutaliyār
  raided the Kōṭṭār palace,
Grabbing the temple vessels
  all the plates and pots,
Gold ornaments and silver belts,
  and necklaces of jewels.
Aḻakappaṉ Mutaliyār took his army,
  a sea of soldiers and umbrellas,
Past Kaḷḷiyankāṭu and Cuṅkāṉ Kaṭai,
  over the Karuppukaṭṭi River
Past Pañcaṅkuḷam and the Villūrṉi temple
  into Ērikuḷam village,
Where they built fences of thorns
  and pitched camp for the night.
The Tampimār drove their army
  past Akkiṉikuḷam and Āṭṭuvāṇiyaṉ Muṭam,
Past Iraṇiyal and into Nālāl Mūṭṭu,
  and there they made their camp,
One army at Ērikuḷam
  the other at Nālāl Mūṭṭu.

* * *

They boomed their big cannons
  all the way to Patmanāpapuram,
Where the raja called his ministers
  and called his army captains,

"Shall we attack
or shall we sit?" he asked.
"Why wait? Our men are many,"
said Kocciravi Mārttāṇṭa Piḷḷai;
"We have Kārakōṭṭu Pēy Kurup,
Kaḷakūṭṭa Piḷḷai and Mārttāṇṭa Piḷḷai.
We have Koccu Piḷḷai
and Nīlakaṇṭan̲ Piḷḷai of Neṭumaṅkāṭu.
We have Ān̲anta Patmanāpa Piḷḷai,
who can wrestle with an elephant."
All these men
and the local temple officials,
Gathered in the palace
to fight the Tampimār.
The raja raised a great army
of soldiers and elephants,
Of cavalry and cannon ball carts
of gun powder and rockets,
Filling the courtyard
and spilling out into the streets.
"Begin the march,"
commanded Raja Mārttāṇṭa Varma.
And the army left Patmanāpapuram
for Tiruvitāṅkōṭu and Takkavāḷai,
Where they camped
and the raja held his sword upright.

* * *

The two great armies,
the raja's and the Tampimār's,
Faced each other,
and then they advanced.
The Tampimār drew their swords
and attacked the raja's soldiers,
Al̲akappan̲ Mutaliyār swung his sword
and rained down vicious blows.
Men fell on the field
cannons exploded everywhere,
Heads rolled on the ground
arms and legs littered the field.
Swords slashed into thighs
into knees and calves.
Fighting close together,
they cut each other down.
Then the Tampimār advanced
and broke the other's ranks,

Scattered the raja's soldiers
  and killed man after man.
Men fell legless and armless,
  without eyes or nose.
The Tampimār struck at the face
  and wounded men in the back.
They slashed and killed
  and quickly killed again.
The raja's men broke ranks
  and the Tampimār cut them down.
Cannon balls scared elephants,
  as men and horses died.
Many died by the sword
  and survivors fled the field.
The raja lost heart,
  "The end has come!" he cried.
His army broken in battle,
  he ran to save his life.
Regrouping at Patmanāpapuram,
  the raja attacked again.
Now the Tampimār's men fell,
  the strong began to falter.
The Kampaḷattār and the Nāyakkar,
  the Maṟavar and the Vaṉṉiyar,
Soldiers and horses
  all died upon the field.
When the elephants fell,
  the Tampimār sprang into battle.
Valiya Tampi chased the raja
  and trapped him near a gate.
Surrounded by supporters,
  the raja fought hard and well,
But when they fled,
  he soon became confused,
Retreated inside the palace
  and shut the four great gates.
Inside the raja rested
  and tried to escape at night.
Out through the northern gate,
  along a mountain path,
Horsemen in front and back,
  four horsemen at his side,
The raja rode in the middle
  out through the northern gate.

But there on the mountain path
  Kuñcu Tampi led a patrol,
Past the northern gate
  along a mountain path.
Back and forth he rode
  and then stopped still to listen.
Suddenly in the dark,
  he saw the raja escaping.
Drawing his magic sword,
  Kuñcu Tampi rode upon him,
And raised his powerful sword
  above the raja's head.
But A̲lakappan̲ Mutaliyār screamed,
  "Stop, Kuñcu Tampi! Stop!"
Kuñcu Tampi heard his plea
  and spared the raja's life.

* * *

Still gripping sword in hand,
  he spoke to the Mutaliyār,
"Look what you have done!
  Now our plans are ruined!"
As they stood there,
  the raja began to scheme,
"I must trick the Tampimār,
  befriend them and kill them."
From the royal treasury,
  like a thief entering a house,
He took two bags of gold,
  to give to the Mutaliyār.
When he saw the money,
  the Mutaliyār rubbed his hands,
Spoke softly to the Tampimār
  and asked that they forget.
He took the hands of the Tampimār
  and the hand of the raja,
And led them inside the palace
  to the temple of Nīlakaṇṭan̲.
He turned to the raja and said,
  "With milk pot and butter churn as witness,
You must make a vow
  never to harm the Tampimār."
But the raja had an evil heart
  and falsely took the oath.

Holding a fly in his fingers,
he repeated the Mutaliyār's words:
"I'll not harm the Tampimār
as long as 'this life' lives."[38]
He touched the butter churn
to make the vow complete,
And then crushed to death the fly
he held between his fingers.
Smiling, he said to himself,
"Now the vow does not bind."
Not knowing the danger to come,
the Tampimār took an oath:
"As long as we shall live,
we'll not harm the raja.
No matter what his command,
we will not oppose it.
We'll not challenge his word,
this much we do promise."
Standing before Nīlakaṇṭaṉ
they took these oaths of peace.
Then the Mutaliyār said to the raja,
"Return everything to the Tampimār."
And the raja returned it all,
all the rights and privileges,
The taxes on land and market
taxes on produce and harvest.

* * *

Then Aḻakappaṉ Mutaliyār
gathered his army and left.
For a time they lived in peace,
the raja and the Tampimār.
The Tampimār had their lands
and their sister Koccumaṇi,
Their mother Kiṭṭiṇāttāḷ
and their uncle Koccumara Piḷḷai.
With Māṭaṉ Poṉṉaṟa Nāyar and Piccaikaipali Nāyar
they ruled the fort at Ciṅkanallūr.
But in the fort at Patmanāpapuram
the raja was filled with hate,
"If I attack the Tampimār
they'll defeat me again.
They'll raise another army
and again destroy the country.
Still, I must kill them,
for they tried to kill me."

So the raja left Patmanāpapuram,
  traveling in procession,
Past Pañcaṅkuḷam, over the Karuppukaṭṭi River
  to the fort at Nagercoil,
Where he rested in the palace
  and called to his ministers,
"Go summon the Tampimār
  and bring them both to me."
Out of the palace they ran
  out of Nagercoil.
The raja's messengers flew
  to the fort at Ciṅkanallūr,
And into the Vēmpaṭivāḷ palace
  where the Tampimār ruled.
Served by Kuñcukāḷi Nāyar
  and their strong attendants,
Valiya Tampi and Kuñcu Tampi
  ruled like proud wild tigers.
The messengers delivered the summons,
  and the Tampimār smiled.
"Immediately we leave,"
  they said and nothing more.
They quickly bathed in a well,
  rubbed themselves with sandalpaste,
Put sacred ash on their foreheads,
  and circled around Lord Śiva.
"Protect us, Nīlakaṇṭaṉ,"
  they asked as they chanted
The five-letter *mantra*
  and the three-letter *mantra*.
Kiṭṭiṇāttāḷ served them food,
  and then they dressed to leave.
Valiya Tampi wore fine muslin
  and a bright Kāñci turban,
Gold chains on his arms
  jeweled rings on his hands,
Priceless shawls on top
  and embroidered cloth below,
Gold belts on his waist
  gold rings in his ears,
Valiya Tampi was a wild tiger
  and yet a fragrant flower.
Kuñcu Tampi wore jewels
  and bracelets on his arms,
Sandalpaste and necklaces
  heavy on his chest,

Diamonds and white pearls
sparkling on his hands.
A dazzling *poṭṭu*
flashing above their eyes,
The Tampimār stood tall
and beautiful.
Valiya Tampi and Kuñcu Tampi
gathered together their servants,
Quickly went to their mother
and asked for permission to leave.
"Listen well, my sons,"
she said.
"Do not challenge the raja.
Go and return at once."
Not knowing what she did,
she told her sons to leave.
The Tampimār went proudly
past Cālamuṭam to Tāḻakkuti
Where Kuñcu Tampi remained
to supervise his rents
But Valiya Tampi went on
past Pañcavarṇakāṭu and Veṭṭuruṇi.
Faster and faster he sped
on and on he ran,
On to Nagercoil
and into the palace,
Where he stood before the raja
who had called him there.

* * *

Valiya Tampi stood at attention
before the raja's darkening face.
"Welcome," he said kindly,
"Welcome, Valiya Tampi."
Bowing slowly to the raja
Valiya Tampi stood with folded hands.
Changing his face to a scowl
the raja began to speak,
"Come, Valiya Tampi,
come here close to me."
Not knowing the danger to come,
Valiya Tampi stepped closer,
Up to the false-hearted raja
who spoke to him again:
"Let me see your sword;
please hand it to me."

Valiya Tampi nodded
  and held out his sword,
Which the raja snatched by the handle
  and drew from its sheath.
He held it high and shouted,
  "No sword in this world,
No weapon upon this earth
  can match Valiya Tampi's."
He swung the sword around
  and flung it through a door;
The door was quickly bolted
  and soldiers surrounded Valiya Tampi.
With Valiya Tampi trapped,
  the raja taunted him,
"Well, my wise friend,
  tell me something now,
It's the month of Mārkaḻi
  time for the Cucīntiram festival.
But where are the temple vessels?
  Where are the temple pennants?"
Valiya Tampi stood tall
  and quietly replied,
"They have been destroyed
  by Aḻakappaṉ Mutaliyār."
Hearing these words,
  the raja snarled at him,
"Huh! that Aḻakappaṉ Mutaliyār,
  is he your 'father' now?"
To this insult
  Valiya Tampi responded,
"If he's 'father' to me,
  he's 'maternal uncle' to you!"[39]

* * *

Mocked by these words
  the raja flew into a rage,
And shouted to his men
  to grab Valiya Tampi.
A dozen soldiers and guards
  went for Valiya Tampi,
But he battled them all
  like a man risen from the dead.
He wrestled with them,
  twisting their arms and legs.
He jumped on them
  like the flying *poṉṉuravi,*

Ran circles around them
  striking from right and left.
He killed four or five
  and wounded more with a knife.
Hour after hour he fought
  but then began to tire;
His mouth went dry
  and his ears began to ring.
"He's getting stiff,
  he's going faint," they whispered.
Valiya Tampi lost control,
  weakened and cried out,
"If Kuñcu Tampi knew,
  at once he would come!
But how can Kuñcu Tampi
  come and kill this raja?"
Pained and confused,
  "My life is over," he thought.
"Only if he comes now
  will I survive this battle."
Suddenly his body stiffened
  and crumpled to the ground.
The raja's soldiers and guards
  rushed to the fallen body,
Grabbed it and dragged it,
  like a tiger would its prey.
They hauled Valiya Tampi's body
  to the doorway of the temple,
Where the raja looked down
  and spit out his words,
"You stood against the raja,
  you scum, Valiya Tampi!
Was it you, you fool,
  who dared talk back to me?
Did you say, my friend,
  you would live out your life?
How dare you oppose me,
  you dog, Valiya Tampi!"
With the guards holding Valiya Tampi
  so he could not move,
Roaring with rage
  and drawing out his knife,
The raja cut the ornaments
  from the body of Valiya Tampi.

Then he slit his throat
  like a chicken's gullet.
His throat was cut
  and Valiya Tampi lay dead,
As the raja stood above,
  smiling with content.

* * *

Valiya Tampi was murdered,
  and his blood freely flowed,
Down the temple steps
  like a sacrificial ground.
The temple oozed with blood
  like a slaughterhouse.
Valiya Tampi lay dead
  and Kuñcu Tampi was in Tāḻakkuṭi;
But those who saw
  and those who heard
Brought the news to him:
  "The raja has murdered your brother!"
"He's been killed?
  Oh, my god!" he screamed.
"He was strong as a bull,
  the one the raja killed."
His brother was dead,
  and Kuñcu Tampi alone;
"No reason to live now,"
  he said to himself.
"Either I or the raja must die;
  there's no other way!"
Hissing like a wild animal,
  Kuñcu Tampi grabbed his sword.
In a second he was off,
  running from Tāḻakkuṭi,
Across the Cītāpālam Bridge,
  past Tirupaticāram and Oḻukaṉacēri,
Through Vaṭacēri,
  to the Nagercoil palace.
The gates of the fort were locked,
  but Kuñcu Tampi kicked them down.
His eyes blazed like fire
  as he crossed the palace courtyard
To the hallway
  where the raja sat in state.

Unsheathing his sword,
  he ran at full speed
To cut down the raja
  who murdered his only brother.[40]

(Here the singing and the possession dance came to an abrupt halt. See also pp. 95–96.)

6

The Marriage of Muttuppaṭṭaṉ

> The Brahmin is younger brother
> to the Paṟaiyaṉ.

Introduction

On its third day the koṭai festival moves away from the ritual depth of death (as in the Tampimār performance) and toward entertainment. This final performance in the festival sequence induces weak possession, if any at all, and involves few rites of worship. By convention, a story of a birth goddess or a story with no ritual links to the temple (the Rāma story, for example) is sung; however, in certain temples the singers present a modified death story, such as that translated in this chapter. In fact, the modifications made in the Muttuppaṭṭaṉ story demonstrate, even more forcefully than a birth story would, the falling away from ritual to entertainment that marks the completion of a bow song festival.

Muttuppaṭṭaṉ is a Brahmin who falls in love with two Untouchable women and changes caste, actually becomes an Untouchable, in order to marry them. The marriage is completed, but on that night Muttuppaṭṭaṉ is called out (in lieu of his father-in-law) to fight cattle raiders and is killed. These themes of cross-caste love and a violent death make Muttuppaṭṭaṉ a standard death story performed in the center of a bow song festival. However, the very popularity of this story has led to the development of a second variant that is sometimes sung in the final slot; the performance translated below is an example. Discussing how and why this variant emerged will reveal from another angle the relation of narrative to ritual that this book has been exploring. It will also lead to issues of patronage and ideology that have not been considered. Let us start by looking at the two variants of the Muttuppaṭṭaṉ story.

In the first, and historically earlier, variant Muttuppaṭṭaṉ leaves his Brahmin family and serves a local raja in Kerala. When his parents fall ill, his six older brothers bring him back home. After the parents' funeral, the seven brothers set out on a journey as merchants; they stop by a river where Muttuppaṭṭaṉ makes a *liṅgam* of sand and mediates on Śiva when, suddenly, he is distracted by the singing of two sisters of the Cakkiliyar (Untouchable cobbler) caste. He asks them to run away with him, but they doubt him (would a Brahmin sincerely love them?) and run to their father (Vāla Pakaṭai) to complain of harrassment by a Brahmin. Wielding a huge knife, Vāla Pakaṭai sets out to kill this Brahmin; but when he finds Muttuppaṭṭaṉ, he forgets his anger and listens to the marriage proposal. At first, Pakaṭai refuses since (like his daughters) he doubts the Brahmin's intentions, but then he agrees on two conditions. First, Muttuppaṭṭaṉ must remove all signs of his Brahmin status: his sacred thread, sacred ash on the forehead, front hair tuft, and silk clothes.[1] Second, he must perform the task of a Cakkiliyar—skin a dead cow and stitch a pair of sandals from the hide.

Muttuppaṭṭaṉ passes these tests and the marriage is celebrated, but that very night he goes out to defend against cattle raiders. Having killed them all, he turns to wash his sword in the river and is stabbed in the back by a man hiding in a bush, and dies. His brides find his body, cry out a dirge, and join Muttuppaṭṭaṉ on the funeral pyre. The three spirits go to heaven, receive boons from Śiva, and return to earth as gods.

This variant, found in the oldest extant manuscripts, is probably the core story.[2] From internal textual evidence it appears that the story originated in western Tinnevelly district sometime in the seventeenth century, when the Cakkiliyar first settled in the area.[3] Today this area remains the heart of the Muttuppaṭṭaṉ cult, where the story is performed in the center slot in the several temples in which he is the chief deity and in others where he is a prominent god. However, the story has also spread beyond this core area and is known in most of Tinnevelly and part of Kanya Kumari districts.

In this secondary area, where Muttuppaṭṭaṉ is not widely worshiped, another variant of his story is sung as entertainment in the final slot of a festival. This second variant differs from the first in one essential point: the caste identity of the sisters whom Muttuppaṭṭaṉ marries. In the second variant, they are not Cakkiliyars, but Brahmins abandoned at birth and later only raised by Cakkiliyar parents. Performances of the second variant, moreover, conclude with the marriage and omit entirely the death and lament scenes. Nullifying the caste conflict, omitting the death scene, and emphasizing the marriage event all combine to move the second variant of the Muttuppaṭṭaṉ story closer to the pattern of a birth story.

The second variant also approaches the birth story pattern by bringing in a mythic world. The change is effected by a motif which I have termed the "substituted birth," or the insertion of a divine origin prior to a human birth.[4] This lifts the narrative onto the cosmological plane of Hindu mythology where it is linked to other narratives, in our case the Tamil variant of the myth of Skanda, the son of Śiva. To atone for the sin of killing the demon Sūrapadma, Skanda sends one of his commanders to meditate in Kailāsa. There his meditation is interrupted by two celestial nymphs whom he curses to be born on earth as Brahmins and to be raised by Cakkiliyars; they, in turn, curse him to be born on the same earth and to marry them. The meditator is then reborn as Muttuppaṭṭaṉ and the two nymphs are reborn to a Brahmin couple (Cuntarakṣi and Cuppu Kuṭṭi Ayyar). The baby girls are abandoned and picked up by a Cakkiliyar couple (Vāla Pakaṭai and Vāla) and later married by Muttuppaṭṭaṉ.

These changes are both cause and effect of the wider distribution and more popular appeal of the second variant. Mythic themes lift the story above local history and the substituted birth blunts the critical thrust of the first variant since Muttuppaṭṭaṉ now marries not Cakkiliyars, but Brahmins. There is some evidence that these changes arose, partially at least, to please high-caste patrons who objected to the cross-caste marriage in the first variant.[5] Given the particulars of the Muttuppaṭṭaṉ story and the nature of Indian society, it is not surprising that caste identities should be at issue. Most of the singers and villagers with whom I spoke recognized these politics of patronage and were quick to explain that the second variant emerged because high castes (higher than the Nadar) supported it. Even those in the core area of the cult who had not heard of the second variant were not surprised when it was described to them: "Oh yes, that's what some people do to our stories," they laughed. One older, high-caste man, who was particularly concerned with the implications of a Brahmin-Untouchable marriage, hit on an ingenious argument to explain it away: since Muttuppaṭṭaṉ actually becomes a Cakkiliyar, no cross-caste marriage occurs![6]

Despite these attempts to suppress it, the theme of a Brahmin man who loves and marries Untouchable women is present, even in the second variant. The substituted birth may insert a Brahmin pedigree for the sisters, but this is only a technical point that does not eliminate the drama. The prior, divine birth does explain that the sisters are reborn as Brahmins, but neither the characters in the story nor the audience in the festival seems to notice. Throughout, the sisters look and sound like Cakkiliyars, and everyone reacts to them as if they were—why else would Muttuppaṭṭaṉ be forced to become a cobbler to marry them?

One reason for the irrepressible popularity of the Brahmin-Untouchable theme, which is found on all levels of Indian literature, is that it expresses a fusion of opposites.[7] As groups, Brahmins and Untouchables are unequal in the material conditions of life, education, and access to power—a fact that individually poor Brahmins and Untouchable members of parliament do not alter. Added to this socioeconomic separation is a ritual opposition since the two caste groups are positioned at either ends of the horizontal axis of purity-impurity. However, because they are equidistant from the ritually nil state of ordinary life in the center, they are also symmetrically related. For example, both Brahmins and Untouchables (in South India) are ritual specialists, but they function at contrasting rites: Brahmins at auspicious times (birth, marriage), Untouchables at dangerous times (death, harmful spirit contact). As opposed but related categories, their union, as in the Muttuppaṭṭaṉ story, produces a satisfying sense of completion, a kind of social analogue to the androgyny in Hindu mythology.[8] This hidden intimacy is the point of the Tamil proverb: "The Brahmin is younger brother to the Paṟaiyaṉ."[9]

It is also true that the theme of Brahmin-Untouchable union can be popular precisely because the groups are *not* in frequent contact (again, at least in Nāñcil Nāṭu).[10] The exclusion of Untouchables from Brahmin settlements is often noted, but in many places Brahmins are prohibited from entering Untouchable areas.[11] Furthermore, Brahmin and Untouchable are pan-Indian castes that are capable of carrying symbolic value beyond the specifics of the locale. This fact stands out when we consider bow songs about conflict between more local castes much closer in status and more frequently in contact—the Nadar and Piḷḷai, for example.[12] Their stories are too close to social reality, too parochial in content, and consequently do not expand beyond a limited area. The story of Muttuppaṭṭaṉ, however, like the gods and demons in Hindu mythology, represents identity within opposition; at the center of even the most severe contrast, it reassures us, lies union.

All this complexity has been drawn out in the performance of the Muttuppaṭṭaṉ story translated in this chapter. First it sets up the opposition between the Brahmin and the Cakkiliyar sisters (Tummakkāḷ and Pummakkāḷ) when the brothers warn Muttuppaṭṭaṉ of dangerous sexual contact from a "snake-eyed Cakkiliyar." Later the religious meditation of the Brahmin is disrupted by the Untouchables' presence. Untouchability itself is dramatized when Pakaṭai (the father) fears to touch the sleeping Brahmin. Opposition is also expressed through the two pairs of parents for the reborn nymphs: the Brahmins (Cuntarakṣi and Cuppu Kuṭṭi Ayyar) spend lavishly in order to have children, but then abandon them; the Cakkiliyars (Vāli and Vāla Pakaṭai) also want children, but can only get what others have cast out. The Brahmins own a calf, whereas the Cakkiliyars are watchmen for the cows of others. And there is humor in poking fun at the portly Muttuppaṭṭaṉ when he lags behind the Cakkiliyar sisters in a foot race.

Then these contrasts are collapsed. If categories of caste separate Brahmin and Cakkiliyar, those of kinship are fabricated to unite them. When Muttuppaṭṭaṉ first sees Pakaṭai, he addresses him as *māma,* the term for maternal uncle and father-in-law. Later, in order to marry the sisters, he strips away all artificial signs of social status, his sacred thread, front hair tuft, sacred ash, and silk clothes.[13] Any remaining differences are then leveled in a food exchange. The Cakkiliyar family offers their new son-in-law betel nut in a cow's skull, and then serves a meal of salted calf's meat and crab salad—and the piously vegetarian Brahmin relishes it all. This culinary conversion signifies the bond between Brahmin and Untouchable even more convincingly than the wedding that immediately follows.

The final wedding scene, however, does underline the transformation of Muttuppaṭṭaṉ through its clear contrast with a scene at the very beginning of the story. In that opening scene, Muttuppaṭṭaṉ sits under a *pantal* (thatched roof) to recite the Rāma story to a crowd of a "thousand Vedic Brahmins." He also sits under a pantal in the wedding scene, but this time the audience is his Cakkiliyar in-laws. If the initial scene leads to Muttuppaṭṭaṉ's departure from his Brahmin home, the final one completes his incorporation into a Cakkiliyar family.

The marriage scene is important also because it illustrates a technique often used in bow song performances: the incorporation of context into text. By bringing the festival context into the story he is singing, the bow singer is able to comment on the festival, especially on his patrons sitting in the audience. Most frequently, this incorporation is achieved by means of a formal acknowledgment of donations to the singers. In addition to the money collected from the temple community at large, the singers also receive individual gifts (of a few rupees) during performance, particularly on the last day of a festival when ritual demands are weak. After the money is given to the singer, he interrupts the narrative and announces the donor's name, village, and the amount given (multiplied by a factor of one thousand).[14] A talented singer will elaborate on this, as in the following example taken from the translation in this chapter. After receiving a two-rupee gift from Nacciyār Aṭimai (a woman of the Untouchable Cāmpavar [Perumāḷ]), the lead singer spoke in formal prose:

> In this great town of Aralvāymoḻi, from the Perumāḷ community which built the high dams across the Cauvery and the Vaikai rivers, in the land of many rains and cool breezes where each banana stem yields two bunches, born in that caste known for generosity, which gives and gives when asked and has given even its own head, in that caste of Cāmpavar, Nacciyār Aṭimai has honored us with a donation of 2,000 rupees.

Then he shifted into the song mode to add the blessing:

> By the grace of Kantaṉ,
>   may you live for a thousand years,
> By the grace of Murukaṉ
>   may you prosper for a thousand more!
> By the grace of the Lord of Nellai
>   may you live happily,
> By the grace of Paṭṭavaraiyar (Muttuppaṭṭaṉ)
>   may you flower forever!

This and similar announcements begin to break down the division between performance and festival and to bring aspects of the context (the donor and her donation) inside the performed text. This allows the singer to use the performance to influence patronage, since by announcing these gifts he calls attention to giving and encourages more gifts. For this reason, donations tend to occur in clusters, one followed by several others. In the performance translated below, ninety-one gifts were made, in ten groups, totaling one hundred and seventy-three rupees. Gifts to singers may indicate appreciation of the singing, but there are other motivations. Even a two-rupee contribution to a performance, which invokes the gods for the benefit of the community, is a small act of *dharma* for which the ordinary villager earns religious merit and public recognition. The blessing tagged on to the announcement also holds out the possibility that the giver may become a recipient of a boon from the gods.

Singers call attention to patronage in more subtle ways, too. In the above excerpt, for instance, the Untouchable Cāmpavar are said to have built a dam, the preeminent act of charity by kings who are the model patrons in

Tamil culture. Next the singer uses a series of images, of monsoon, banana trees, and breeze, that connote prosperity and yield; then, almost as a part of this natural world, he adds that the Cāmpavar have given their own lives. So, too, has Nacciyār Aṭimai given to these bow singers.

This identity between bow song donor and royal patron was reinforced in a later announcement in the same performance. When a man from the Ācāri (carpenter) caste, one of the five artisan castes collectively known as Viśvakarma, offered two rupees, the lead singer spoke in formal Tamil:

> In this famous town of Aralvāymoḻi, born in the Viśvakarma caste, kings even to kings, best of all people, possessing the highest good, the caste who fashioned the rays of the sun and made this square earth, who made crowns for poets and lion-thrones for kings, who created humans, rajas, and the elements of the natural world, and who makes the *tāli* [marriage pendant], born in this caste and bearing the sacred name of Kanpam, Kaṭampam, Poṉi Malaiyaṉ, Tiru Malaiyaṉ, Tiru Centūr Āṇṭavar, and Civacupramaṇiyaṉ, Śrī Cuppaiya Ācāri honored us with a gift of 2,000 rupees. For him and all his family,
>
> By the grace of Murukaṉ
> may you prosper;
> By the grace of Pecci Ammaṉ
> may you be eternal like Kailāsa.

Here the bow singer, like other oral performers in India, plays the role of genealogist and elevates the carpenter Cuppaiya to a descendant of the Vedic god Viśvakarma, who "made this square earth." The carpenter is also identified with other artisans who honored poets and kings. This analogy flatters the singer as well, since he says, in effect, "You celebrate me with this gift just as your ancestors celebrated other poets with crowns." [15]

Other singers move the performance context more completely into the sung text. Often the temple, the festival, and even the local community become part of the story. This incorporation of context is inevitable in the performance of birth stories since they conclude with a scene in which the god or goddess arrives at the particular temple in which the story is being performed (the name of the temple is changed to suit each festival, but the general events are fixed for all performances). This nearly total absorption of context by the text is illustrated in the following excerpt from a performance of the Kāḷi Ammaṉ story at a temple controlled by the Nāyakkar caste in the village of Māvatikāḷ.

> On the wake night of Amavāci, the people of Māvatikāḷ decided to go to Courtrallam to worship Śiva there. They went in a caravan of twenty-one

> carts, worshiped all the gods and goddesses, and spent the night. In the morning, they were preparing to return, but Kāḷi Ammaṉ, who had watched the entire night, said to herself, "They worship everyone, but they don't honor me. They show me no respect. This must change!" And so, she took the form of a young child and came back with them to Māvatikāḷ. When she arrived, she let out the kuravai cry in the village streets, caused disease and dirt to fall like rain. People were confused and called the diviner who beat his drum and said, "It's not a ghost or evil spirt; it's Kāḷi Ammaṉ herself. Build her a temple, and hold a festival for her." Everyone got together and built a temple in the middle of Māvatikāḷ; they put Vairavaṉ on the north and Cuṭalai Māṭaṉ on the south. Then, in the month of Tai, on the third Tuesday, they celebrated a koṭai for Kāḷi with bow songs and dance. Kāḷi and the other gods came to reside there and protect the people from harm.

Here text and context have been completely merged. Temple, goddess, community, and festival have been lifted out from the performance context and set within the performed text. Even the date of the actual performance (the third Tuesday in the month of Tai) has been used in the text. And when the last lines of the excerpt above were sung, Kāḷi appeared in the festival and possessed her medium. As in the "scripted" performances, although less overtly, the text directs performance, the narrative cues ritual.

A still more detailed incorporation of context into text is found in the Muttuppaṭṭaṉ performance of this chapter. This merger is achieved by exploiting the natural identity between the marriage festival in the text and the koṭai festival in the context. The excerpt below picks up the story when Pakaṭai has finalized the dates for his daughters' marriage with Muttuppaṭṭaṉ. He is proud, but realizes one problem remains.

> As the day for the wedding got closer and closer, Pakaṭai got more and more worried. He had no money. No cash in hand and no one to loan him any. Not a rupee anywhere! But, I ask you—is that anything to get worried about? Well . . . is it? Of course not. All you need to do is *collect* money. And where do you start? Go to every house and ask for it? No, there's no time for that. Better to begin right here, right in this festival; better to ask everyone sitting under this pantal—all you women and men, sisters and brothers.

With these words, the lead singer widens the frame around his text to include the listening audience. Not coincidentally, this occurs at the very point in the story where the issue of patronage arises, at the preparations for Muttuppaṭṭaṉ's wedding. By describing the difficulty and necessity of financially supporting that wedding, the singer obliquely comments on the patronage that keeps him on the platform where he is now singing. This conflation of wedding with bow song festival is then completed by detailing how the items necessary for both are contracted.

> Luckily we've got a little cash on hand so we can start to make arrangements. Now, who's the first person you need for a [wedding] festival?
>
> [Audience:] "A pantal man."
>
> Exactly! We need a pantal man, and luckily we don't have to go very far to find a good one. Right here in Aralvāymoḻi there is Paramacivam Piḷḷai.

Paramacivam Piḷḷai, who did in fact build the pantal under which he and the singers and the audience are sitting, is now a character in the performance. He beams with pride as the lead singer continues.

> And so we'll go up to him and say, "Mr. Pantal man, we're going to have a wedding and we need a pantal. How much do you want?" Now Paramacivam Piḷḷai is not one to make a big thing of money, and he'll say, "Money? Don't talk about it now. Let's get the work done, then we can talk." So we agree and give him . . . say . . . eleven rupees as an advance.

The same scene, with minor variations, is then repeated for the food, lights and loudspeakers, and temple music required at both a bow song koṭai and a wedding. In each scene, the person who performed the service for the present bow song festival becomes a character doing the same for Muttuppaṭṭaṉ's wedding; and each person, like Paramacivam Piḷḷai, appears disinterested in financial gain. The bow singers do not appear in their story, but the implication is that they, like other recipients of temple patronage, are motivated by religious devotion and friendship, and not by money. Here, as in the earlier excerpt from the Kāḷi Ammaṉ story, the performed text is a mirror in which the singers and audience see themselves in idealized roles—the unselfish performers and generous patrons.

The total incorporation of context into text in this Muttuppaṭṭaṉ performance is somewhat unusual in the bow song tradition. However, its exaggerated nature only clarifies the "textualization" of context that is less pronounced, but nonetheless present, in all performances. Here we see yet another aspect of the text's primary role in bow song performances. The text, from the performers' point of view, is extremely important because it is the only part of the total performance that they (even partially) control. By bringing the context within their textual grasp, the singers can manipulate it for their own ends, for example, to stimulate patronage.

Narrative texts, however, do not have a free rein in the bow song tradition.

The ritual pattern, as we have seen, requires performances in each slot to omit, expand, or otherwise alter the narrative to conclude with specific events. The force of this ritual patterning on narrative was clearly illustrated toward the end of the performance of the second variant of the Muttuppaṭṭaṉ story translated in this chapter.

The performance was sung, properly, in the final slot of a festival held in a temple belonging to the Kōṉār caste. Muttuppaṭṭaṉ is not worshiped in this temple, but he is worshiped in several other temples in the area and many in the audience were thus familiar with the story as sung in the center slot when it culminates with the death of the hero and the lament of his wives.[16] As the performance in the Kōṉār temple drew to an appropriate close with the wedding scene, some men in the audience jumped up and shouted, "Sing the death scene, sing the death scene!" The singers were momentarily caught off guard and argued weakly that they could sing those scenes only if possession occurred. But the protesters reversed this logic and said (as is generally believed) that possession would occur only if the death scene were sung. Then the singers put the matter more bluntly: "It isn't right (*cari illai*) to sing them now"; and this appeal to the canons of context proved persuasive. The festival officials stepped up and announced that the festival should conclude with a "good event" (*nalla campavam*). The last verses of the wedding scene were sung, bringing the performance and the festival to a proper close.

The lead singer of this long and complicated performance was K. Patmanāpaṉ, a young man whose burly chest shone with the bronze pendants his patrons have donated to him (see Plate 9). A good singer, he is also a superb storyteller who played the roles of all the many characters in this story. He begins with the invocation.

Performance Translation

God of the victory spear!
  Murukaṉ,
  protect us from evil.
Help me sing this magic music,
  make my tongue eloquent.
The *paṭalai* and budding *mutalai*
  tiṭulai flower, tiny *tuvarai* seed,
  grains and young fruit—
All this, Murukaṉ,
  I offer to you.
Milk, water, sugar,

tender coconut, mango,
sweet foods and areca nut—
I offer these to you.

Murukaṉ of the Red City!
who by the grace of Śiva,
released the gods from imprisonment.
Guru and poet,
who kindly taught me
music and rhythm on the bow
with heart generous as a king,
Palacuppiramaṇiyā!
I worship at your feet.
Kumarā!
your powerful spear
held back the sea
and destroyed the demons!
God with six heads
and matted hair,
Majestic Murukaṉ,
All-Knowing One,
wish-granting *karppakam* tree,
keep us from harm.

Gaṇapati!
I'll not forget you,
or my guru.
Āṟumukam! Sarasvati!
help me sing this song.
Murukaṉ!
husband of that forest girl,
lovely as a dark peahen,
Come rest in my throat,
come bless my words.
Older brother to Kantaṉ,
born before Vēlaṉ,
Gaṇapati! Vināyaka!
come bless me.

Goddess!
I sing of you,
I worship you.
Wandering in this southern land,
I searched for you,

you who danced with Śiva
  at the beginning of time.
Garland of shining light!
  come to me now,
  come quickly,
  bless me as I sing!
Protect me, Great Goddess,
  as I sing of Muttuppaṭṭaṉ
  in the temple of Corimuttu Ayyaṉ,[17]
Destroyer of demons
  and son of Śiva,
  Lord of the eight directions.

In the best of all lands,
  in the land poets praise,
Land where rains pour
  and cool breezes blow,
Where light rains fall
  and sweet pepper grows,
Where the monsoon pours
  and dry lands yield fruit.
Land where rains dance
  and clouds drizzle,
Where rains fall in Māci
  and deer herds roam,
Land of tamarind and turmeric
  where black lilies bloom.
Land of sugar cane
  of sweet ripe bananas,
  of red and white paddy
  standing rich and tall.
Land where cow and tiger
  play at the water hole,
Where the snake and mongoose,
  cats and mice
  live peacefully.
Land of spreading peacock fans
  and swans' graceful dance,
  where cow herds graze
  and the deer run free.
Land of spreading mango trees
  and dense forest groves,
Land where fighting with cows
  sends one to hell,

Where fighting with horses
  brings suffering,
A land where kings
  fight only with elephants,
That good Āriya Nāṭu![18]

In the land where they use only elephants in war, in the beautiful Āriya Nāṭu, lived seven Brahmins, the *paṭṭaṉ* brothers: Appāpaṭṭaṉ, Kuppāpaṭṭaṉ, Āṉantapaṭṭaṉ, Cōmaccipaṭṭaṉ, Cōmaliṅkapaṭṭaṉ, and . . . the youngest of them all, the good Muttuppaṭṭaṉ.[19] His brothers raised precious little Muttuppaṭṭaṉ with tender care, and he grew up quickly—one, two, three, four, and five years passed. Then his brothers decided they should train him to become a learned man, a great scholar. To this lofty end, they enrolled him in the very best school in the area, and there Muttuppaṭṭaṉ began to learn:

Aaaaaaaa . . .
    the letter "ā,"
  aaa . . .
    the letter "a,"
Iiiiiii . . .
    the letter "ī,"
  iii . . .
    the letter "i."[20]

And so on—the entire alphabet, mathematics, the *Mūturai,* astrology, wrestling, pole fencing—Muttuppaṭṭaṉ learned all these valuable things. From the age of five (when he first became aware of the world) up to sixteen, he learned all the Hindu arts—the four Vedas, the six *śāstra*s, the eighteen *purāṇa*s, the sixty-four literatures, the ninety-six philosophies, the 108 *Ākama*s, and all the old poems. He mastered them all, every single one! Then his brothers looked at him and said,

"Good! . . . Our Muttuppaṭṭaṉ has learned even more than we had hoped for. But there is something else—he must now become as *brave* as he is intelligent. Courage! That's what he needs." Now for that they also have a special school, where Muttuppaṭṭaṉ began to learn:

The pole, the knife, and spear
  one by one
The sword and small dagger,
  he learned them expertly.
If a tiger attacked,
  he'd leap ninety feet away.
If someone attacked from behind,
  he'd jump seventy feet away.
Elephant riding and horsemanship
  and all the arts of war,

When he was twenty-one,
  Muttuppaṭṭaṉ knew them all!

He could fight riding on top of an elephant or riding on a horse, and direct a battle from his palanquin. He knew it all. Again his brothers thought to themselves,

"Well, he's learned all there is to know, and he's only twenty-one. But something still remains; he's educated, but we don't really know what he's learned. Let's set aside a day and have him recite a story. And we shouldn't be the only ones to hear it; we'll invite the whole village!"

Now it was already the month of Māci when, during Śivarāttiri, everyone would stay awake through the night. So they decided to ask Muttuppaṭṭaṉ to read something on that night.

"Little brother, come here a minute. C'mon, it's something important."

Muttuppaṭṭaṉ rose and approached his older brothers, who said,

"You know it's the month of Māci and during Śivarāttiri everyone will stay awake, so we want you to recite something for us on that night. You see, we haven't enjoyed the benefits of your education. We're inviting the whole village and making the arrangements."

"But . . . what story should I read?"

"What do you mean 'what story'? There's only *one* story—forget the others. Read us the *Rāmāyaṇa*!"

Muttuppaṭṭaṉ agreed, and when the day for the recital had arrived. . . .

Muttuppaṭṭaṉ looked beautiful,
  mango leaves hung everywhere,
As a thousand Vedic Brahmins
  gathered to hear the Hari-Rāma story.
Villagers sat in groups
  to hear Paṭṭaṉ tell the Rāma story.
Into this crowd of thousands,
  into the very center,
Muttuppaṭṭaṉ walked and sat down,
  to tell the Rāma story.
Fearing that evil would come
  if he outshone his brothers
  by reciting perfectly,
Paṭṭaṉ told the Gōvinda Rāma story
  but garbled all his words.[21]
In the very first word
  he made nine mistakes,

in the second word
he made twenty more.
In the third word
there were thirty-four mistakes,
in the fourth
he made forty-four.
In the fifth word
he made fifty-four mistakes,
in the sixth
there were sixty-four.
In the seventh word
he made seventy-four mistakes,
the eighth
had eighty-four.
In the ninth word
there were ninety-four,
And after the tenth word
every sound was wrong.

Sitting in the middle of that crowd, Muttuppaṭṭaṉ recited the story with mistake after mistake; and the old men, women, and children who had come to gain religious merit by hearing the story, soon began to talk,

"Hey! What is this? Appāpaṭṭaṉ made such a big deal of his younger brother, saying that no one else in the village could match his learning. He boasted and boasted, but his brother can't even recite a well-known story like the *Rāmāyaṇa*. He's chopping it to bits! You know the saying, 'Many know the story, few know its meaning.' Let's leave. There's nothing to hear from him."

With these words, most of those standing and even some who were sitting down left the crowd. Appāpaṭṭaṉ wanted to know what people were saying—would they say, "Well, not bad; he's doing fine" or would they criticize him? He wrapped a towel around his head so that no one could recognize him, and circled around the crowd while Muttuppaṭṭaṉ was reciting. When he heard what was said, he was crushed! He glared at Muttuppaṭṭaṉ and screamed,

"Is this our reward for all we've done for you? You fool! Do you know what everyone is saying? This is your education, huh? You've been studying since you were five years old and now you're twenty-one. That's a lot of education, but where is it? And do you know how much it has cost us? We spent piles on you! We poured it out. Look what you have done! You repay us by acting like this, disgrace us in front of the whole village! Dishonor us in public! Peabrain!"

The brothers got madder and madder until Appāpaṭṭaṉ, forgetting that they were in public, went up to Muttuppaṭṭaṉ and bop! smacked him on the head.

Then the other brothers—Kuppaṉ, Caṅkaṉ, Caravaṉ, Cōmacci, Cōmaliṅkam—looked at each other,

> "Hey, let's get out of here. It looks bad."

And so they left. But Muttuppaṭṭaṉ, who had been hit in public, felt terrible:

> "Who hit me? My oldest brother Appāpaṭṭaṉ? Well, that's not so bad, but the others could have done something, at least come over and taken me home. Someone should have helped. Ah, who cares about them? At least my mother and father are here; surely they'll come and take me home."

Muttuppaṭṭaṉ sat there for a little while and waited, but even his parents did not come up! He was very upset:

> "Alright! That does it! There's no point in living any more with such people—these brothers and parents. I can do perfectly well without them. I'll just go off and live by myself."

He was feeling bad because he knew that saying "The youngest is doomed." As the youngest, he thought he should leave his family and live somewhere else. But where to go?

Join the Pāṇṭiyaṉ raja?
  there's money but no status.
Go to the Cēra raja?
  there are no victories.
Or to the Cōḻa raja?
  there's food but no happiness.
With no other place to go,
  Paṭṭaṉ headed for Kōṭṭāra.

Muttuppaṭṭaṉ went strait to Kōṭṭārakarai, to the palace of Rāma Raja, where he thought he might gain a position and some status.[22] But as he neared the palace, he began to think,

> "Now, let's see. Can't just march right into the palace, to the raja and say, 'Hi, Raja! Please give me a position in your palace.' He might be in a bad mood and scowl at me, 'Hey, who are you, wandering around like this looking for work? What would I give you? Ask somewhere else.' He might just dismiss me that fast. Anyway, a person is paid according to his skills, so I better show mine first. Even if I am not personally respected, at least my skills will be and then the raja will give me a position. But where to demonstrate my talents? Not in the middle of this town, a big crowd would gather, and cause trouble—they'd stop traffic, and I'd be arrested, taken to jail, and then . . . well, only those who have experienced that would know. No, better go to some isolated place, like the seashore, the ocean. It's wonderful there, nothing to bother you—no cars, no busses, no trucks; a little boat now and then, but that's all."

So Muttuppaṭṭaṉ went to the seashore and . . .

Fixing his sword upright in the water,
he spun around like a wheel.
Spun around,
looked to the south,
and saw a crowd of men.
Spun around,
looked north,
and saw a crowd of gods.
Spun around,
looked east,
and saw a crowd of *sādhu*s.
Spun around,
looked west,
and saw a crowd of men.

When Rāma Raja saw him spinning around on his sword in the middle of the ocean, he sent a messenger who said,

"Sir, you have been summoned by Rāma Raja. Please follow me."

Muttuppaṭṭaṉ heard this request and thought,

"Good, things are going as planned."

Then he climbed down from his sword, followed the messenger, and came to Rāma Raja. The raja greeted him with a *namaskāram* and Paṭṭaṉ did the same; they exchanged introductions and Rāma Raja asked,

"What path led you here?
where is your home, my friend?
why have you come here?
what is your goal?
What's your name?
what's your village?
What's your father's name?
and your mother's name?
What land are you from?
tell me these things, my friend."

When asked who, what, where, and why, Muttuppaṭṭaṉ thought,

"Hmmm . . . what to say? If I say that my parents are alive, that I've got five brothers, a comfortable life, land, livestock, and more, and that I came here because of a fight, and that I want a position in the palace—if I tell the truth—the raja is bound to wonder about me and think 'This guy's here because of a problem at home; he'll leave as soon as it is cleared up; better not hire anyone like that.' He'll tell me there's no work and get rid of me."

To avoid that disgrace, Muttuppaṭṭan̲ hid the truth and answered with a total lie,

> "Raja!
> Āriya Nāṭu is my home,
> Kṣatriya is my caste.
> But I have no brothers,
> no one for support,
> no mother and no father,
> no relatives at all.
> Born under an unlucky star,
> I travel alone."

And the raja said,

> "No brothers, no parents, no one to help you? You must be an orphan, wandering around like this. But no need to wander any more; I'll give you a post in my palace—you can be a minister. There's only one thing you must tell me, that's your salary. What do you require? This sort of thing is best settled at the start. If not, then you'll go along thinking, 'Well, the raja gives what he gives; I'll take it and not complain.' And I'll be thinking, 'What a loyal minister; he just takes what I offer without complaint.' If we go on thinking like that, there'll be an argument before long. To avoid any kind of suspicion or confrontation, it's best to settle this salary business right at the start."

Then Muttuppaṭṭan̲ spoke up,

> "Raja! If I am to be one of your ministers, this must be my salary: 1,000 for the *veṭci* flowers I wear in front, 1,000 for those in back, 1,000 for my sword, 1,000 for its sheath, and 1,000 for my words of advice. Plus 50 gold pieces in advance."

Rāma Raja thought over his demand,

> "My god! He's asking 5,000 plus 50 gold pieces. How can I give it? On the other hand . . . when you consider his beauty and his strength, even 6,000 wouldn't be too much! With him I won't need anyone else in this palace. He'll bring so much fame and status to me I'll give whatever he asks. But I better put it in writing, because if I just say it, there'll be trouble later. Besides, it will confer honor on him."

So the raja made it official.

> By formal proclamation
> Paṭṭan̲ was honored
> and named first minister.
> He rode an elephant in procession
> he rode upon a horse,
> And viewed the city from a palanquin.

As first minister, Muttuppaṭṭaṉ was just and compassionate. And remember, only when an official governs justly are the rains frequent and the harvests good. Under Muttuppaṭṭaṉ's rule, the land prospered as never before, and the people were amazed,

"This is wonderful! We used to get rain, but not like *this*. Now it rains and rains and rains. It's green everywhere, all the time!"

One, two, three,
rain three times a month.
One, two, three,
three harvests every year.
All the thieves and murderers . . .

You see, before this crime was rampant—mugging, breaking into houses, through walls, through windows, through doors, murders—crime had become normal, an everyday event. But under Paṭṭaṉ's just rule, well . . . there wasn't a single crime anywhere. There was peace, harmony, order,

All the thieves and murderers,
liars and trouble-makers,
Were safely put away.

Muttuppaṭṭaṉ brought unknown prosperity, peace and bountiful harvests. As minister of the raja in the Kōṭṭārakarai palace, he became a famous man. But back in his birthplace, in Āriya Nāṭu, things were different. His parents' situation had gone from bad to worse; in desperation they called the brothers together:

"You are here, my sons,
but where is the youngest?
Without him,
what good is life?
where is my little baby,
my sweet sugar cane?
Where is my pretty boy?
my dear pet?
Go now,
search for him,
and bring him back to us."
The brothers traveled far
searching high and low,
They looked in every place,
except where Muttuppaṭṭaṉ was.

After looking everywhere and not finding a trace, they sat down exhausted.

"What are we going to do? We've tried everywhere and can't find him."

Then Caṅkaṉ, the second oldest, said,

"Look, it's simple. When he left, he was really mad, and we don't have many relatives where he could go. So wherever he went, he must have committed suicide. There's no other explanation! He certainly couldn't have made it on his own; he was too shy even to speak with strangers. How could anyone like that manage? No, he must have killed himself. If he were still alive, we would have found him by now. Let's go home, and when our parents ask about him, we'll say, 'Mom . . . Dad . . . you see . . . your son . . . he died.'"

The brothers turned to go home, but went first to a cremation ground to get some ash and pieces of bone—they needed evidence for their story. Once home, they said,

"Mother, Father . . . our brother Muttuppaṭṭaṉ . . . has died."

And they gave them the ashes and bones, but their parents yelled,

"Fools! Do you think if he had died we wouldn't know about it? What kind of a dirty trick are you trying to pull with this story? If he had died, we wouldn't remain alive for even a second! We're alive only with the hope that we will see him again. If it weren't for that, we'd have died long ago. But one thing I'm sure of: wherever he is, he is doing fine. Go look again and bring him here. Don't come back alone!"

After these harsh words, the brothers looked at each other,

"Now we're really in a mess. If we don't do something quick, they're going to die and we don't need that sin on our heads. Let's go look another time. If we find him, fine; if not, well . . . we'll just do what he did—we'll go off and never return."

In the dense forests,
  in every town,
  in land after land,
They looked
  but found no Muttuppaṭṭaṉ.
Finally,
  with no place to go,
  they came to Malayalam country.

*[Bearing the sacred name of our Gōpāla Kṛṣṇa, of lotus-eyed Viṣṇu, of the great-souled Nārāyaṇa, Śrī Perumāḷ Kōṉār has honored us with a gift of 3,000 rupees. To this scion of the Yādava community, this jewel of the Āy caste, and to his family and relatives,

By the grace of Kaṇṇaṉ,
  May you prosper as the *karppakam* tree.

*Here the singer announces a donation from the audience.

By the grace of Achuytaṉ,
  May you flourish like a lotus.
By the grace of Perumāḷ,
  May you endure like Vaikuṇṭaṉ.]

In the Malayalam country the brothers went to Kōṭṭārakarai.

"Well, we've looked everywhere and still can't find him. But we can't go home now. Let's rest here and start off first thing in the morning, but where's a good place to spend the night? Can't lie down in one of these mango groves; the watchman would report us, the police grab us, and then . . . well, only those who have had that experience know. No, better go off to some isolated place where no one will ask any questions."

They looked around, spied an old, crumbling *maṇṭapam* and decided to sleep there. As they lay down in the *maṇṭapam,* and closed their eyes, Muttuppaṭṭaṉ came that way.

On an elephant in a royal seat,
  beneath umbrellas and jewels,
  a silk shawl on his shoulders,
Riding high in procession
  Paṭṭaṉ saw the old *maṇṭapam.*

Muttuppaṭṭaṉ called to his ministers and gently said,

"See those people sleeping in that *maṇṭapam* over there? Are they thieves or murderers? Better find out. Go grab them and bring them to me."

The ministers brought the brothers to Muttuppaṭṭaṉ, but he didn't recognize them:

"Where are you from?
  where is your home?
  who are your parents?
Why have you come here?
  tell me, please."

When the five brothers heard the raja speak, they didn't realize who it was and answered,

"Raja! Great lord! We are from Āriya Nāṭu, the sons of Cōmaccipaṭṭaṉ and Civakāmi. We were seven brothers and lived together happily. Then a problem arose between us and our youngest brother, Muttuppaṭṭaṉ—nothing serious . . . just a little dispute—but because of that, he cursed us and left the house. Now we have no idea where he is. Meanwhile, our parents are upset, very upset. It's so bad that if we don't bring him back, they're going to die of grief! We've looked for him everywhere, but don't have the slightest clue. It got dark, so we decided to sleep in this old *maṇṭapam* and leave in the morning. Then your men came and dragged us in front of you, and here we are."

When Muttuppaṭṭaṉ heard this, he knew they were his brothers. He felt terrible that he had caused all this trouble, and that he was riding on an elephant while they, his older brothers, were standing below him. Unable to hold back any more, he cried out,

"Brothers! My brothers!
I did not recognize you.
We are flesh and blood,
born of the same mother!"

Appāpaṭṭaṉ, the oldest, looked at the person speaking to them from the elephant and then turned to his brothers,

"Hey, Kuppaṉ! Caravaṉ! Caṅkaṉ! Do you realize who this is? Take a good look, a real good look. It's him—our little Muttuppaṭṭaṉ!"

When Appāpaṭṭaṉ pointed this out, the others shrieked,

"Muttuppaṭṭaṉ! Little brother!
where have you been?
we searched everywhere.
Our parents are dying of grief;
if you don't return,
they'll surely kill us too!"

Hearing this, Muttuppaṭṭaṉ was deeply saddened and decided to leave immediately, to see his parents. But then he looked back at his brothers and felt even worse because they obviously hadn't eaten in days—their stomachs had shrunken to a pea! First he must feed them; so off they went and on the way, Paṭṭaṉ began to think,

"I can't take them into the palace, since I've already lied about having no family, no brothers, and so on. They'll ask questions, and that would be awkward. Better go into town and eat there."

Muttuppaṭṭaṉ took his brothers to the bazaar, where they saw a little shop with a board hanging in front:

Meals Ready: Janata Meals—1 rupee.[23] Standard Meals—1.50 rupees.

Muttuppaṭṭaṉ read these details and thought,

"Hmm . . . Janata meals for 1 rupee. But that won't do for these stomachs. And the Standard Meals? That's still too little. These brothers of mine know no shame when it comes to food! They'll eat everything in sight. I'm not going to do this cheaply; that's a sin I don't need."

So he called out to the shop-owner,

"Listen, I've brought six people here to eat. Feed them till they're stuffed. Don't hold back. Just send me the bill, and I'll take care of it. And the regular food won't do. Serve them the best stuff, including *vaṭai* and *pāyacam.*"

The brothers sat down and really enjoyed themselves. They ate and ate—downed everything that was brought to them. When they finished, Muttuppaṭṭaṉ let them rest while he went off alone to the raja to announce that he was returning home.

"Raja! King!
listen to my words:
My brothers have arrived,
my parents are dying of grief.
Total up my salary,
and send me on my way."

Listening to this, the raja remembered what Muttuppaṭṭaṉ said when he first accepted the position in the palace—"no brothers, no parents, no supporters anywhere"—now where did these brothers and parents come from?

"Muttuppaṭṭaṉ, you say your brothers have come. Bring them here, I want to meet them."

Muttuppaṭṭaṉ brought his brothers to the raja, but they couldn't keep quiet,

"Raja! Figure out our brother's pay and send him off with us. You see, we have urgent work back home, and our parents are very ill. Please don't delay. Give him a nice send-off."

But Rāma Raja got angry,

"What business do you have with me? This is between my minister and me. Listen here, Muttuppaṭṭaṉ, I'll give only *half* of what you've earned. That's all. And what's more, you may go home, but you must return as soon as possible."

These words angered Muttuppaṭṭaṉ. He was so mad he couldn't control it. The raja had faithfully fed and supported him for a long time, but Muttuppaṭṭaṉ spoke without the slightest trace of gratitude. He was insolent,

"Listen here, Raja!
give me that money or else;
Give it to me
or fight me in a war!"

To this the raja responded with a curse,

"You come to my palace,
and then insult me!

For this you will die
  at the hands of Cakkiliyar women!"

Still, the raja gave him his full salary and quickly told him to go. Taking the money, Muttuppaṭṭaṉ counted it down to the last coin and then, when he was sure it was correct, tied it in a bundle, put it on his head, and left with his brothers.

When they reached home, the brothers entered the house silently, but Muttuppaṭṭaṉ called out for his parents. When his parents heard his long-absent voice, they wanted to cry out to him. But what good is wanting? When they opened their mouths, no sound came out. Muttuppaṭṭaṉ continued to call for them, and they wanted to take him in their arms. But what good is desire? They moved their arms, but were too weak to lift them. Finally Muttuppaṭṭaṉ found them, but when he saw their condition, he was shaken. No one should be kept alive in such pain, he thought. So he went to the bureau, took out a little gold cup and filled it with cow's milk; then he fed them by dipping cotton into the milk and squeezing it into their mouths.[24] Immediately they went to Śiva's heaven, and the brothers performed the necessary rites. Time passed until one day Appāpaṭṭaṉ called the others and told them of a plan,

"You see, if a woman,
  a Cakkiliyar or anyone else,
Cooks our meals for us,
  it is never enough.
We must start a business
  and eat what we earn.
In the Malayalam country,
  we'll buy cheap goods,
Sell them in the Pāṇṭiya land
  and make a little profit."

The seven of them took what money they had and set out for the Malayalam country where they bought dried ginger, pepper, cardamom powder, coffee powder, and all sorts of jewels at cheap prices. Then the older brothers tied it all into six bundles, and said to Muttuppaṭṭaṉ,

"Little brother, now listen. We're going to trade this stuff in the Pāṇṭiya country. Go home and watch over the house until we return,"

But Muttuppaṭṭaṉ was not pleased,

"You can't just leave me all alone. How do you expect me to manage? I'm not used to it. If you go, then I go too."

To which his brothers responded,

"Now look, there's no problem as far as we are concerned. It's only for you that we say this. If you come, you'll probably get hurt. It's really nothing to be afraid of, but . . . well . . . the Malayalam country is bad enough, but the Pāṇṭiya country is really dangerous. Something terrible might happen, you see . . . it's just that

A false-eyed Cakkiliyar
  will call you to her side,
A deep-eyed Cakkiliyar
  will trick you with her powders,
A snake-eyed Cakkiliyar
  will give you the eye,
A dark-eyed Cakkiliyar
  will catch your eye with hers,
A lovely-eyed Cakkiliyar
  will fall in love with you,
Muttuppaṭṭaṉ, you're a prince
  a hero beautiful to see.
Carrying a spear,
  you look like Bhīma,
Carrying a knife,
  you look like Karṇa.
Wearing a loin cloth,
  you are Lord Śiva himself!"

The brothers continued:

"Listen, Muttuppaṭṭaṉ, do you understand what we're telling you? We've always told you not to dress up so much because you're handsome just as you are. But you don't listen, do you?

You dazzle with your *kumkum*
  and bewitch with your *poṭṭu*.
You can escape a stone prison,
  but not a woman's eyes."

The brothers tried to dissuade Muttuppaṭṭaṉ from coming with them, but he got angry,

"Obviously you've already made up your mind to leave me here alone. Alright, but when you return, you'll not find me . . . alive. That's all I can say. If you really want to leave me . . . well . . . well, then just go ahead."

This worried the brothers,

"He's really upset. If we leave him, he might even commit suicide."

So they took the six bundles, opened them, and redistributed the goods into seven bundles and then set off together with Muttuppaṭṭaṉ following behind.

Over forest-covered mountains
through groves of mango
where the monkeys play,
through teak and ironwood forests
Through the tall bamboo forest
and red areca nut trees,
to Āriyaṉ Kāvu they went.
They worshiped and left in the morning,
past the high Sabari peak
past famous Potikai mountain
They prayed "Protect us, Lord of Potikai."
They bathed in the Akattiyaṉ *tīrttam,*
the Varṇa and the Brahmā *tīrttam,*
the Ēka, the Cula,
and the Cakara *tīrttam.*
They crossed the Kōvari River,
past Kuttumayil and Palikai,
past Paṭṭaṉ Kāṭu and Paṭṭaṉ Puli,
past Maylati and Nīlakaṇṭavacam,
Along the Āriyaṉ Kāvu-Potikai path,
past Alaṅkāravacam and Eṭṭumalai,
past Nallukāl Maṇṭapam
to Talavāykōṭṭai,
Where they laid their bundles down,
at the temple of Corimuttu Ayyaṉ
and there they slept the night.

In the morning they walked to the western entrance of the Corimuttu Ayyaṉ temple, took a ritual bath, and then performed *abiṣēkam* for the deities there: Corimuttu Ayyaṉ, Tōkumuttumalai Ammaṉ, Kṣetra Nātaṉ, Kṣetra Pālakaṉ, and Caṅkili Bhūtam. While his brothers lit oil lamps, laid out coconut leaves, and did pūjā, Muttuppaṭṭaṉ worshiped the gods within his heart,

> "Corimuttu Ayyaṉ! Pūrṇapporkalai Ammaṉ! Kṣetra Nātaṉ! Kṣetra Pālakaṉ! Caṅkili Bhūtam! Wherever I may die, I ask that you offer me a place at the northern entrance of this temple."

Just then he heard the sound of a cricket off to his right, and knew that this wish would be fulfilled.[25] When he rejoined his brothers, they traveled on.

Leaving Corimuttu Ayyaṉ temple,
past Pāl Ōṭai and Talavāykōṭṭai,
past Paṭṭaṉ Pāṟai and Kuntari,
past Kaiveli and the Muttu Ammaṉ temple,
Across the Kaliyāṇi *tīrttam,*
past Āṉantakōṭṭai and Āṉai Kuṟavai,
past Turaipuri and Pāpanācam

To the Tambraparni River
  where they bathed,
  made offerings at the Perumāḷ temple,
And continued to Vikkiramaciṅkapuram,
  to the Civanti Appar temple,
  along its northern wall,
  where they sat down to rest.

When they began to chew some betel nut, Muttuppaṭṭaṉ looked at his brothers and said,

"You go your way, but I'm going to worship at the 1,008 Śiva and 108 Viṣṇu temples in this Pāṇṭiya country."

But his oldest brother didn't like this idea,

"What are you saying? Off to the 1,008 Śiva and the 108 Viṣṇu temples? Are you crazy? Do you know how long that would take? We've got to finish our business and can't wait for you to do all that. Besides, we came here as seven brothers and we should return as seven. If you go your way and we ours, that isn't right. How about this: instead of going to all those temples, just go to Pāpanācam temple, the temple that 'destroys sins.' You know, where Lord Śiva came and gave *mokṣam*. Let's go there, to the Tambraparni River and make an offering."

"Alright. You are my older brother, and I won't act against your wishes."

With those respectful words the matter was decided, and they slept well that night. However,

Muttuppaṭṭaṉ closed his eyes
  into a world of dreams:
At the foot of a hill
  he laid a net for deer;
  and into the net
    two women fell.
He saw them in his dreams.
On the bank of a river
  he placed a net for quail;
  and into the net
    two women fell.
He saw them in his dreams.
On the edge of a pool
  he placed a net for heron;
  and into the net
    two women fell.
He saw them in his dreams.

Seeing this in his dreams, Muttuppaṭṭaṉ rose, went to a garden, and gathered flowers for his morning pūjā. Then he took a copy of the *Rāmāyaṇa* and the *Tiruppukaḻ* and went to the Tambraparni River, where

He made an altar of sand
  a *liṅgam* on top,
  a *liṅgam* of Bhagavāṉ.
Holding the *Rāmāyaṇa* and *Tiruppukaḻ,*
  he closed his eyes
    raised his arms
    faced the east
  and sat in meditation,
Calling on the Lord,
  "Araṉē! Śivaṉē!"

Muttuppaṭṭaṉ meditated on Lord Śiva in the deepest recesses of his heart and did not waver in his concentration. Meanwhile, as he was sitting there on the banks of the river,

In Vikkiramaciṅkapuram,
  a wealthy Brahmin couple,
Cuppu Kuṭṭi Ayyar
  and his wife Cuntarakṣi,
Lived without worry
  and prospered happily.

But one day Cuntarakṣi turned to her husband and said,

"It's true we have land and money, but what's the use of all that if we don't have children? What's the point if we don't have someone to repeat our name after we die?"

Being childless, Cuntarakṣi was ridiculed by the village, and she tried to explain this to her husband:

"The door of a childless house
  never sees respected elders,
  never sees a Brahmin,
  or a married woman.
Living in this childless house,
  I'm a barren sinner.
How miserable!
  no water in my pot
  no child to bathe with me
  no child to stretch his hands
  for the curry that I cook.
In the rain-soaked courtyard,
  no child to play in the mud,

no child to grab my sari
  with his muddied hands.
My bowl is filled with rice,
  but no child eats with me.
On banana leaf or metal plate,
  I always eat alone.
Eating rice when you're childless,
  is like eating worms;
  rice to a barren woman
  tastes as rough as sand!
No, there's no child
  to play in the courtyard
  and scatter my *kōlam* drawing."

Cuppu Kuṭṭi listened to his wife and tried to console her,

"Come on, now. Why get so upset about this? Is it something we control? Remember, a child is a gift given by Lord Śiva, a boon from him. Only he can fulfill your desires; there's nothing we can do about it. Besides, who knows what sins our ancestors might have committed, or what sins we might have done unintentionally.

Have we ever insulted a woman?
  used the short measure?[26]
  adulterated rice or killed a deer?
Have we ever mistreated a priest?
  cheated or beaten a *sādhu*?
Denied a calf its mother's milk
  and drunk it all ourselves?
Have we ever spoken the lie
  that says there is no god?
Ever insulted a storyteller?
  or underpaid a singer?
Have we ever defaced a temple?
  ever stolen, lied, or killed?"

Cuntarakṣi said to her husband,

"We've done none of these things; even so, who knows what we have done unknowingly. Of course, even if we have done sins, there are ways to counteract them. We can perform acts of *dharma*."

And so Cuppu Kuṭṭi and Cuntarakṣi decided to do as many acts of *dharma* as possible. First they took lots of money (not to waste on stupid things, but enough for meritorious acts) and then,

Every mile along the road
  they built stone platforms
  for travelers to rest their loads.[27]

Cows and gold and land
  to the *sādhu*s they gave.
But all these acts of *dharma*
  brought them no reward,
No matter what they did,
  no child was born to them.

This Brahmin couple gave every kind of gift to *sādhu*s—food, gold, cows, and land. But when they didn't receive the boon of a child, Cuppu Kuṭṭi said to his wife,

> "Well . . . we certainly haven't skimped on money, have we? We've spent a lot—more than I could even count! We have given and given. But then, boons don't just come; they come only when the time is right. So don't give up hope yet. I'm sure we'll get a child."

He tried to console his wife, but no matter what he said, she felt depressed. With a heavy heart she looked at him.

> "Tell me, do you really think I'm going to feel better because of your words? The reason I'm so upset is this: you're about forty-five, and I'm almost forty. If we don't have a child now, our chances in the future aren't good. It's like this:

The snake-eyed tamarind tree
  and the spreading banyan tree
  stand without flowering—
Why should I,
  poor sinner,
  stand here and grieve?
The young tamarind tree
  and the strong banyan tree
  stand without blossoming—
Why should I,
  poor sinner,
  stand here and grieve?
Had I been born as soil,
  at least now
  I'd be an earthen pot.
Had I been born a tree,
  at least now
  I'd be a temple door.
Had I been born a jewel,
  at least now
  I'd be a raja's throne.
All the gods and goddesses
  from the many heavens
  would come to me for *darṣan*.

Had I been born a stone,
at least now
I'd be an image
standing in Murukaṉ's temple
at Tiruccentūr
where crowds would gather,
pour oil and coconut milk,
and worship me.
But I was not born
soil or stone
jewel or tree,
I was born a woman
to suffer."

And after she said all this, Cuntarakṣi looked at her husband and softly cried,

"If I don't get a child, if I remain barren like this, well . . . I can't go on. Suppose you die. You know what they'll call me: 'Barren bitch' or 'childless hag.' I just can't take those insults. If you die, then I'm going with you; I'll join you on the funeral pyre."

At this point Cuppu Kuṭṭi interrupted and shouted angrily,

"Shut up! Whatever you say, don't you ever repeat those words again! That phrase 'I'll join you on the funeral pyre' has a story behind it. You see, once a man and his wife were living in a village and had the same conversation that we are having now. The woman said, 'If you die, I'm going with you; I'll join you on the funeral pyre.' And she didn't say it just once—she kept repeating it all day . . . every day! Her husband wondered what had gotten into her, and finally he got an idea. He was pretty well off, so he took out one hundred rupees, went to Kerala, and said to a *mantra* specialist,[28]

'I've got one hundred rupees here and it's yours. All you have to do is teach me a *mantra* that will put someone to sleep for about half an hour. Just teach it to me, that's all.'

"And he put the money in his hands. Well, everyone needs money (especially *mantra* specialists), right? So he took the money and taught him the *mantra*. On the way home the husband went through Trivandrum and Nagercoil to the market at Vaṭacēri, and bought a nice bird there. A real fine bird . . . a chicken, that is. When he got home, he said to his wife,

'I'm really tired after running all around Kerala today doing business. Here, take this chicken and boil it up with some rice. I'm going to take an oil bath and rest. Call me when the food's ready.'

"He tossed her the chicken, and she put it in a pot of water and began to prepare the rice. When she went out to get some hot water for his oil bath, her husband realized that the time had come for him to test the *mantra*—if he let this chance go, another might not come. He took his bath, rubbed oil all over his body, and then lay down on a cot. When his wife returned, he was fast asleep, and she was confused.

'What's this? He's never slept after an oil bath before. This is strange.'

"She put the water down and called his name—no response. She went over and shook him—no response; she poked him, but still nothing. The *mantra* had worked! After his bath, he had said it to himself and gone off into a deep sleep. When his wife shook him and shook him and he still didn't wake, she began to think that maybe he had died. But she wanted to test him more, so she went over to the chicken pot, tore off a nice tender piece and put it under his nose. Even then he didn't move! Frantic, she put the chicken into his mouth, and still he didn't move. Finally, she put it right on his tongue, but he lay there sound asleep; then she knew:

'Well, there's no doubt about it now. He's dead, dead as a door nail! But what about the chicken and rice? Can't let all that go to waste.'

"So she locked the door—lest someone walk in—sat down and devoured the whole chicken and the pot of rice. When she had eaten it all, she remembered something:

'Because I have no son, his relatives are going to say that all the stuff in this house is theirs—better hide it fast.'

"She looked for a place to hide it all and saw a space above the rafters. But there was no ladder. 'No problem. We'll just make ourselves a ladder,' she thought, and went over to her husband, dragged him by his feet over to the wall, and stood him up against it. She put his one leg to this side and the other to that side, and made *him* into a ladder. She climbed up, put the things above the rafters, climbed down, and then she realized something else: 'I better do a little lamenting. After all, he is dead.' Normally a wife sings with at least a *little* respect for a dead husband, but the way she sang . . . he wanted to kill her.

'How miserable,
married to a dying man!
How terrible,
married to an invalid!'

"When his wife sang these lines, the husband couldn't stay quiet any longer and keep his self-respect, so he opened his mouth and said,

'Hello, sweetheart. Now what is it you're crying about? What's all the sniffling for? Is it because I'm dead? Well, I'm *not* dead. I died, but I'm not dead. I went straight to Kailāsa and had an audience with Śiva. He called me and said, "*Bhaktā*! You know what happened down there? Your wife has all that chicken and rice, and she's crying because you died. You came here on an empty stomach; go back there and eat and come back." So cut out the crying and open the pot. Let's eat.'

"Now the wife had to think fast,

'Well, you see, when you fell asleep, I took the chicken and rice—without touching even a bite of it, mind you—and sent it all over to Muttu's house.'

"Her husband snapped back,

'So I have to call Muttu, huh? What's he—some kind of saint? There won't be any rice or chicken now. And you can't get back what's gone, can you? This is too much! I ought to kill you! And to think that you went around saying, "If you die, I'll join you on the funeral pyre." How many times did you say that? And now look at you!'

"And he continued,

'You witch!
put the chicken on my tongue,
but ate it all yourself!
You bitch!
touched the rice to my lips,
but gobbled the pot yourself!'

After Cuppu Kuṭṭi told this story to his wife, Cuntarakṣi, he said to her,

"So you see, don't say anything about joining me on the funeral pyre. Don't worry, we'll have a child. Somehow it will happen."

But words couldn't soothe her.

"I am worried because we are getting older and older. In the palace yard,

A tree,
a tree gives *cāvi* fruit—
If it gives no fruit,
it sinks into a pool.
Will I bear fruit
or lie sunken in a pool?
In the garden,
a tree,
a tree fruits every year—
If it gives no fruit,
it sinks into a pool.

Will I give fruit
  or lie sunken in a pool?
At the water's edge,
  a tree,
  a tree gives cardamom fruit—
If it gives no fruit,
  it sinks into a pool.
Will I bear fruit
  or lie sunken in a pool?"

To his wife's worries, Cuppu Kuṭṭi responded,

"That's silly, about getting old and not having children. Besides, we're not very old anyway; in fact, we're probably about the right age for kids. Don't worry. Look at all the acts of *dharma* we've done. I'm sure they'll bring us a child. And if not, well then, let's forget it altogether."

Still Cuntarakṣi was not assuaged.

"You're just putting me off again. You don't listen to what I'm telling you—you've *got* to do something. Don't leave any act of *dharma* undone. Do them all!"

And so the Brahmin did whatever he hadn't done already. He built roads from Kāsi to Kanya Kumari and planted trees along them. He began preparations for a highway to the sacred bridge at Rāmesvaram, but even then no child came. Cuntarakṣi was desperate,

"Listen, you haven't liked most of what I've said about this problem, but I think you may like this idea. I don't know what is wrong with me—maybe I was born at an inauspicious time or something—anyway, I am not pregnant. But in our caste there are plenty of houses with women. So let's look for a big house, one with lots of kids, find a nice woman and . . . well . . . you know . . . you should get married . . . take a second wife. Then maybe she, or maybe I, will have a child. That's the only solution—take a second wife."

Cuppu Kuṭṭi didn't like this suggestion.

"A second marriage! Are you crazy? What about the inheritance? Who would get it? Just tell me that! I've seen what happens in these situations, and it's not nice. Even leaving the inheritance problem aside, it's a mess. Besides . . .

In a thousand women,
  none is as beautiful as you.
If they gave me a million women,
  none would be faithful like you.

No matter how beautiful,
no woman could match
your loyalty, your softness . . .

"But aside from all that, there is something else.

What Śiva wrote for us that day,
he'll not erase today.
Whatever Bhagavāṉ has arranged
that's our destiny.
Who and what and when
Śiva wrote long ago.
If you were born a barren woman,
fate cannot be changed!"

Cuppu Kuṭṭi tried to console his wife by telling her not to worry about desires over which she had no control. But she, in turn, said to him,

"You ask me to be brave, but if I had that strength, I wouldn't have said all I've said so far. The real problem are the insults I must endure. You see . . .

Women of my age
have mothered seven children,
Or they are married women,
carrying their first child.
Young full coconut trees
fruit abundantly;
They swell with maturity,
but what good am I?
With my friend
I go to the tank,
But at the water's edge
they insult me.
This I cannot endure . . .

"If I go to the tank or to a well or anywhere, women make fun of me. 'Hey there, lady! What's the big hurry? We're the ones with children, children in our arms and around our legs. Where's your kids? In your arms? At your feet? Or maybe in your mouth? What makes you think you should go ahead of us?' They scream at me like that.

It's a battle,
a raging war
against a childless woman.
It's a battle,
an outright war
against a barren woman.

"That's the way it is. They hate me because I'm childless. Of course they ridicule all barren women, but I just can't take it any longer. I think I might go crazy . . . but you don't listen, or you won't change your mind. You just keep saying what you've already said. If there's something you haven't done, do it . . . do it now!"

"There's nothing left undone. I've done it all. Now it's in the hands of Lord Śiva."

"Well . . . in that case, there is something else I want, and you can at least do that."

"What's that?"

"This problem of a child is making us miserable. Let's forget it for a while. If we get a child, fine; if not, well . . . in the meantime, instead of a child, let's raise a calf, a young calf."

"No sooner said than done! How could I refuse you this? Just go and get some money."

He was rich, but she handled the money! When she gave him five hundred rupees, he packed a meal of curd, rice, pickles, a little vegetable, and some chili paste and went to buy a calf. He went straight from Vikkiramaciṅkapuram to the market at Melapāḷayam, bought a nice calf, and, holding it by the tail, walked it home. The two of them raised that calf, instead of a son or daughter, with all the tenderness and care of a parent. Then one day,

In Ambasamudram town
  in the Akattiyar temple,
  to the annual Paṅkuṉi festival
  to the eighth-day celebrations,
  Cuppu Kuṭṭi and Cuntarakṣi went,
But then remembered
  the calf they loved like a child.

They didn't want to leave the calf alone, and besides, it was a dangerous, stormy day. So they found a little boy who herds cattle and said,

"Now listen, we are going to Ambasamudram to see the eighth-day festival. Take care of this calf until we return. If we aren't home when you're finished grazing, then tie it near the house. But tie it well. We'll take care of it after we return."

Cuppu Kuṭṭi gave the calf to the boy and then left for the festival. When the boy grazed his cattle, he was so careful with the calf that he carried it in his arms. But then he thought,

"Gee, they say this eighth-day festival is really something. When will I ever get a chance to see it? Maybe I'll just take a peek."

He's only a kid—can't expect him not to have such desires. Still he took the calf to the Brahmin's house and very carefully put a rope around its neck and then tied the rope to a stone pillar. After he left, the storm got worse. Lightning began crackling and flashing everywhere, and the calf got scared and starting jumping around. Because both the rope around its neck and the stone pillar were new, little by little the rope began to fray, and finally it broke. Freed of its tether, the calf began to jump even more wildly and came near a well where it smelled water. Going to the edge, it peered down and saw its reflection; thinking the image was another calf, it jumped down the well. And there, at the bottom of the well, the poor calf died. Now when Cuppu Kuṭṭi and Cuntarakṣi returned home from the festival, the calf was gone. Seeing the broken rope, they realized what had happened; they looked everywhere around the house, in the garden and near the well, but couldn't find the calf. When it got dark, they decided to sleep and try again in the morning. They laid down, but were so anxious they couldn't sleep a wink. Before the sun rose, they got up and went to the cowherder boy's house and called him. The little boy came out, looked at the Brahmin, and said politely,

"Yes, *cāmi,* what is it? What is so important at this hour?"

"Yesterday we gave you a calf to look after—now where is it? What did you do to it?"

"Nothing, *cāmi,* I brought it back to the house and tied it to the stone pillar. That's all."

"Yes, but the rope broke, and now we can't find the calf anywhere."

"In that case, don't worry. The calf must be around somewhere. Let's have a look."

The boy and the Brahmin searched for the calf; they looked in every possible place—on the road to the mill, over the hill near the tank, even near the big rocks outside of town. But they found nothing. When the sun got hot, Cuppu Kuṭṭi returned home exhausted. He took a bucket and went to bathe, but when he threw the bucket down the well, he heard a strange sound. He hauled it up and threw it even harder, but again it made the strange sound. Then he looked down and saw the calf, lying there like a sack.

"Oh my god! We've killed the calf. How did this happen? How can we ever rid ourselves of the sin of killing a cow? Where else but in Kāsi can one wash away this sin?"

He ran to his wife and spoke excitedly,

"The calf is dead, and now I have to go to Kāsi. There's no other way. Do you hear me? I'm going to Kāsi!"

Wearing a special loin cloth, a fancy *vēṭṭi,* and an ochre shawl, he went to holy Benares.

Five months passed, and then one day, Cuntarakṣi went to the well to bathe.

Hair freshly oiled,
Face sweetly powdered.
a water pot on her hip,
she walked to the water's edge
where the women looked at her
and snickered to themselves,
"Look sisters, look.
It's the first Tuesday of Āṭi,
time for the Auvaiyār fast,[29]
but she wears fancy make up."

When she heard these words, Cuntarakṣi spoke,

"Can you do this fast,
my friends,
in a house without a man?
My man has gone to Kāsi
for the sin of killing a calf.
Tell me, my sisters,
can I do the Auvaiyār fast?"

So the women decided to help Cuntarakṣi: they went home, cooked a meal for their families, and when their husbands were deep asleep, started the fast. The first thing was to pound rice. Of course, they don't do it today like they used to. Traditionally during the fast no man—from a little boy to an old grandfather—would be allowed to see any of the preparations. They did it with real *bhakti* too. But now it's different. Women get together in groups of ten or even twenty and meet in a big house so they can sit or lie down, or gossip, or even sleep. In the past each woman made her own food to eat after the fast. On the morning before the night of the fast, she would wait for her husband to wake up, and then ask,

"Are you going out? Well . . . when you do, buy me a nice coconut and bring it back."

At this, the husband would suddenly open his eyes,

"What's that? A coconut? Do you know what a coconut costs these days?"

"Now, just listen to me. I'm not asking you to buy one for nothing. I'm going to do the Auvaiyār fast tonight, and that requires a coconut, right?"

"Auvaiyār fast? Oh . . . I see. Sure, I'll get you a coconut."

Meanwhile, he would be thinking to himself,

"Why not? If I buy her a coconut today, tomorrow morning, I'll get some of those rice cakes."

So the husband goes out and buys a coconut, and not just any coconut. He buys a Malayalam coconut, or even a huge Yāḻpāṇam coconut. When he hands it to her, it is so heavy she can hardly hold it. Then she counts how many people are in the house, say seven, and divides the rice into seven equal portions, ties it in a bundle, and runs off to the rice mill. And she doesn't just stand there waiting to be served; she shouts for the manager,

"Hey, you! Pound up this rice for me!"

"Are you crazy? I can't even pound up the rice that was brought here yesterday. You've got to wait in line. And then there's the electrical power shortage. Wait if you can; if not, go."

Then she gets even more angry,

"Listen here! Do this rice for me or I'll stop my Auvaiyār fast, and the sin will rest on your head!"

But he won't give in, and so she runs back home. She has to pound the rice herself, but the problem is that today women can't pound rice like they used to. In the past, a woman could pound a couple bushels in no time, but today she can't even do those seven little portions in a day! No, she has to call the other women in the neighborhood to help her.

"Hey Kamala! Hey Maṅgu! Hey Kasturi! Nali! Rukku! C̀ampaka! Rani! Baby! Cānti! Vijay! Muttu! Come here and grab a pestle."

Immediately all these younger women come and pick up a pestle and pound away. Wham! Wham! Wham! They really go to it because they're going to make those tasty rice cakes; they really want those little cakes! And it doesn't even matter whether they serve them to Auvaiyār or not—they'll eat them anyway! Even during the fast their little hands get restless and the cakes start to go. By morning, there's none left. So they pound away, make the cakes and fast until morning. Her husband eats his breakfast before going out, while she hides behind a curtain eating a few more of those cakes. Now he knows what she is doing, but knows also that if he mentions it, she'll get mad. So he hesitates, beats around the bush, and then, as if he didn't know anything about the fast, asks,

"Say, what's that you're eating? Your mouth's been moving ever since I got up."

"What do you mean? Now don't make fun of me. You know I did the Auvaiyār fast last night; I'm eating a few cakes, that's all."

"Come on, sweetheart. I bought that coconut yesterday, didn't I? How about a couple of cakes for me?"

"Don't be stupid! You know you shouldn't eat these things. Your eyes will go weak or something. Just wait a day. Tomorrow, I'll make you some nice lentils."

"Just one or two cakes, please? Be fair."

Not wanting a fight, she'll give in and throw him a couple of cakes which he scrambles for and gulps down. That's what's become of the Auvaiyār fast these days. You know in the past it used to be performed only three times a year: in the months of Tai, Āṭi, and Māci. But now, any month will do—all you need is a taste for those cakes. As soon as you've got that, the fast is on! At least they still stick to Tuesdays. The other thing is the food they used to make. In the past they mixed two or three high-grade rices, made it into the cakes, and then steamed them just right! But now . . . well, it's different.

After the women had cooked all the sweet cakes for Auvaiyār, they went to Cuntarakṣi's house and called her.

"Cuntarakṣi! Come on, bring your cakes for Auvaiyār. It's getting light."

But Cuntarakṣi stayed inside her house wringing her hands, as they continued to call. Finally, realizing she would have to tell the truth, she went outside and said,

"What's an Auvaiyār fast anyway? I've never heard of it before. It's not a tradition in our house."

"You're telling us this now? We've all come here for the fast, and now you say you don't even know what it is? What can we do at this hour? If you told us earlier, we could have asked one of our relatives to prepare the cakes for you. My older sister has come for the fast from our father's house—I could have asked her to do it. Or my aunt who's come from my uncle's house could have done it. My sister-in-law has come from my brother's house, and there's my grandmother, too. Any one of them could have done it for you. But what can we do now? It's too dark to go outside. Look at my ear, at the earring—it's diamond. I don't care about the diamond, but some thief'll take off my ear with it if I go out. And there's this necklace. I can lose it, but I don't want to lose my honor with it."

"You don't have any cakes? Look, Cuntarakṣi, listen to me. Instead of making an offering to Auvaiyār, just take some flour and turmeric and make an image of her; then take some of what we have brought—the food and flowers—and offer it to the images.[30] Simple, but there's one very important thing: get up before the sun rises and take all this stuff and throw it in the river. And don't let any man see it. Remember that!"

With this warning the women took their things and went back to their own houses. Cuntarakṣi did as she was told and then lay down to sleep, and slept right through the morning. When she got up, the sun was high, almost 10 o'clock and she didn't know what to do.

"I can't throw this stuff in the river like they told me now; it's too late. Something bad might happen."

So she simply patted everything into a ball and tossed it in her mouth. She ate the whole thing! And then . . .

> Swallowing the flour ball
>   she was pregnant at last!
> Forty days passed,
>   one, two, three months.
> In the fourth month she weakened
>   called her servant Ceṅkamālai
> And said, "I'm pregnant,
>   but my husband isn't here.
>   If he comes home now,
>   he'll tear me to pieces.
>   He'll cut me up, brand me
>   and send me to the heroes' heaven!"

"Ceṅkamālai! What am I to do? He'll beat me when he returns. Not just me, but you too. Since you are with me, he'll figure you had something to do with it. Tell me what to do!"

When she heard her mistress say this, Ceṅkamālai was stunned. She just stared, eyes wide open, her head spinning round and round. Cuntarakṣi was impatient:

"What's the matter with you? Staring at me like that. Are you possessed or something? If you've got an idea, tell me, but at least control yourself!"

"Sorry. I was just scared, that's all."

"Well then, calm down and help me. Or at least be quiet. Now, of course, there is one way . . .

> Take that special medicine
>   and kill off the fetus.
> Drink some poison
>   and destroy the child."

"Don't do that, Cuntarakṣi! It's dangerous. You say you're in the fourth month, right? (Anyway, you look like it's about the fourth month.) The medicine could be dangerous. If something happens and you die, then your husband would be miserable. Now listen, I've got an idea. He's not going to return for about seven or eight months, and you're in the fourth month so there's only about six left until the child comes. We'll just cover everything up and then in the tenth month, when the child is born . . . well . . . we'll take it and leave it somewhere. When he returns, he won't know anything."

"That's a great idea! But there's only one problem. How can I stay inside the house all day? If I go out for a walk, that Paṅkajum next door, or that Indira down the street, or Muttu across the way—they'll make fun of me: 'Hey girls! Take a look at Cuntarakṣi. Her husband's away, but check out her stomach! It's pretty big! And her face is all pale, and she looks weak. How about it huh?' They'll tease me night and day."

"Why worry about that? They won't know anything unless you go outside. If you're inside, there's no problem. So you leave all the outside work to me, and you look after the work inside. And there's one more thing. If someone stops by the house while you're inside—you know, to talk or something—don't stand up! If you do, your stomach will show. As long as you stay seated, nobody will know a thing. Don't forget that."

They followed Ceṅkamālai's plan, and the months passed until the tenth month came and Cuntarakṣi gave birth to two girls. But they didn't tie up the umbilical cord, or wash them, or even feed them—they just put them in a cloth and then in a basket and carried them out of the house. They went toward Tampattu near the temple of Cūliya Tāyār and left them near that rocky hill there and returned home. Since they were all alone, the babies cried and cried until a five-hooded snake in a nearby hole heard them and came out to look around. When the snake saw the newborn babies, and wondered why they had been left alone, it opened its divine eye (it had the powers of Viṣṇu, you understand) to see what had happened in the past:

When the god Cuppiramaṇiya was born in the Sravana Lake to kill the demon Sūrapadma, he was raised by the celestial women, and then given the name Kārttikai, six heads and twelve arms. Gathering nine warriors, he killed the demon, and then one of the warriors went to Kailāsa to atone for the killing. In Kailāsa, he closed his eyes, held his arms above his head, and entered into deep meditation on the name of Lord Śiva. At that time, the nymphs Urvaśi and Dēvarambai were on their way to pick flowers for Śiva's pūjā. When they saw his powerful tapas and beautiful body, they wanted to marry him. So they went up to him and, without the slightest respect for his tapas, pulled on one of his legs. His tapas ruined, the man opened his eyes and cursed them,

"Since you have come to this sacred spot and disturbed my tapas, you will be born on earth and raised by a Cakkiliyar family."

But the nymphs countered,

"We will endure your curse. But now listen to ours: On that same earth you will be born and then marry us."

Now the snake knew that according to the first curse the two women were born on earth as these abandoned children, and that by the second curse the warrior was born in Āriya Nāṭu as Muttuppaṭṭaṉ to marry them. Trying to feed the babies, the snake slithered over to a honeycomb and rolled it back with his tail, thinking,

"Can't feed them from my mouth because it's poisonous, so I better use my tail."

Scooping out the honey with its tail, the snake fed the children and then spread its large hood above them as a shield against the sun. Now at that time . . .

In Aṭicanallūr town
Vāla Pakaṭai and Vāli,
a Cakkiliyar couple
tended cattle for a high-caste man.
Vāli turned to her husband.
"Listen to me," she said,
"A childless woman,
I am miserable,
my life full of pain.
Other women ridicule me,
call me 'barren' and 'witch.'"

"I want a child so badly; isn't there anything we can do?"

"You shouldn't worry about not having a child, because that's not something we have any control over. It's all in the hands of Lord Śiva; it's a boon he gives. Besides, if you get worked up about it, you'll get sick. If we were healthier, our bodies could take a little worry perhaps, but we're weak and worn. When people like us get worried, the mind falters, the veins shrink up, the skin starts to peel off, and then you're a bag of bones . . . you don't even have the strength to pick up a grain of rice! We have to take care of ourselves, so forget your troubles and go on with life. You know why I say this—we don't have much: no money, no garden, no groves, no wet or dry lands, no livestock, no cattle, no goats, no buffaloes—nothing. Every day we have to earn what we eat. That's the way it is."

Saying all this, Pakaṭai started off to work, to watch over the cow pens,

"I'm off to the pens; go cut some greens for fodder. At noon bring me some lunch and don't be late. Even though we don't have much land or anything, I like to eat on time. And it doesn't have to be fancy—a little salt mixed with cold rice and pickle, maybe some lentils or a little vegetable. And if nothing else, just a green chili to bite on. That'll be fine. But bring it on time, because my mouth starts to water at noon."

When he left, Vāli quickly finished her work and

Went to cut greens
bag in one hand
sickle in the other.

The Untouchable woman Vāli
walked along the path,
Stepping aside for cows
and avoiding strangers.

In order to bring lunch to her husband on time, she had to hurry, so she ran along the path,

To the Cūliya Tāyār temple,
where the snake guarding the children
saw her coming and thought,
"These children are without parents,
she is without a child!
If I give her the children
she'll protect them
Like an eyelid
protects an eye!"

But how could the snake let Vāli know where the children were? The best way would be to draw her attention to them, hide away, and let her take them. But how? Well, this wasn't any ordinary snake—it was the diadem of Viṣṇu.

"All I have to do is to get the children to cry—if she hears them, she'll come over."

Coiling up its great tail,
it smacked them on the head.
And smarting from the blow,
the kids began to wail!

Vāli heard their cries, looked around, and soon found them lying all alone. She picked them up and kissed them on both cheeks. She was overjoyed! So thrilled that she cut enough fodder for not one, but two sacks. She put it all on her head, held a child on each hip, and walked back home. Inside the hut, she threw the fodder in the corner and began to play with the kids, and totally forgot about her husband and his lunch! The poor man was waiting right up to 12 o'clock, thinking "she'll come in a minute; she'll come any second now." But she didn't come. And when the sun passed the noontime mark, he got mad—really mad!

His anger was wild!
His two eyes danced.
My god how they flew!
Reddened with rage,
his eyes raced away!

"That witch of a wife!" he fumed,
"She'll never come."

Grabbing his butcher knife
  and his hunting dogs,
Driven by a ferocious anger
  he raced toward his home.

On the way Pakaṭai passed a liquor shop, stopped, and called for the owner,

"Hey friend, give me four or five *muṇṭa.*"

"What? Who are you? 'Four or five *muṇṭa?*' Imbecile! It's been years since we used *muṇṭa*s! We even changed from the *cīr* measurement years ago. Now everything's in liters. Tell me how many liters you want, and I'll serve it."

"Brother, I don't know liters from letters. All I know is that I used to drink *muṇṭa*s and *cīr*s. *Muṇṭa* or *cīr,* give me one or the other."

"Watch it! This is not a booze joint, not a *kaḷḷu* shop; it's a liquor store, a *carāyam* shop. If you want *carāyam,* fine."

"Listen, I don't care whether it's *kaḷḷu* or *carāyam.* Just give me something to drink. The problem is that I'm hungry and I'm angry. I need a little *kaḷḷu* for the hunger and something to feed my anger. Give me whatever you've got."

Now the shopkeeper knew just what to do; he was experienced in these matters.

He took one kind of *kaḷḷu*
  and mixed it with another;
Pakaṭai drank the first
  and his eyes ran red,
He drank the second
  and his head spun around.
Off he ran in a stagger
  and reached his little hut,
Blind with rage and drink
  until he heard children's voices.

Hearing them, he slowed down, calmed himself and quietly entered the hut. When he saw the children, he said.

"Hey Vāli, what's going on here? What . . . who . . . are these children?"

"I went to cut the fodder like you said, and I found them there."

"Really? Great! But don't say you 'found' them. Better to say 'Lord Śiva gave them.' See what I mean?"

Once Pakaṭai had corrected her wording, the two of them did the necessary ceremonies. They tied up the umbilical cord, bathed the children, and fed them their first milk. Pakaṭai was so excited he got out his money and counted it—not much, but enough—and ran off to a cloth shop and bought two silk saris. Back home, he tied them up as cradles and put one child in each. With Vāli swinging one cradle and Pakaṭai the other, they sang a lullaby:

Ra ri, ra ri,
   ra ra rooo . . .
Golden ones, precious one,
   born in this Cakkiliyar family.
Ra ri, ra ri,
   ra ra roooo . . .
To feed the poor
   and uphold justice,
My child,
   my glittering gem,
To take up a stylus
   and write on palm-leaf,
   you were born.

Now that's how women *used* to sing lullabies in the past. Those women could really sing, and in whatever style they wanted. But today . . . they might get an idea to sing a lullaby, but . . . well . . . let's just say they do what they can. They sing like this:

Driving a cart of cucumbers,
   to Tirunelveli,
      your father sells it there
      and brings you a sack of sugar.
Driving a cart of pumpkins
   to Pulliyaṅkuṭṭi,
      he sells it there
      and brings you sugar cane.

That's how they sing today, because kids love those sweets. If you sing about them, they'll keep that image in their minds and fall off to sleep. Other kinds of songs are sung by women who sold everything in their house, went off to big temples to do tapas and then got a kid; they sing with tremendous pride:

Your uncle, my child,
   sells flowers in Cochin.
He'll return, my sweet,
   with a fine anklet for you.
Your uncle, my child,
   sells jasmine in Madurai.
He'll return, my sweet,
   with ripe mangoes for you.

There's another style in houses where the child's father goes to work rain or shine—then the mother sings with even greater pride:

Riding in a railway car,
your father goes to Calcutta . . .

Ordinarily, if someone wants to ride the railway to Calcutta, they get on at Tirunelveli station. But sometimes, they don't get any farther than the next station at Talaiyūttu. You see, there's a story behind that: once there was a husband and wife who never left their house and didn't know anything about the world outside. At that time the train had just come to their area, and when this guy somehow found out about it, he turned to his wife,

"Hey, you know what? There's this thing they call a 'train'; you can get on it and go anywhere you like. I don't know any places to go to, but I really want to try it."

"Fine! But don't think anything is free. You'll need some money. Better go do some work today and get your pay, and then take the trip."

So he went out and got his pay—in those days it wasn't much, only six annas—and came home. His wife took two annas and gave him four,

"Here's money for a ticket. Go ahead and see the sights. You know . . . the zoo and all, and come back."

Holding the money tightly in his hand, he entered the station and, remembering the warning about a ticket, went up to the booth and said,

"Give me a ticket, please."

The man inside the booth looked at him,

"Sure. To which place?"

Now, this fellow didn't know the names of any places, so he stood in silence, and the man in the booth raised his voice,

"Where to?"

And still our friend was unable to speak. Finally the man in the booth tried another tack,

"Look. How much money do you have? Let me see, and I'll give you a ticket for that much."

The fellow opened up his hand, gave the other man his four annas, and received a ticket for Talaiyūttu. With the ticket he went into the station and looked around. But because he didn't know a thing about a "train," he went up to the only other person in the station and asked,

"Excuse me, friend, but they say a 'train' will come here. Tell me what it looks like."

The other person couldn't believe his ears.

"What are you? Some kind of an idiot? If you don't know what a train is, what are you doing here? Go away and don't bother me."

"Please, sir. Tell me something about this 'train.'"

"It's black, puffs out smoke, and you climb on it. Now scram!"

Our friend was thrilled with this information, and he repeated it to himself,

"It's black and blows smoke. Oh boy! I can hardly wait!"

The actual train was about to arrive, so a porter came onto the platform, wearing a coat—a black coat—and smoking a pipe. Our friend saw him and thought,

"This is just what that man told me: it's black and blows smoke. It must be the 'train,' but it's going too fast; if I jump on the front, it might run me over!"

He let the porter pass and then suddenly realized,

"Looks like it's not going to stop. No problem, I've got my ticket. I'll just jump on the back."

And with a leap he sprang onto the porter's back, throwing his arms around his neck.

"What the hell is this? Off of my back!"

"You think I got on without a ticket, don't you? Well, I paid four annas for this ticket! Anyway, what makes you think you can stop this train? What right do *you* have to cause a delay on public transportation?"

"Look, mister. I'm not a 'train.' That comes on those little steel tracks over there. Now get off!"

Finally realizing his mistake, the man went shamefully home. But this is the husband that those women sing about with such great pride in their lullabies. You know what they sing? . . .

Riding in a railway car,
  your father goes to Calcutta.
He travels a great distance
  and sits on a hill,
Picking lice from his hair . .

That's the kind of husband they praise in lullabies! As if that wasn't enough, there are other women who sing without even knowing the right words! It's so bad that they use cinema songs. Remember that one a little time back? . . .

Oh my sweetie, my little fruit,
  my sugar from the south . . .

Other women use another more recent cinema song . . .

Gee, honey, you look sweet,
  bathing by the pool!

Yeah! They actually sing *that* as a lullaby! Of course, there's that new song . . . you know . . . well, maybe we should forget that one.

Anyway, at least Vāli and Pakaṭai knew how to sing; they could really sing! They sang and sang for the children, cuddled and pampered them. Then they wondered what names to give them, and that's when the fight started; Pakaṭai spoke first,

"If I die, everything in this house goes to these children, so they should be named after *my* parents."

"Listen. I found them, and they will bear *my* parents' names!"

They argued and argued until, disgusted with each other, they turned their backs and sulked in the corners of their hut. Soon the children began to cry, and each ran to pick one up, and Pakaṭai said,

"Well, I guess we can learn from this not to fight over these kids. You know that story about the couple who had a fight and then ended up killing the kids? Let's forget our parents' names and give them new names. We'll call one 'Pummakkāḷ' because we found her on the earth [*pūmi*] and the other 'Tummakkāḷ' because we found her in the dust [*tum*]."

With these names,

Hour by hour, day by day,
  they grew tenderly,
One, two, three months
  little faces began to laugh.
Four, five, six months
  they called "mom" and "dad."
In the seventh month
  they stood up
  in the eighth they walked.
One, two, three years
  their hair was cut,
  their ears were pierced.
Ornaments put in their ears
  a kāppu string on their wrists,
  silver belts on their waists.
In their fifth year
  when their mother passed away,
Pakaṭai raised the girls
  with even greater care,
Until their sixteenth year
  when they matured as women.

At sixteen Pummakkāḷ and Tummakkāḷ were fully developed flowers—like water lilies opening out, they had blossomed. And they were truly beautiful . . .

More beautiful than any woman
  beautiful as dark-blue peahens,
Their hair was black
  like dark mountain clouds.
Their thin eyebrows
  were long margosa leaves,
Eyelids flashed
  like black fluttering birds.
Their shapely bodies
  were red *kumuka* fruit,
Their ears decorated
  like white *tittiri* flowers,
Two teeth in front
  were strings of pearls.
The other rows of teeth
  like small *eccum* dates.
Their wide eyes
  flashed like gold,
Their beautiful necks
  were slender areca nut trees.
Their hands
  like ripened banana fruits.
Graceful fingers
  like bananas about to fruit.
Stomachs gently turned
  like soft banyan leaves.
Waists tightened by saris
  like the little uṭukkai drum.[31]
Bodies lovely and dark
  like a serpent's hood,
Their tiny feet
  curved like a turtle's shell,
Their ten toes
  sparkling with gems,
They were beautiful women,
  finely wrought jewels.

Trembling like the water lily, shimmering like water, and wearing the shining Tiruccentūr *poṭṭu,* Pummakkāḷ and Tummakkāḷ grew up in Pakaṭai's house. When you saw them, you'd think,

Even Pārvati
  has a few blemishes,

Lakṣmi at least four or five,
  and Sarasvati some faults.
Indrāni has spots on her hips,
  dancing girls marks on their stomachs;
And beneath running water
  the sand is often black.
Now the moon
  is a bit tarnished,
  the sun is sometimes stained,
But these women,
  except for jet-black hair,
  have no darkness anywhere!
Not a flaw in front
  not a flaw in back,
Like a perfect shape
  molded in the blacksmith's forge,
They were pure gold
  formed in the goldsmith's fire.
Their sandalwood *poṭṭu*
  sparkled and shone,
And the smell
  was won-der-ful!

No woman in the world was more lovely than Pakaṭai's daughters, Pummakkāḷ and Tummakkāḷ. And Pakaṭai himself had changed. Instead of spending money on everything—liquor, *ganja,* snuff, tobacco—now he began to save it. Since the day his daughters appeared, he hadn't even touched a betel nut. He had become that practical! It's all a stupid waste of money anyway, and he stopped it completely. As a result, of course, he ended up with more money. Now what do you think he did with it? Right! Off to Ambasamudram to a jewelry shop to buy lots of jewels for his daughters. When he got home, he dressed them from head to foot in jewels.

Pins and rings
  and combs for their hair,
A crescent moon
  hanging above their eyes.
Fans and wheels in their noses
  and rings in their ears,
Gems green and red
  and gold on their bodies,
Diamond and gold necklaces
  sparkled on their necks,
Coral and pearl garlands
  dazzled on their breasts,
Heavy copper bracelets
  a kāppu upon their arms,

Bangles of red and blue
  shining on their arms,
Rings of lapis lazuli
  of topaz and green,
Rings of white and red
  sparkled on their fingers.

But that wasn't all. Pakaṭai bought bells and chains and bracelets for their feet, and rings for their toes. Yet even this wasn't enough for Pakaṭai—he got more money and went back to the jewelry shop and bought more jewels:

Necklaces and pearl strings
  and ornaments of gold,
    gold bangles on their arms
    gold rings on their fingers.
They made the heart flutter
  and the mind go wild!
Heavy studded necklaces
  and silk Kāsi saris,
    saris with gold borders
    that weighed more than they!
In their nose a pin
  worth 3,000 pieces of gold,
    and in their hands
    a silky silver fan.

Pakaṭai put all these jewels on his daughters, and still he wasn't satisfied. Knowing that if you run into bad times, these jewels will be useful . . . you sell them little by little to get cash . . . he bought more,

Diamond pins and rings
  and jewel-studded chains,
  only a thousand eyes could see!
Heavy gold bracelets
  and red, red stones
  only a thousand eyes could see!
Red gems and white gems
  silver belts around their waists,
To see it all
  you'd need a thousand eyes!

Finally, fearing something evil might occur if he put any more jewels on them, Pakaṭai stopped. Of course these three had their everyday lives, too. Pakaṭai still waited for his food while he watched the cow pens, but now, ever since their mother Vāli had died, Pummakkāḷ and Tummakkāḷ took the food to their father. One day, they were trying to decide what to cook for him and thought,

"Mere sambar and rice
he will not touch,
Even mixed with ginger
he won't eat a bite."
So they cooked sweet tamarind rice
and boiled a fat chicken.
Fried up salted veal,
buffalo and beef,
Mixed in crabs and fish
and stewed it all.
Then made a special dish
with a Brahmin's chick.

That dish with the little chick is really great! You get one raised by a Brahmin, cut it up, then mix it with a lot of cow's milk and boil it. You have to taste it to believe how good it is! Anyway, they packed all this food carefully, added a little *carāyam,* some *kaḷḷu,* cigars, and high-quality betel nut. They were ready to go, but first they dressed up a bit. After all, they were going outside . . . so something special.

Combing their jet-black hair,
they plaited long braids.

They combed and twisted their hair, and put flowers in their braids—white jasmine, blue jasmine, the fragrant jasmine, the dense jasmine, and big roses—enough flowers to fill a basket! Then they rubbed sweet-smelling oils on their bodies, so they smelled wonderfully and they looked lovely! Their jewels tinkled softly as they walked.

Through Ālaṭiyūr and Aṭicanallūr,
by Muttumaṇṭai and Maṭṭukaḷḷu,
Across the Paḻaiyakōṭṭai River,
into a mango grove.

In that grove, the older sister Pummakkāḷ picked up a little piece of mango, turned to her sister and said softly,

"Listen, sister,
listen as I sing;
this mango piece
means a husband soon.
This slice of mango
will get us married
will bring a man to us.
But this mango has a nut
and surely means a fool
a dunce for a husband!"

When Pummakkāḷ sang this song, her younger sister Tummakkāḷ laughed,

"Are you saying we're going to get a husband just because you picked up that mango piece? Listen. Last night I had a dream . . .

"I saw a banyan tree, sister,
our husband-to-be.
I saw him with his father,
in my dreams,
sister, in my dreams.
I saw a mango tree, sister,
in my dreams, in my dreams.
I saw him with his friends,
in my dreams,
sister, in my dreams.
I saw him drink
from the Tambraparni River,
in my dreams,
sister, in my dreams.
I saw him
tie on the tāli,
in my dreams,
sister, in my dreams."

As the sisters were singing to each other, Tummakkāḷ said,

"Pummakkāḷ! Why is it taking so long today to get to the cow pen? What's different about today?"

"Don't know. But why not sing some of those field songs you know. Then time will fly. Just one song will take us there."

"Not now, I'm too tired. Well . . . alright . . . just for you, sister. I'll sing a song, one you've never heard before."

Along the path,
ailasa, aiyelasa,[32]
a tiger prowls.
Through the flowers,
ailasa, aiyelasa,
it stalks.
In the running stream,
ailasa, aiyelasa,
little, little stones.
Little by little,
ailasa, aiyelasa,
they make a bridge.
Over that bridge,

ailasa, aiyelasa,
our husband walks.
In the river,
ailasa, aiyelasa,
he drinks.
That handsome man,
ailasa, aiyelasa,
with silk turban and shawl.

Tummakkāḷ's song made her sister ecstatic! She brimmed with happiness, but Tummakkāḷ was too thirsty to share her feeling.

"Remember what I said when we left home: we should eat some of the leftover rice and add a little pickle or *dāhl* or something. But you said no, and cooked up that big chicken meal. And what a meal! All that salt—I couldn't tell if the meat had salt, or the salt had meat! Now my tongue and mouth are dry. Let's stop to drink."

"Fool! If you drink the foul water around here, you'll get sick with a fever and headache and be in bed for days. And who is there to take care of us? Mother's no longer alive and though Father's there, he's not able to do much at his age. He leaves us to wander all around in the sun and dry fields. If he left us while we are still unmarried, that would be it. No marriage at all. Anyway, forget about the water here, because besides the fever and headaches . . .

Drink from a well,
you'll get the runs!
Water in a canal
is so unclean,
In a standing pool
it's much the same.
Let's go on
a little farther
on to the Tambraparni.
And drink
its clean, pure water."

When they reached the Tambraparni, they put down their food packets and stepped into the water, as beautiful as the Ganges. After washing their hands and faces, they drank by cupping their hands and scooping up a little water, and this sent tiny waves which . . . remember our Muttuppaṭṭaṉ was doing pūjā on the banks of the same river . . . well, the waves washed away the sand *liṅgam* he was worshiping.[33] The *liṅgam* gone, Paṭṭaṉ opened his eyes but couldn't see a thing—the light was blinding! He had to close his eyes again. Then, putting his hands over his eyes, he tried to peer out through the cracks, but Pummakkāḷ and Tummakkāḷ were standing there like the rising sun. And who can look directly into the rising sun? Well, Paṭṭaṉ couldn't either, and so he tried to get a look at the light by shielding his eyes. He kept thinking, "What *is* this light? This is incredible!" But the light from the sisters' sparkling jewels and gold ornaments was still too powerful. Finally, turning his head and looking from the corner of his eye, he saw them. That did it—he forgot all about his pūjā! Who could think about anything after seeing them?

Blinded by love,
  Paṭṭaṉ stopped his pūjā!
He forgot about the Lord
  and wanted those women!
Paṭṭaṉ gave up Śiva
  for the Cakkiliyar sisters!
Love-struck,
  he ran to them
  and stood in their path,
Babbling the first words
  that rushed from his mouth . . .

That Brahmin Muttuppaṭṭaṉ stood before them and asked the important questions . . .

"Tell me,
  Who are you?
  Who are your parents?
Don't be afraid,
  wait a minute,
  and speak a word with me.
Don't run,
  I'll catch you
  if you try."

To which the sisters replied,

"Make fun of us, Brahmin,
  and we'll knock out your teeth!"

But they were taken by him and said to themselves,

"Sister, he looks like Śiva, like the Great Lord himself!"

And then to him,

"Cāmi, you are like great Śiva,
  we are Cakkiliyar.
This world of ours—
  will it allow us to touch?"

Paṭṭaṉ responded sharply,

"Who says that? Who will swear that you are Cakkiliyar? There's only one person in this world who knows your true origin, and that's me. You see, your mother is my aunt, and your father is my uncle. That's the truth!"

"What's this? He claims he's our cross-cousin, the one we should marry![34] This guy's not going to let us go easily; he's serious. Pummakkāḷ, say something to get him to listen. Make him see the problem."

"Sir, you seem to have lost your way, like a calf looking for its mother. There's nothing here for you. Go back the way you came."

"No, no. I'm just a little thirsty; my mouth is parched. If you'd bring me a little water with your hands . . ."

"This one's not going to listen. He's out of a bad dream! And about to grab us, I think."

Worried that he might force himself on them, they skipped off.

> "Here we go, mister,
> catch us if you can!"
> And off they pranced
> through the thorny brush.

The dazzling women were gone, but Paṭṭaṉ didn't stand around—he ran, he really ran. He ran, he jumped, he leaped—this man was love-sick! But there was a problem here: they were Cakkiliyar women and could fly, but he . . . well, he was an ordinary Brahmin and couldn't go very fast. In fact, in his first burst of energy he was totally exhausted, went dizzy, and fell down—plop! in a mango grove. You should have seen him try to run—he couldn't even *walk* if he had to! With Paṭṭaṉ collapsed in the grove, the sisters ran on.

> Dropping the curry and rice
> they fled through the brush.
> Frightened and calling for help
> they ran toward home.
> Hearing their shrieking voices,
> Pakaṭai ran home too.

Reaching the hut, Pakaṭai heard his daughters inside heaving and gasping for breath, and called to them,

"Pummakkāḷ! What happened? What are you running from? Tummakkāḷ! Tell me, girl, what's the matter?"

Trying to straighten their saris, loosened from running through that rough country, the sisters came out of the hut to answer their father. Still, when Pakaṭai saw them, he was shocked.

> "Your sari is loosened
> your arms and legs bruised;

young lovely doe,
what happened to you?
Your untouched body
now is streaked with sweat.
Pearl tears stain your eyes,
your face is pale grey.
Your eyes a sea of tears,
your body exhausted;
young lovely doe,
what happened to you?"

Pummakkāḷ answered her father,

"We were bringing your lunch along the path when Tummakkāḷ started making trouble. She was thirsty, so rather than drink the bad water there, we went to the Tambraparni where someone was sitting down, facing east, and doing some pūjā. He came over to us and asked what caste we were. 'Cakkiliyar,' I said. 'Doesn't matter!' he said, 'I'm going to marry you. I'll elope with you or have a traditional marriage—anything you want. But I'm going to marry you.' When he said that, we threw everything on the ground and ran away. Only with the help of god did we escape."

Hearing this, Pakaṭai was livid with rage.

"Is there anyone that low! So vile even a dog wouldn't touch him? Approaching you in a forest so thick even a crow wouldn't fly there! So dense even a sparrow couldn't enter! Show me where he is right now, or I'll cut you up like an animal!"

So the sisters led their father.

With one hand
Pakaṭai grabbed a butcher knife,
With the other
his hunting dogs.
His daughters ran ahead,
leading along the path.
They took him to Paṭṭaṉ
asleep in the mango grove.
Boiling over with rage
his knife held high,
Pakaṭai charged
to slice up the Brahmin!

But when he brought down the knife and saw Muttuppaṭṭaṉ's glowing beauty, he was stunned . . . and drew back. Confused, he began to wonder if his daughters were fooling him; he yelled at them,

"Don't play games with me! Can't you tell by his beauty that he's some raja, some prince? Probably came on a hunt and now he's just sleeping in this grove to avoid the heat. You're stirring up big trouble with him. You fools! How can I even *approach* him?"

He was about to beat his daughters when they cried out,

"No, father! I swear. I swear on Aiyaṉār: it was he and no one else."

Since they would never lie with an oath like that, Pakaṭai knew they were telling the truth. The only way to figure out what had happened was to wake the fellow up and ask him. Pakaṭai walked up to the sleeping body and called,

"Sir! Sir!"

But there was no response. He tried three or four times, but still Muttuppaṭṭaṉ didn't move. Pakaṭai was caught in a bind, like the proverb says: "If you touch him, it's wrong; if your shadow touches him, it's a sin."[35] How to wake him up—obviously he wasn't a light sleeper—in the least offensive way? Then Pakaṭai got an idea:

He clapped his hands
  and lightly tossed a pebble.
"Who are you?"
  the startled Brahmin asked.
"Oh Raja," Pakaṭai replied,
  "at the Tambraparni river
  my daughters stopped to drink,
And some lust-crazed Brahmin
  spoke insulting words.
When I find that bastard,
  I'll cut him in two,
Make him into mincemeat
  and feed him to the jackals!"

When he heard Pakaṭai speak these words, Muttuppaṭṭaṉ knew he was a Cakkiliyar; then he saw Pummakkāḷ and Tummakkāḷ behind him, and put it all together. This was the person he must ask for permission to marry them. But how could he, a Brahmin, ask a Cakkiliyar? What form could his request possibly take? Then it hit him: he had to use a kin term, treat him as his maternal uncle, his potential father-in-law, and address him as "Māma." Muttuppaṭṭaṉ looked right at Pakaṭai and spoke clearly,

"Māma!
  O Māma,
  I'm in love with your daughters.
I cast aside my pūjā
  Māma,

I left everything
to follow your daughters.
Let me marry them, Māma."

"Māma! I've left my mother and my brothers for your daughters. I left everything for them. If you agree to this marriage, without any thought of caste, I'll do anything you ask."

Pakaṭai answered calmly,

"Sir, you can't be saying this. What about our castes? You are a Brahmin and we are lowly Cakkiliyar. Even if you put a ladder between us, we wouldn't touch. What's the matter with you? Someone from a high caste like you can't want a person from a low caste like my daughters."

But Muttuppaṭṭaṉ cut him off,

"What is this talk of 'high' and 'low' caste? Where have you been? Sitting in your hut all your life? We live in a society that says all are one caste. Don't go back to the old days when we used to talk about this caste and that caste, high and low. Do you want to count bars in jail?[36] Keep any caste thoughts to yourself and don't speak of it again."

After Pakaṭai heard Muttuppaṭṭaṉ's lofty words, he thought to himself,

"Hmmm . . . can't even talk to this Brahmin. I'd better try something else. I know, I'll tell him about the disgusting practices in our caste. That should drive him away pretty fast."

And Pakaṭai spoke again.

"You want to marry into our caste? Alright, but first you better know about our customs.

We eat crabs,
we eat little fish,
and all kinds of snails!

"That's right. We eat crab, little fish, and even snails. If there's time, we boil the snails; but when we're in a rush, we eat them raw! Just remember that, friend!"[37]

Since these words had no effect on Muttuppaṭṭaṉ, Pakaṭai continued,

"Listen, sir,
we put rice in our vēṭṭi.
and eat it in the streets.
We eat goat's meat
and cow's meat,
drink *carāyam* and *kaḷḷu*.
We have to scrape and bow . . .

"Scrape and bow! You see, boy, no matter how educated they might be, people always treat you as a servant. Some will look at you and say, 'Hey you! Come here!' Others say, 'Hey dog! Over here!' And still others, 'Move scum!' And no matter what they call you, you must address them with respect: 'Yes sir' or 'Cāmi, I am at your command.' You've got to bow and bend to them, and hold everything inside. It's rotten, the life we lead! You know the sayings, 'Life is a bow,' 'Obeisance is survival.' That's the way it is! A life of bowing and bending. Just try to live with your head held high—you'll be destroyed! You'll lose even the little you've got. No, better to be careful. Humility! Patience! Silence! That's what they want."

When Muttuppaṭṭaṉ, undeterred, asked for more details, Pakaṭai softened and agreed to the marriage—but with conditions:

"Take off
  your sacred thread,
Shave off
  your Brahmin's tuft;
Wipe off
  your sacred ash,
Wear this dirty cloth
  around your soft waist,
And start growling your words
  like a Cakkiliyar!
Find a dead cow
  and skin it,
Cut it up
  and serve us Cakkiliyar!

And remember, when you cut it up, be careful with the meat. Not even one tiny piece should be wasted! Got that?"

Muttuppaṭṭaṉ was undaunted,

"What's the hurry? You don't have to tell me all this now. Let's get on with the marriage and then if there's some problem with my work, we can discuss it."

Pakaṭai was stunned at his words and thought,

"He *is* determined. Guess there's no way to make him change his mind!"

Muttuppaṭṭaṉ spoke again, in a gentler tone,

"What's the problem, Māma? Maybe you haven't heard, but . . .

Caste, Māma?
  what is caste?
  a confusion in the mind!

In the beginning,
 in the very beginning, Māma,
That great poet Vyāsa
 was the son of a fisherwoman!
Caste, Māma?
 what is caste?
 it's a category of the mind!
And Atri's son, the sage,
 was the son of a Cakkiliyar!
What is 'caste,' Māma,
 but a division in the mind!
That great sage Nārada
 was a washerwoman's son,
 the son of a *vaṇṇāṉ!*
And that learned teacher, Kaṅkaiyaṉ,
 was the son of an ass,
 only a donkey's son!
All this 'caste,' Māma,
 it's only in the mind.
Who was that saint, Māma,
 who gave his eyes to Śiva?
It was a tribal's son,
 the child of a Kuṟavar.[38]
Who gained *mokṣa,* Māma,
 upon this very earth?
It was Nantaṉ, Māma,
 the son of an Untouchable!
What is caste, Māma?
 but a confusion of the mind."

When Pakaṭai heard Muttuppaṭṭaṉ say all this, he was moved,

"You have spoken well. What more can I say? Maybe your luck is with Śiva. We'll see. First, go to Vikkiramaciṅkapuram—your brothers are there, right? Get their permission and then stitch me a pair of leather sandals. If you do that, my daughters are your wives. Now hurry off and don't delay."

Paṭṭaṉ agreed, but had something to say himself,

"Fine. I'll do what you ask and come back as soon as possible. But one thing I ask of you: when I return, don't you say, 'Well, you see . . . they're already married. Their cross-cousins came all of a sudden and there was really nothing I could do.' If you plan to get rid of me with that trick, tell me right now because I'm not playing around. When I come back, my hands won't be empty. I'll have your sandals for you! And if I don't, then you have my promise—I'll rip out my tongue!"

With all this said, Paṭṭaṉ left and went directly to Vikkiramaciṅkapuram where his brothers were staying. When they saw him, they couldn't believe it and called to him in anger and joy,

"Where have you been? We were sleeping by the Tambraparni River, and in the morning you were gone. What happened? C'mon, out with it!"

But Paṭṭaṉ could only stammer,

"Bro . . . ther . . . brother . . ."

"Cut out the 'brother' stuff! Where'd you go?"

"I . . . I . . . went to look for a wife."

"Where'd you do that? Anyway, we already have a wife selected for you. You know, Uncle Śeṣu's daughter, Rukku? You see, it's 10,000 rupees in dowry for us. Of course, you're not supposed to talk openly about dowries, so we did it very quietly. Now, when we've got a wife like her set up, what are you doing looking for one?"

"Bro . . . ther . . ."

"I said cut out the 'brother' stuff! Where'd you go to look for a wife? Tell us!"

". . . Near the village of Ālaṭiyūr, in the hamlet of Vermaipuram . . ."

But Appāpaṭṭaṉ interrupted with a shout,

"You fool! There's no Brahmin *agrahāram* there! It's . . . it's a bunch of Cakkiliyar huts! That's not an *agrahāram!*"

Muttuppaṭṭaṉ decided to forget the details and make it brief:

"I'm marrying two women,
two Cakkiliyar.
They are Cakkiliyar,
and I'll become one too!
Leave me, my brothers!
don't waste my time.
I'm marrying two women,
two Cakkiliyar."

Appāpaṭṭaṉ was shocked! He thought his brother had actually lost his mind.

"You little fool! We've raised you since you were five years old! We raised you carefully and sent you to school till you were almost twenty-one. Where is all that education now? How can you say you are going to marry into the Cakkiliyar caste? Have you forgotten caste? Who are we and who are they? You sound like you've gone crazy. Are you sick? Tell me, what's wrong with you?"

"What kind of a question is that? I'm fine. I'm not crazy; I'm just speaking my mind."

"Not crazy, huh? But a Brahmin and a Cakkiliyar? Don't talk nonsense."

Then Appāpaṭṭaṉ made a quick decision and turned to his other brothers.

"He's just a little . . . well . . . different, that's all. You better take him and lock him up somewhere for his own good. Don't misunderstand me. Remember he's done a lot of studying . . . even the Vedas, right? That's why his tongue gets twisted a bit. Nothing serious."

The others grabbed Muttuppaṭṭaṉ and put chains on his arms and on his legs, all over his body. Locking twenty-one chains on him, they led him into a stone room, shut the door and left. Inside the room, Paṭṭaṉ began to think about Pummakkāḷ and Tummakkāḷ and called for them in a slow, halting voice,

"Pummakkāḷ! Tummakkāḷ!
Where are you now?
Can I hold you
in these chained arms?
Can I offer wedding garlands
with these bound hands?"

At exactly the same time, in the hamlet of Vermaipuram, Pummakkāḷ and Tummakkāḷ were thinking of him! The younger sister spoke her heart.

"Tell me, sister! That Brahmin we met the other day, isn't he the most beautiful man in the whole world? Will we ever find another like him? He's a flower, and I want to wear him in my hair right now! I'd marry him today! Our cross-cousins who came and asked for us, huh! We got rid of them pretty fast, didn't we? Remember how we insulted them? But now maybe we'll never get married, and if we don't before father dies, well . . . then there's not much hope. But if we *do* get married, I want it to be that man, that Muttuppaṭṭaṉ!"

Back in his stone cell, Muttuppaṭṭaṉ was howling away. It was so loud that the Brahmins in the nearby houses came to Appāpaṭṭaṉ and complained,

"He's making a racket! What's going on here, anyway? He's calling someone's name over and over: 'Pummakkāḷ-Tummakkāḷ, Tummakkāḷ-Pummakkāḷ.' He's at it day and night. The night isn't so bad, but in the day his bawling is unbearable! We can't even tell the difference between night and day anymore. What are you doing with him, anyway? Can't you make him come to his senses, or is he crazy?

Appāpaṭṭaṉ relented and told his brothers to free Muttuppaṭṭaṉ. After all, he was their brother, and there was no excuse for causing trouble to others. The whole thing was such a mess! He regretted the day he let him come with them to the Pāṇṭiya country.

However, when they went to unlock the cell and let him out, Paṭṭaṉ had already . . .

Snapped the chains on his legs,
  snapped the chains on his arms,
    twenty-one chains
    broken effortlessly!
Springing like a tiger
  to the Tambraparni River,
He hurled 1,008 *liṅgam*s
  into the clear waters,
  and destroyed his pūjā place.
He tore off his sacred thread
  shaved his Brahmin's tuft,
  wiped off his sacred ash
  and shed his fancy clothes.
Wrapped in rags
  slurring his speech like a Cakkiliyar,
He called on Viṣṇu
  at the Pāpanācam temple
  and made this vow:
"Listen to me, Perumāḷ,
  I'm going to be a Cakkiliyar!"

Muttuppaṭṭaṉ ran off to the Saturday market at Ambasamudram, bought some animal skin, and carried it to Pakaṭai's hut in Vermaipuram, where he called softly to Pummakkāḷ and Tummakkāḷ,

"Bring me the cobbler's tools so I can make the sandals."

The sisters gave him what he needed—a little knife and a punch—and Muttuppaṭṭaṉ took them under a tree near the house to work.[39]

He cleaned and cut the skin,
  and then stitched the soles,
Tied fancy colored tassels
  on the leather straps.

Muttuppaṭṭaṉ made a magnificent pair of sandals! He took them in hand and walked to the hut, but then he hesitated:

"If I give these sandals to him myself, he might think I didn't really make them. He'll think I bought them ready-made in some shop. But if he discovers them himself and is impressed, he'll seek out their maker anyway."

Paṭṭaṉ put the sandals just above the door to the hut so that they would fall down when the door was opened; then he withdrew. Soon Pakaṭai appeared, dead tired after a long day's work; and when he banged through the door, the sandals fell right in front of him! Surprised, he picked them up and turned to the sunlight outside to examine them. Squinting as he looked them over, he was amazed.

"Hey! *Who* made these sandals? Pummakkāḷ! Who did these? Tummakkāḷ! Do you know?"

But the sisters were too shy to speak, and they just stood there squirming and giggling. Then Pakaṭai raised his voice,

"Now look here! I asked you a question. Answer me!"

But the sisters could only speak word-by-word:

"That . . . man . . . who . . . came . . . to marry . . . us . . . He did it!"

"Really! Why didn't you say so right away? Where is that son-in-law of mine? Where's your husband-to-be?"

Now, Paṭṭaṉ was lounging outside the hut under a tree as if he knew nothing. Pakaṭai ran out to him, trembling with joy, and said,

"Son-in-law, those hands that made these sandals . . . ah . . . let me see them—just a peek."

Paṭṭaṉ was a bit embarrassed—how do you show your hands? But Pakaṭai assured him,

"Now c'mon, just a little look at your hands. Put them out for me."

Paṭṭaṉ did, and when Pakaṭai saw them, he beamed with joy! What a pair of hands! Hands to make any father-in-law happy. Yes sir, a fine pair of hands! Pakaṭai led Paṭṭaṉ back into the hut, sat him down, and thought to himself,

"I better give him a final test to see if he can stand the food we eat. If he gets disgusted, better now than later."

With this plan, the family began to prepare a feast for their Brahmin guest.

They sat him down
upon a cattle skin,
Served him betel nut
in a cow's skull.
And poured him hot water
in small *kaḷḷu* bowls![40]

Then the sisters called to their father,

"Come and eat, and tell him, too."

Pakaṭai turned to Paṭṭaṉ, who was a little stunned, and said,

"Alright, son-in-law, food's ready. Go wash up."

The sisters gave him some water in one of the *kaḷḷu* bowls, but he didn't move.

"Come on boy, wash up."

Slowly the Brahmin washed his face and hands, went over to where the food had been spread out, and sat down. He looked over the dishes closely—goat meat, cow meat, sweet young calf meat, salted meats, and even a sauce made from crab meat! He felt totally undone and cursed himself,

"So this is what lust brings! I desired these women and now this degradation!"

He just stared at the food and, without even knowing it, tears ran down his face. When Pakaṭai saw this, he was curt:

"That does it! Out! I tried to tell you about this before you came into this hut. You were warned what it would be like, but you didn't listen. And now, just looking at our food, your eyes are smarting! You better leave, and leave quickly!"

"Don't get me wrong, Māma! You don't understand. It's not my lands, my goats, cattle, gardens, groves, or even my family that I'm thinking of. It's just that I always put sacred ash on my forehead before eating. But you said I couldn't wear it—remember? I've never sat down to eat before without it. And without my ash, I feel like my *bhakti* has been ruined. That's the reason for my tears."

Listening to this, Pakaṭai wondered whether Paṭṭaṉ might be doubting their own religious devotion,

"Alright, sit down. Pummakkāḷ! Get the ash box from the wall and bring it here."

Pummakkāḷ grabbed the box and gave it to her father, who held it out,

"Here, son-in-law, take some."

Paṭṭaṉ stood there; he looked at the box, then at Pakaṭai, and again at the box. Finally he took a big handful of ash and smeared it over his entire forehead! Fortified by all that ash, he took a second look at the food. When his eye caught a funny-looking dish, he asked in an uncertain voice,

"Māma, what is this? . . . this one with . . . all these pieces?"

"Now, son-in-law, that's goat curry. Just take a bite and tell me what you think."

Paṭṭaṉ hesitated, then slowly lifted out a small piece of the curry and put it on his tongue.[41] Then he knew!

"Wow, Māma!
this goat curry,
is absolutely great!"

Then Paṭṭaṉ asked about another dish,

"Ah . . . what's this . . . with all the lumps in it?"

"That? Oh, that's cow curry. Try it and see if you like it."

Cow meat was a little too much for Paṭṭaṉ, but he bravely fished around in the curry until he got a little piece of it. Lifting it, he touched it very lightly to his tongue.

"Wow, Māma!
this cow curry
is very tasty, too."

He looked at a third dish.

"Māma, what's this dish with all these dark things?"

"Just try it."

And he did.

"Great, Māma!
this calf meat
is sugar cane to me!"

Paṭṭaṉ looked once more at the food,

"Māma, what's this one? With the . . . mustache and beard?"

"Let me explain something to you. In your rich villages you can make lots of different sauces—mango, tomato, ginger, orange—all those great sauces. But here in this poor area we don't get any of that. We can only make sauces from field crabs. But give it a taste and see what it's like."

Paṭṭaṉ was willing and tried to grab a piece of the crab, but he didn't know you can't pick it out like a piece of meat. He fished around and around without success and then . . . in desperation . . . stuck his fingers into the sauce and licked them!

"Oh, Māma!
this crab sauce,
I love it most of all!"

Son-in-law and father-in-law finished their meal and relaxed with some betel nut. Then Pakaṭai called a Vaḷḷuvar astrologer to check his daughters' and Muttuppaṭṭaṉ's horoscopes. Amazingly, their horoscopes corresponded on each of the twenty-one points; so the Vaḷḷuvar wrote out an announcement on palm-leaf fixing the wedding for the eighteenth of Paṅkuṉi during an auspicious asterism. Pakaṭai was very happy, but as the day for the wedding got closer and closer, he got more and more worried. He had no money! No cash in hand and no one to loan him any! Not a rupee anywhere! But I ask you, is that anything to get upset about? Well . . . is it? Of course not. All you need to do is *collect* money. Now, where do you start? Go to every house and ask for it? No, there's no time for that. Better to start right here, right in this festival. Better to ask everyone sitting under this pantal—all you women and men, sisters and brothers! We can go to each one and collect money for a wedding. That's the only way you can do it these days. You know, it takes 1,000 rupees or 2, 3, 4, 5—up to 10,000 to put on a wedding! Now, we don't have to do it that extravagantly. Still, even for a simple marriage you need 500. What kind of a wedding are you going to put on for less than that? Couldn't even call it a wedding for less than 500! So we've got to come up with at least that much. We'll have to buy new clothes for the boy and girl, right? Luckily we've got a little cash on hand so we can start making arrangements. Now, who's the first person you need for a festival?

[Audience:] "A pantal-man."

Exactly! We need a pantal person, and luckily we don't have to go very far to find a good one. Right here in Aralvāymoḻi, there's Paramacivam Piḷḷai. We'll go to him and say,

"Mr. Pantal-man, we're going to have a wedding for our daughter, and we need a pantal. How much do you want?"

Now, Paramacivam Piḷḷai is not one to make a big thing of money, and he'll say,

"Money? Don't talk about it now. Let's get the pantal up, then we can figure it out."

So then we'll give him, say, eleven rupees as an advance. Let's see, who's next?

[Audience:] "Mic-set man."

Right, a microphone man. And no need to chase all around to get one, because right here in Kanya Kumari district there is the famous electrical company, Love's Sound Service. We'll go to them and say,

"Mr. Mic-set man! Our daughter's getting married, and we need a mic-set and lights and all. The tube lights, mind you, and those automatic . . . whatever they're called . . . We want you to do it in a special way. How much will it cost?"

Now, he isn't one to worry about money either.

"Forget about the money for now. I'll put it up and then ask you for it."

We'll give him an advance of eleven rupees too. Who's next?

[Audience:] "Mēḷam!"

Right. We need a mēḷam ensemble. Again, we have a good group right here (where's he from?) . . . right here, the mēḷam from the coffee shop, Ratnam's mēḷam. We'll say to him,

"Ratnam, Mr. Mēḷam-man! We're putting on a wedding, and we want you to play. How much do you want?"

"No need to talk about that now. I'll do my best and then we can talk money."

And then we'll have to give him an advance of 101 rupees.

[Audience:] "101 rupees?"

Well, remember something: Ratnam may be local, but he's got to travel and contact the others, and then they have to travel to get here, so it costs more. Now, the next thing we need is a second kind of mēḷam, an *urumi mēḷam*. Without that, people in some castes won't call it a wedding! For this we have to go north of Caṅkarakōvil, to the village of Ūttumalai, to Krishna,

"Krishna! We need you to play at our daughter's wedding. What's your fee?"

"Fee? Don't worry about it. Just give me a little advance, then we'll figure it out."

So we'll give him also 101 rupees. Then you have to hire workers for the wedding. You can fix a contract with them from fifty to one hundred rupees and even give an advance of ten rupees, but it won't do. They want something else, don't they? C'mon, what do workers want? If you give them an additional five rupees, they'll run to a shop and eat, right? So what do you have to give them?

[Audience:] "Food."

That's right. You have to arrange meals for them, so we need a person to supply food. Now this person is very important, because he can keep us hungry or make us happy. You've got to have good food, so it pays to look around, but we don't have to look far—right here in Aralvāymoḻi there is a man bearing the divine name of Achuytaṉ, Gōpālaṉ, Hari, Nārāyaṇa, Paramatma, the Protector of this Wide Earth, Mr. Krishna Piḷḷai. We'll say to him,

"Mr. Krishna, we're having a wedding, and we want you to supply the meals. No goat or cow meat. Only *pure* vegetarian food. How much do you want?"

"Don't worry about the money. Vegetarian, right? We'll do it first-class. Here's the dishes you'll get:

"Eight different sauces,
  vegetables and pickles,
Eight kinds of potato,
  six kinds of lentils,
Cabbage and drumsticks,
  all cooked just right.
Even foreign vegetables . . ."

All those English vegetables! There's so many more of them than our Tamil vegetables. Carrot, beet root, beans, lettuce . . .

Even foreign vegetables
  and sweet potato, too.
Tasty vegetable mixtures
  and thick buttermilk sauce.
Plenty of sweet lentils
  pickles and seasonings.
It will smell wonderful
  and satisfy your stomach.

"There'll be ten kinds of curry, eighteen different sauces, and all the nicest preparations. We'll make it the best meal you ever had!"

Then Pakaṭai gave him an advance of 101 rupees—remember he has to go and buy lots of things, all those seasonings and vegetables.

By now everything was arranged for the marriage of Pakaṭai's daughters, but they still needed money, so he decided to ask the caste elders. Plucking up his courage, he said,

"Sirs . . . we're marrying my daughters and . . . I need a little money."

They looked at him quizzically,

"Wedding? What wedding? When? This is awfully sudden, don't you think? We haven't even seen the boy! Who is he?"

"Well . . . he's my sister's son. When he was young, he left home in a fight, and now he's returned. As I said, he's my eldest sister's son; we have looked into their horoscopes, and they are perfectly matched. We've already fixed the date for the marriage; that was four or five days ago."

"Now look here, Pakaṭai! We haven't even seen this groom. You bring him here first!"

So Pakaṭai grabbed Muttuppaṭṭaṉ and brought him in front of the elders. When they saw his radiance, they were amazed.

"*He* is the groom . . . well . . ."

Following the proverb, "Better than money that fills the hand is a groom that fills the eye," they gave Pakaṭai everything![42] Expensive wedding saris, silk clothes, coins, and cash! Pakaṭai brought it all back home and began to prepare for the big event. Paramacivam Piḷḷai put up the pantal, and it was something else!

Like a palace,
  flowers were everywhere,
Bright *icci* and *vaṉṉi,*
  coconut and banana fronds.
Betel nut was sent to the locals,
  palm-leaf messages to those afar.

Music came from the mēḷam
as guests filled the pantal,
Into the crowd walked Pakaṭai
leading that Muttuppaṭṭaṉ
Followed by Tummakkāḷ and Pummakkāḷ
those tall, lovely queens.
As they sat beside the Brahmin
and the women cried the kuravai,
The tāli pendant was lifted
from its inlaid box
and given to Muttuppaṭṭaṉ,
Who called on Lord Śiva
and tied it on their necks.
The tāli was tied!
the kuravai was heard!
Brides and groom were covered
with heavy flower garlands;
Singing the blessing songs,
the girls joined them hand-to-hand
Then led them three times
around the marriage fire.
Muttuppaṭṭaṉ and his brides
cut the marriage-room ribbon,
Stepped past the women relatives
and sat on colored mats.
Milk and fruit were given
as the girls sang to them:
"May you be blessed
with a son
and daughter, too.
May you know happiness
and a long, long life."

When the blessings were over, Pakaṭai entered and sat by his son-in-law, took out a stylus and wrote down his dowry rights.

Your rights are to five places:
the Parumaṉai Hill, and its base,
the Kōpparai Hill, the Big Hill,
and the Koḻuntaṉ Hill.
And on all dead cattle
you have rights, too.

When the dowry was written out, all the young girls gathered in the marriage pantal and sang the *kummi* wedding song to Muttuppaṭṭaṉ,

Come girls!
  beat out the *kummi*
  for our Muttuppaṭṭan̲
    born in Āriya Nāṭu,
    the youngest of seven brothers.
Beat out the *kummi,* girls,
  for our learned Paṭṭan̲!
Move along, girls,
  beat out the *kummi*
  for our Muttuppaṭṭan̲,
    with curly mustache
    and pearly teeth.
Beat out the *kummi,* girls,
  for our beautiful Paṭṭan̲!
Come on, girls,
  beat out the *kummi*
  for our Muttuppaṭṭan̲,
    with moon cool face
    and golden sun body.
Beat out the *kummi,* girls,
  for our gentle Paṭṭan̲!
Come on, girls,
  beat out the *kummi*
  for our Muttuppaṭṭan̲,
    tie the wedding tāli
    on his wide chest.
Beat out the *kummi,* girls,
  for our Muttuppaṭṭan̲!

7

Conclusions: Death and Ritual Narrative

With the celebration of Muttuppaṭṭaṉ's marriage we reach the end of a koṭai festival, as represented by the performances translated in the previous three chapters. In this concluding chapter, I want to develop two major themes that were introduced earlier and then illustrated by the translations. The first is the ritual center on death in the bow song tradition; the second is the ritual role of narrative.

The structure of a bow song festival, as outlined at the close of Chapter 3, is an enclosure, closing around a death story sung in the middle slot. It will be remembered also that these performances of death stories are the ritual center of the festival (indexed by markers of ritual depth) and, moreover, that the death scenes within those songs are the points of greatest ritual depth in the entire tradition. What, then, is the meaning of this correlation between ritual depth and death in the bow song tradition?

At the outset it is important to note that this ritual center on death is not unique to the Tamil tradition. Even the sparse literature on folk religion in South Asia indicates that the worship of the deified dead is widespread in this cultural area. Cults of the deified dead form a continuous band along the southwest coast of India, from Udipi to Kanya Kumari, where they meet the bow songs. In particular, the *teyyam* cults of northern Kerala and the *bhūta* cults of southwest Karnataka are very closely related to the bow song. A second group of cults of the deified dead has been reported from western India (Gujarat and Rajasthan); these include the *khambha, bhomiyā, sāgati,* and *jhūnjhār.* In Sri Lanka, the *yak tovil* and the Pattini cults, both of which are major traditions of folk Buddhism on the island, show strong similarities to these Hindu cults of the dead.[1]

None of these cults (apparently) contains the bow song distinction between birth and death stories, and it is uncertain if anything like "birth" stories exist; however, the death stories, especially in the Hindu cults, are remarkably similar, almost uniform. Their heroes and heroines are born as ordinary human beings; a conflict develops over the control of land or a woman's sexuality; the heroes or heroines are cruelly killed (or commit suicide), are deified, and finally take revenge; later, they are worshiped in a local festival, and a cult begins. Variation exists within this basic pattern (revenge may precede instead of follow deification), but the overall thematic unity among these death stories is such that a *bhomiyā* story from Rajasthan (with appropriate changes of place and personal names) could be sung in a bow song festival.

Like the Tamil death stories, moreover, these narratives are sung to honor their hero-gods in a local festival involving spirit possession. Again there is variation: in some cases the roles of singer and dancer are taken by two separate persons (bow song); in other cases, the two roles are assumed by a single performer (*teyyam, bhūta* cults). The crucial commonality, however, is that the performance of the hero's story in most of these cults is centered on the death event. As in the bow song, possession and other rituals are closely linked with this narrative episode.

This ritual center on death is not limited to the Hindu cults of India; it runs beneath religiocultural boundaries and surfaces in the folk Buddhist cults of Sri Lanka.[2] The long exorcistic ceremonies on the southwest coast (*yak tovil*), for example, are poised on the symbolic death of a demon; and this demon, "Great Cemetery Demon" or Mahasona, is himself a figure of death (Kapferer 1983, 162–63 passim). The ritual dramas of the Pattini cult in the central highlands are likewise focused on the death (and resurrection) of Pattini's consort, Kōvalaṉ. Although that event (*marā ipäddīma*) is only one-sixth of the total performance, the entire "ritual drama is called *marā ipäddīma* owing to the centrality of that text in the events enacted" (Obeyesekere 1984, 245). The resurrection, which is crucial to Obeyesekere's conclusion that the Pattini ritual dramas have a West Asian origin (ibid., 474–82, 530–35), also makes sense as a Buddhist functional equivalent of the deification of the hero in Hindu cults. In fact, as Obeyesekere notes (ibid., 590–92), Kōvalaṉ is deified and assimilated with a Hindu god in some areas of Sri Lanka with heavy Tamil influence. Whether deification or resurrection, this return from the dead is important to an interpretation of the ritual center on death in the bow song, as we will see shortly.

Cults of the deified dead are not only widespread on the local level, but are also, I believe, at the core of certain larger, regional religious traditions in India. Two book-length studies of oral epics, the Tamil epic of Aṇṇaṉmār

(Beck 1982) and the Telugu epic of Palnāḍu (Roghair 1982), are cases in point. The narrative core of each epic is that a human hero suffers a loss of land and rights to the kingdom, war ensues, and the heroes (or son of the hero, in the Palnāḍu epic) die on the battlefield. Today the dead heroes are worshiped by singing their stories in an annual festival that has a ritual center on death. In performances of the Aṇṇaṉmār story, Beck notes (1982, 37–49) that the heroes' deaths are enacted by a number of men who lie down and then (like Pattini's consort, Kōvalaṉ) are resurrected by the magical power of a woman. The festival of the Palnāḍu epic is similarly focused on the heroes' deaths, which are sung on the climactic fifth day of the seven-day ceremony (Roghair 1982, 26–30). Without assuming any direct evolutionary process, one can see that these oral epic traditions represent an expansion of a death story and its accompanying cult.[3] In developing from local death story to regional epic, the narrative has been changed to appeal to a wider circle of patrons and audiences: the violent death has been muted, and the heroes have been homologized with higher status, Sanskritic figures. However, the ritual center on the death event points to the local death story at its core.

Unfortunately, the study of Hinduism has overlooked the importance of these cults of the dead, so that what we know is largely a Hinduism of birth stories and birth deities. The Indological tilt toward pan-Indian deities, stories, and concepts has guided even most studies of "village Hinduism" toward the local goddesses identified with Sanskritic figures.[4] Part of the reason for this lack of knowledge of death cults is that they are obscure, often found in only a few villages, and explained away even by their own patrons as pale reflections of higher status, regional or pan-Indian Hinduism. More research is needed before the true role of these death cults in India is known; already, however, it is clear that they are widespread and perhaps the substratum of folk Hinduism.[5]

In any case, the following explanation of the bow song's ritual center on death is one approach toward a general understanding of folk Hinduism. Let me state the negative case first. Bow song cults of the dead cannot be explained by any theory based either on pre-death relations between worshipers and deified dead or on a fear of death. The pre-death relation is crucial both to standard theories of ancestor worship, which claim that such worship extends social relations into the afterworld to ensure the continuity of power and wealth, and to certain psychoanalytic explanations of spirit worship and possession, whose theoretical chain of hostility, guilt, and eventual appeasement begins with an emotional bond formed prior to death.[6] It is significant that no such pre-death bond exists in the bow song cults. The early stages of some cults may be kin-based, but this is not true for the fully developed cults described in this book. In the Tampimār cult, for example, worshipers, patrons, singers, and dancers have no kin bond with the deified heroes. In fact, in most bow song cults, worshipers and heroes do not belong even to the same caste. Whether or not there was some personal contact between the original worshipers and bow song hero-gods is impossible to ascertain, but certainly there is no such contact today.

One major explanation for the worship of the dead that assumes no prior bond between god and worshiper is based on the concept of liminality. During the interim between death and incorporation into the ancestor world through funerary rites, the disembodied "soul" or "spirit" floats in ambiguity, belonging neither to this nor quite yet to the other world. This ambivalence, according to the liminality theory, creates anxiety in the living and prompts them to placate the dangerous spirits with worship.[7] Liminality and danger, furthermore, are compounded if the death is premature and cuts short the normal life span. The liminal and therefore dangerous spirit is known throughout the Indic cultures of South and Southeast Asia, often by the term *preta*.[8] Generally speaking, all deaths produce the disembodied *preta* that is potentially malevolent until transported by proper mortuary rituals into its role as *pitṛ* ("father" or ancestor). If the funeral is not or cannot be performed, the *preta* can roam freely and attack the living, who must somehow ward them off with offerings.

This liminality-*preta* theory is potentially applicable to the bow song cults because it is based not on a pre-death relation but on a general condition of the dead: the ambiguity epitomized in the premature deaths of the Tamil death stories. However, it fails to explain the correlation between death and ritual depth in the bow song cults for several reasons. First, not all who die prematurely or who fail to receive mortuary rites are deified and worshiped; conversely, some who are given proper funerals are deified and worshiped. Second, death deities in the bow song tradition are not liminal, ambiguous, ambivalent spirits. They are fully integrated into the local pantheon as major gods and goddesses. Third, these death deities are not malevolent spirits; they do cause harm, but almost always as just retribution for their own death.[9] Malevolent, *preta*-like spirits who wantonly attack, and cause illness and disease are called *pēy*. Far from causing these malevolent attacks, death deities are called on in the festival to prevent or cure them.

Thus the bow song's ritual center on death stories and deities cannot be explained by a fear of death. This point cannot be overemphasized because so much of the literature on the worship of the dead rests on the premise of a fear of death. Even bow song performance, wrapped around the ritual center on death, might be interpreted as a cushion against death.[10] However, if this were the goal, it could be accomplished far more effectively by not singing the death stories, for (one must remember) there is no independent "need" to perform them or to conduct the complex koṭai festival. But bow song performance is not structured to act as a buffer against dangerous contact with death. On the contrary, I believe it works toward the opposite goal. It positions death in the center not to avoid contact, but to demarcate a ritual realm for contact with it.

To understand why that contact with death should be desirable, we must turn back to the factor that all explanations of the deified dead overlook: the narratives themselves. If, as this study has attempted to demonstrate, narrative is the ground for the ritual pattern in the festival, then the worship of the dead cannot be separated from death stories.

The central theme of these stories, the "generative point" of the narrative and the cult that develops around it, as well as the ritually deepest point in performance, is the death of the hero. Moreover, the essential element of that death (whether murder or suicide), the unchanging fact, whatever the variations in detail, is its violence. A violent death, I would argue, generates a cult not (as the liminality-*preta* theory holds) because it truncates a life span, but precisely because it is violent, and powerful. The link between violence and deification was noted earlier (p. 92) when discussing how the violated woman is transformed into the violent goddess (Icakki Ammaṉ and others). By the same principle, a violent death transfers its power to all death deities. Driven inside at the moment of death, that power then becomes a source that can be summoned to counteract other elemental forces of disease, disaster, or even death. Birth deities also have power, but theirs is a gentle, somewhat abstract goodness that fosters fertility and prosperity. Death deities, on the other hand, have a power as raw and violent as death itself.

Deification of the dead is a recognition of their power. It is not simply an honoring of the dead, but a category transfer that makes possible contact with them. Unlike the ordinary dead, the violently killed are not made into ancestors; they are more powerful and are made into gods at the very center of the bow song festival. Birth stories form auspicious borders around that center, but they are not a buffer against death as much as a frame to highlight it by contrast. The structure of bow song performance, thus, has very little to do with fear or with ancestors. It is shaped, instead, to provide access to the power of the deified dead.

In the end, this deification and worship of the violently killed is a celebration. By summoning the death gods and their power to the worshipers, the performances at the ritual center of the koṭai celebrate a minor triumph over death. When men and women, the victims of murder and suicide, return as gods and goddesses to dance and speak through their mediums, then death has been beaten back, its finality denied. Whether Kōvalaṉ is resurrected in Buddhist Sri Lanka or the hero is deified in India, the effect is the same: as the singers describe the revival of the dead heroes in performances of the Tamil epic of Aṇṇaṉmār, "the dead men *have* come back to life" (Beck 1982, 39). In the bow song tradition, worshiping the deified dead signals not a grim resignation to the powerful grip of death, but a partial victory over it.

The ritual center on death, as we have just seen, is based in the narrative event of the hero's violent death. Bow song narratives not only underlie ritual in this way, but also play an active ritual role, which is the second issue I wish to discuss here. First, however, in order to appreciate the full complexity of the relation between ritual and narrative, let us recall that ritual also shapes narrative.

Developing Turner's etymological suggestion that performance is a "furnishing," I described bow song performance as a ritual rearrangement of a narrative world. It positions the two terms of the birth/death contrast into the three slots of the koṭai festival. A further shaping of narrative occurs within each slot as performances alter the story to fit the ritual demands of its particular slot. Each of the three performances translated in this book demonstrates this process of altering story content. The Śāstā/Vallarakkaṉ text is performed only to its midpoint where the singing closes with the birth of Śāstā. The performance of the Tampimār story is curtailed at the brothers' death in order to coordinate that event with the tīpārātaṉai and the possession dance. Even more instructive is the performance of the Muttuppaṭṭaṉ story, which concludes with the marriage and avoids the ritually deeper death scene, as is appropriate in the final slot.

Rearranging and reshaping the narrative world does not, however, replace it. As the ground upon which ritual lines are drawn, narrative remains the basis of the bow song tradition and exerts a reciprocal influence on ritual, evidence of which has been noted at various points in this book. Bow song texts lead to cults, and their cast of characters determines the clusters of deities in a temple. Bow songs are sacred histories that invoke gods, and their manuscripts control performances at the ritual center of the festival. Finally, narrative events (birth, death) are the catalyst to possession, without which the koṭai would be a failure: if Śāstā were not born in his story, if the Tampimār were not killed in theirs, these gods would not appear and speak through their mediums.

This power to summon gods is the most important aspect of the bow songs' ritual role. This is a power often discussed in studies of ritual language, but bow songs are narrative, whereas ritual language, almost by definition, is considered nonnarrative, low in semantic load and high in formulaic ("ritualistic") features, such as repetition and redundancy.[11] Ritual language has thus been identified with "religious" genres: prayer, invocation, chant, devotional song, sermon, and so forth. Some studies have analyzed ritual language that is narrative, but their emphasis has been the description of metaphor, parallelism, condensation, and other formal features.[12] Myth, of course, is a narrative, religious genre; however, most literature on myth has examined it outside the ritual context (as charter or exegesis) and not as ritual language. In short, little thought has been given to how narrative works in ritual, an omission that reflects the general approach to performance discussed in the Introduction: to treat performance as event and to downplay text.

If the bow song tradition reveals a textual basis for performance, it demonstrates also that ritual language can be narrative. More than this, I would argue that bow songs possess the essential property of ritual language: not the ability simply to repeat, but to name. Ritual naming, once again, is normally associated with short, nonnarrative genres. The best known examples are probably the African "praise-poems."[13] But these namings (as Opland's 1983 study of Xhosa eulogies makes clear) actually narrate, inasmuch as the names explain deeds, usually heroic exploits.

Ritual naming is also common to Hinduism, and like the African traditions, Hindu namings are narrative. The standard verbal form of worshiping a deity is to recite his or her many names, which are often derived from episodes in that deity's mythology. Kṛṣṇa, for instance, is called Dāmōdara ("rope-belly") after a story in which the child-god was tied to a mortar.[14] Similarly, Śiva is known as Tripurāntaka ("Destroyer of the Triple City") because he razed the triple city of the demons.

Bow songs are namings, too. They are the unfolding of events condensed into names. Bow song performances, then, are simply extended invocations that summon the gods because they name them through recounting their histories. It is important to note that many religious texts in India are "histories" (*caritra,* or its derivations): *Rāmcaritmānas, Buddhacaritra, Palnāṭiviracaritra,* to mention only a few. If naming is narrative, then history becomes panegyric.

This ritual naming might be explained by reference to the iconic theory of language found in India, at least on the conceptual level of the mantra and other techniques of realization. Since, according to this theory, words are cosubstantial with the things they denote, to name a thing is to make it manifest. However, the appealing wholeness implicit in the notion of iconicity can, if taken too literally, lead to unwarranted explanations, as Stanley Tambiah has warned (Tambiah 1968, 187). Such caution is appropriate for an interpretation of the naming power of bow song narratives. These stories (or names) of local gods do not conjure up nonexistent or distant things, or transport them through space. They summon gods who exist already, and invite them to reside in a particular spot.

It is not, then, the magical power of words that summons gods to a koṭai. Śāstā, the Tampimār, and the others, come because they are called when their stories are correctly sung on the bow. This is why the lines of a bow song performance are relatively fixed. Fixity, however, is more than the repetition and invariance said to be characteristic of ritual language. In the bow song tradition, fixity is a form of veracity. There is only one true version of the Tampimār story and that version must be faithfully learned, copied, and then sung, even read, in performance. Most important is the singing. It must be precise, for only narrative accuracy ensures ritual efficacy.

This last statement typifies the influence that the narrative world of the bow song wields over the entire tradition. In particular, we know that the core of the tradition—the ritual center on death and the temporary triumph over death—is grounded in narrative events. Perhaps this Tamil tradition is somewhat unique in that its narratives play such a primary role; yet it is difficult to imagine that stories sung in a religious setting anywhere would not possess similar power. In the Tamil case, bow songs exert the doubled force of narrative as ritual. They tell stories that summon gods.

Notes

INTRODUCTION

1. Burke 1969; Turner 1974; Goffman 1974. Other major influences on the development of the performance concept in folkloristics and anthropology include Abrahams 1968, Bateson 1972, Ben-Amos 1972, and Hymes 1975.

2. See, for example, Kirschenblatt-Gimblett 1975 and Abrahams 1970.

3. Here Lévi-Strauss explains that myth structures are grammar (*langue*) not speech (*parole*).

4. See, for example, the essays in Stolz and Shannon 1976. Haymes 1973 provides a bibliography of scholarship derived from Parry and Lord's oral theory.

5. Ben-Amos 1983.

6. Bauman's recent book (1986) speaks of reciprocity between text and performance; following Bakhtin, he writes of the "interdependence of narrated event and narrative event" (ibid., 2). Bow songs demonstrate less this ontology of the event and more the power of narrative to affect its own performance.

7. See the references in notes 11 and 12, Chapter 7.

8. Most of the work was done in a portion of Kanya Kumari district traditionally known as Nāñcil Nāṭu (see Map 2), although I also worked in neighboring Tinnevelly district, where the bow song is also strong (Reiniche 1979; Kōmatināyakam 1979). Particulars do vary from region to region, but the broad patterns of the bow song described in this book represent the tradition as a whole.

CHAPTER 1

1. These lines, a conventional opening in many bow song performances (see pp. 152ff.), aptly describe Nāñcil Nāṭu, which translates as "the fertile land."

2. Kōmatināyakam (1979, 5) suggests that the *vilyāḻ* mentioned in the *Perumpāṇāṟṟuppaṭai* (A.D. 300–400?) is the bow played today; for an opposite opinion, see Veḷḷaivaraṉār 1961. Aruṇācalakavuṇṭar (1968, 362) claims that the bow song is referred to as the "song sung to Ayyaṉ (Śāstā)" in a list of folk song genres in a thirteenth-century (A.D.) commentary on the earlier poem *Cilappatikāram* (see *Cilappatikāram,* p. 97).

3. This earliest literary reference to the bow song is in *Tevyaccilaiyār Viṟalivitutūtu* (Vāṉamāmalai 1959, 27; see also Kōmatināyakam 1979, 77–78); another reference, about a century later, is found in *Mukkūṭal Paḷḷu,* pp. 114, 118. Published

literature on the tradition is scarce. The late Tamil folklorist Na. Vāṉamāmalai edited two texts (1971, 1974), and a book recently appeared in Tamil (Kōmatināyakam 1979). Other information on the bow song is found in an article in English (Hameed 1956), a French ethnography of a Tinnevelly village (Reiniche 1979), and a few short articles in Tamil journals (Asirvatham 1978, Piccai Kuṭṭi 1969); or books (Makārācaṉ 1962, 51–58; Perumal 1982, 92–100, 112–16).

4. Mateer 1870, 200.

5. Ibid., 215.

6. See also Caldwell 1849; Abbs 1870; and Mateer 1883. A. A. Bake's recordings of bow songs in the 1930s (now housed in the National Sound Archives, London) make it clear that basic musical patterns have also remained stable. The only identifiable diffusion of the tradition since the mid-1800s has been to the mountains in Kerala where Tamils have migrated to work on tea estates.

7. The cultural geography of the Tamil country has yet to be drawn, though some outlines are now becoming clear (see Stein 1980, Murton 1975, Ludden 1985). The northern border of the bow song tradition is fairly abrupt: on the western side it continues right up to Srivilḷipputtūr where it suddenly thins out so that one performing group serves larger and larger circles of villages, and then disappears altogether about ten miles north; the same is true on the eastern side around Āruppukōṭṭai. The reasons for this northern border are not readily apparent; perhaps it represents the point where Pāṇṭiyaṉ-Nāyak influences from the Madurai court stop and more local cultural traditions begin. The southern border is roughly coterminous with the Tamil-Malayalam language border; nevertheless, Tamil (and some Malayali) castes all the way up to Quilon, and even beyond, continue to patronize the tradition, often by bringing singers from Nāñcil Nāṭu to perform at their temples.

A Malayali bow song tradition still exists in parts of southern Travancore. One of its forms (*taḷḷu kavi*) influenced the Tamil tradition, but its most popular form today ("modern bow song" or *naviṉa villaṭiccaṉ pāṭṭu*) is entertainment-oriented, uses theatrical elements (stand-up delivery of lines, props, costumes), and is seldom performed as worship. The Malayali tradition received a boost during the 1970s when student groups around Trivandrum performed pieces of Russian literature (especially scenes from *War and Peace*) on the bow.

8. The early references are found in ancient Tamil poems (*Puṟanāṉūṟu* 137, 138, 139, 140, 380) that praise a local ruler called Nāñcil Vaḷḷuvaṉ or Nāñcil Porunaṉ (K. K. Pillay 1953, 17; Kailasapathy 1968, 21).

9. Krishna Ayyar 1966, 150. This historical survey of Nāñcil Nāṭu also draws on Nagam Aiya 1906, 1, chap. 6; K. K. Pillay 1953, 13–54; Jeffrey 1976; Ibrahim Kunju 1976; Ramachandran 1975.

10. The first European (on record) to enter interior Nāñcil Nāṭu went through this mountainous gap, and not without difficulty. When the Prussian missionary Tobias Ringletaube attempted to cross from Tinnevelly in 1806, he was stopped because the guards said the land would be desecrated and the gods would not take *pūjā* (Robinson 1908, 45). Later Ringletaube was allowed to set up a small hut about twenty miles from the border where he preached and converted until his mysterious death ten years later.

11. The Tamil flood myth has generated a body of scholarship almost as interest-

ing as the myth itself; see Tampy Pillai 1913, Aravamuthan 1932, Bharati 1935, Joseph 1958, Zvelebil 1973a, 45–49, 1973b; Shulman 1978.

12. Nagam Aiya 1906, 2:24; India 1903, 194ff.

13. One foreign observer said in 1854 that "Malayalam was the language of the courts and of the domestic circles among Sudras and Brahmins. Tamil is the language of the Bazaar and of the lower castes" (quoted in Jeffrey 1976, 22). During field work, I found a truly hybrid language community only on the far western edge of Nāñcil Nāṭu (see also Karunakkaran 1972; Subramoniam 1958). A hybrid script, combining Tamil and Malayalam characters, was apparently used in Nāñcil Nāṭu from A.D. 1300 to 1900 (Desikavinayagam Pillai 1931).

14. In southern Travancore, certain modifications in standard Malayali matrilineal inheritance were made such that a portion of a man's wealth, acquired after marriage, would go to his wife and her children (Jeffrey 1976, 244ff.; Mateer 1883, 176).

15. Hardgrave 1969a, 270.

16. This assimilation to Malayali culture effectively split the Piḷḷai caste into two factions. Later this split became the focus of a reform movement in the early twentieth century in which Tamil-speaking, patrilineal Piḷḷais sought to remove any Malayali influence (particularly matrilineal inheritance) from their community and reassert its Tamil character. During this period, a well-known Tamil literary figure published a Tamil tract bitterly denouncing the fate of a Piḷḷai woman married into a matrilineal family (Tēcikavināyakam Piḷḷai 1974). For other castes that likewise split into Tamil and Malayali factions, see Nagam Aiya 1906, 2:371–72, 375–78, 389–91, 399–402; Mateer 1883, 108–9; Hayavadana 1915.

17. See Hardgrave 1969a, 270–71; India 1966, 266. Slightly less than half of the Nadars in Nāñcil Nāṭu are Christian.

18. Hardgrave 1969a, 22; Umaitāṇu 1966, 22–23; Mateer 1870, 41; Jeffrey 1976. This information was confirmed in conversations with Nadars in the area.

19. For accounts of the "breast cloth controversy," see Mateer 1870, 277–82; Hardgrave 1968, 1969a, 59–70; Jeffrey 1976, 57–87. The only analysis to focus on the importance of Piḷḷai-Nadar tensions, however, is Paktavatcalaṉ 1973.

20. These middle- and low-level castes are the Īḻavar, Malayali counterpart to the Nadars (except that they climb coconut and not palmyra trees); the Kōṉār, small landowners and livestock breeders; and the Cālaiyar, a weaving caste that has gained an economic standing in Nāñcil Nāṭu above that of other weavers in Tamil Nadu. A few castes slightly higher in status and fewer in numbers (Ācāri, carpenters; Kurup, Malayali peasants and small landholders; and Tēvar, peasants and small landholders) support the bow song only sporadically: some of their temples host performances; some do not.

21. These Untouchable castes (Cerumāṉ, cobblers; Vaṇṇaṉ, washermen; Paḷḷaṉ and Cāmpavar, both field laborers) have contributed some gifted singers, however. Other low-status castes whose temples sponsor bow song performances only irregularly are the Paṇṇaiyār (salt makers) and the Ampaṭṭaṉ (barbers).

22. The Kaṇṇikar, who practiced slash-and-burn agriculture (and now work for wages) in the hilly forests, and the Kuṟavar, itinerant hunters and diviners, are groups too marginal to local Hindu society to have any association with the bow song tradi-

tion. In the past, however, it is possible that such groups did contribute to the tradition: two groups of gods (vātai and māṭaṉ) worshiped today appear to have been borrowed from the Kaṇṇikar (Mateer 1883, 69), and the Kuṟavar (according to local legend) once ruled Nāñcil Nāṭu (Nagam Aiya 1906, 1:261–62; *Kerala Society Papers* 7:19; Nīlakaṇṭaṉ 1973).

23. Middle- and low-level castes also support the bow song tradition in Tinnevelly district; because the Nadars do not dominate there, the singing and patronage is more evenly divided between them and Maṟavars, Tēvars, Piḷḷais, Kōṉārs, and a special group of singers called pulavar (see p. 27).

24. A similar slippage occurs when Nadars convert to Christianity (and conversions continue even today) since they worship new gods without the bow. I did contact two families of Christian Nadars who, even after their recent conversion, continued to play on the bow in a large festival at the healing shrine of the Christian goddess Vēlaṅkaṉṉi (in Tanjore district).

CHAPTER 2

1. To Curt Sachs (1940, 57), the "strangest of the musical bows is the gigantic instrument of some tribes of southern India." In his worldwide survey of musical bows, Henry Balfour (1899, 57) called the Tamil vil an "aberrant form." Certainly none of the reported forms of the musical bow corresponds to the Tamil bow in playing style or length; the closest parallel appears to be a bow used by the Tanjongs of Sarawak (Balfour 1899, 69; see also Marcuse 1975, 178–83). Another variety that is close to the Tamil one (but not mentioned in these sources) is found in Japan (Blacker 1975, 19, 105–7). In India, musical bows have been reported in Assam (Marcuse 1975, 178–81), in the tribal belt around Chota Nagpur (Balfour 1899, 56–66; Joyce Flueckiger, personal communication [letter], 1985), and in Kerala (Menon 1933, 3:252, 447). The Chota Nagpur bows are long like the Tamil bow, but not (according to the published descriptions) played in a group; the Kerala bow is shorter (about 3 feet), but like the Tamil vil it is played as an accompaniment to other instruments during temple dances.

2. Indian varieties of the hourglass-shaped drum are discussed in Kothari 1968, 33–34 and Sachs 1940, 158–59.

3. See Hart 1975, 146; Beck 1982, 73–78; Marcuse 1975, 122, 124–25, 144–45.

4. This special rhythmic effect is discussed in greater detail in Blackburn 1986.

5. On these individual donations, see also pp. 145–47.

6. Per capita income of peasants in Nāñcil Nāṭu in 1977–1979 may be estimated at 800–1000 rupees (see India 1965, 82).

7. Training of singers in African traditions also appears to stress individual creativity (Merriam 1973, 260–1; Nketia 1973, 87–90; Ben-Amos 1975, 34–42).

8. This excerpt is from the opening verses to the Muttuppaṭṭaṉ performance translated in Chapter 6.

9. A combination of mōṉai and etukai is also a common rhyme scheme in classical Tamil poetry (Zvelebil 1975, 33; Hart 1975, 208).

10. A consummate use of the antāti device is the classical Tamil poem *Tiruvāymoḻi* whose more than 1,000 verses are linked internally in a chain that turns back and connects the very last verse with the first (Ramanujan 1981, 167–68). See Tedlock 1972 for an antāti-like technique among the Zuni.

11. Although bow singers memorize their lines (contra the oral formulaic), the process of oral performance produces the same absence of necessary enjambement as in the South Slav tradition (Lord 1960, 54). When orally performed, a story is understood easily if the units of delivery (the musical phrases) are also discreet units of text.

12. For the opposite position (emphasizing improvisation) in Indian oral epic traditions, see Roghair 1982, 59–61; Beck 1982, 59–83; Wadley n.d.

13. Finnegan 1977, 73–87.

14. For more recent clarification of the nature of the formula and improvisation, see Lord 1974 and n.d. The subtleties of fixity and creativity are also explored in Abrahams 1978. See note 11, this chapter.

15. Prior composition was apparently the method for producing Tamil *purāṇas* ("myths"), at least until the late nineteenth century (Shulman 1980, 37–39); a poet, commissioned to write a *purāṇa* for a temple, orally composed and then dictated verses to a scribe who immediately wrote them on palm-leaf.

16. To appreciate the fixity in the bow song tradition, one need only compare it with other traditions, for example Xhosa oral poetry (Opland 1983), in which free improvisation is the norm.

17. In an almost uncanny parallel, a shadow puppet singer turned a three-minute summary into a three-hour performance for television in Malaysia (Sweeney 1978).

18. Even today, the name Perumāḷ is used only by educated Nadars, but is common among Piḷḷais.

19. This man, to whom this book is dedicated, assisted me with many aspects of my research, in particular collecting palm-leaf manuscripts.

20. Mateer 1870, 219; Nagam Aiya 1906, 2:393; interviews with Nadars in Nāñcil Nāṭu. Privileged Nadars in Tinnevelly were also known as nāṭāṉ (Hardgrave 1969a, 56).

21. An account of the music and musicians at the Travancore court is given in Nagam Aiya 1906, 3:252–59 and in L. Pillay 1918.

22. Palm-leaves were used for most official documents in Travancore until 1884 (Menon 1933, 3:225). In general, they were used more widely and in more ritual contexts in South India than in North India, where they began to be replaced by paper from about A.D. 1300 (Shah and Shroff 1959, 48; Losty 1982, 5); on the use of palm-leaf in Tamil village schools in the 1800s, see Ramakrishna Piḷḷai 1911, 35.

23. An example of a scripted performance is that translated in Chapter 5; a parallel to this kind of bow song performance is epic recitation in northern Sumatra (Siegel 1979, 208).

24. Printed pamphlets began to appear in Tamil, and other Indian languages, about 1835 when Indians were permitted to own presses (but see Vināyakamūrtti [1978, 128] for two Tamil publications of folk literature from the eighteenth century). Bow songs, however, were not printed until about 1950 when a version of the Gandhi story, popularized by N. S. Krishnan (a resident of Nagercoil and later a film

star in Madras) appeared in print. Since then, first in Tirunelveli city and now in Nagercoil, only a limited number of these bow song pamphlets have been printed.

25. Printed pamphlets of vil pāṭṭu texts are viewed with skepticism by singers and others; since they are distributed outside the closed distribution network of palm-leaf and handwritten copies, they are thought to contain changes resulting from both human error and design. However, when I compared a few pamphlets with the palm-leaf manuscripts upon which they are based, I found them to be faithful, nearly syllable-for-syllable, to the original. The invocatory verses at the beginning of the palm-leaf texts were often changed to include more local deities, but this is in no way unusual and occurs in performance, too.

26. The effects of printing on a folk narrative in Bengal are discussed in Nicholas 1978.

27. Basso (1974) has made the case for an ethnography of writing; see also the essays in Goody 1968.

CHAPTER 3

1. Turner, however, was not much interested in texts; like others, he preferred to use text as a metaphor for events.

2. In the wider classification of oral narratives in Nāñcil Nāṭu, both birth and death stories are "god-stories" (*cāmi katai*) as opposed to "king-stories" (*rācā katai*). The only "king-story" regularly performed on the bow is the *Rāmāyaṇa* (or portions of it); since Rāma is not worshiped publicly in Nāñcil Nāṭu, his story is not a "god-story."

3. Conforming to standard definitions of folk genres, both birth stories (as myths) and death stories (as legends) are believed to be "true"; the "king-stories," by contrast, are considered fictive, like the folktale.

4. Childlessness is also the generative motif in other Indian folk literatures (Roghair 1982, 65; Wadley 1975, 76–79, table 5; Beck 1982, 14). Cf. Propp 1968, 119.

5. A similar strategy is used by a midwife in a Telugu oral epic (Roghair 1982, 155).

6. The role of the birth motif is evident also from the fact that another widespread birth story, Cuṭalai Māṭaṉ, has seven variants, each distinguished and identified (by the singers) by a different kind of birth for the god.

7. *Muttu* also means "sweat" and "pearl."

8. See O'Flaherty 1980a, 66–68.

9. This figure first appeared in Blackburn 1985.

10. Growing interest about folklore in Tamil Nadu has now brought the bow to festivals and conferences in the capital of Madras; it is also sometimes played at secular functions in Tinnevelly district. Special note should be made here of the talented S. M. Gorky, who has sung on the bow for meetings of the Communist Party of India in the villages of western Tinnevelly since the 1950s.

11. Hinduism in Nāñcil Nāṭu also includes direct worship of pan-Indian deities, but only in large temple complexes with Brahmin priests, high-caste patronage, and

usually governmental control. Bow song temples, by contrast, depend on local patronage, collected from the resident community, and employ non-Brahmin priests from the same caste as that which controls the temple.

12. The pītam, a unique part of the bow song tradition, is found also in southern Kerala where the bow is played.

13. In a reversal of the architectural plan for high-caste temples, which by convention face east, most of the bow song temples (thirty-seven of the fifty-three for which I have complete plans) face north. The same is true for local temples in the Koṅku Nāṭu region of Tamil Nadu (Beck 1972, 87).

14. Consistent with these examples, most bow song temple communities in Nāñcil Nāṭu comprise a single caste. This applies also to the eastern seacoast (*teri*) of Tinnevelly where Nadar villages dominate, but not to the western riverine parts of the district, where the multi-caste composition of the villages is reflected in the temple communities of bow song cults (see Reiniche 1979, 150–72, 187–99; see also pp. 208–11, for details on koṭai expenses).

15. Tuesday and Friday appear to be special days for worship in South India generally (Whitehead 1976, 69, 72, 75, 76, 144, 149; Thampuran 1936, 90; Thurston 1975, 2:500–501; Perinbanayakam 1982, 52), and probably in North India, too (Mahapatra 1972, 141–42; Wadley 1975, 156; Babb 1975, 111–12). Some of these sources also mention an association between the goddess and Tuesday (based on the malevolence attributed both to Mars and women), but a consistent correlation of goddesses with Tuesday and gods with Friday appears unique to the bow song tradition.

16. Another variation on the three-day festival occurs when a single family sponsors a one-day koṭai, called a ciṟappu ("special"), in fulfillment of a vow. See p. 51.

17. Tradition holds that each temple contains twenty-one deities—even if only three or four are visible, people can quickly point out spots on the ground and walls that add to up twenty-one. For the same numerical convention in another part of Tamil Nadu, see Dumont 1957, 357–66; for Chattisgargh, see Babb 1975, 129.

18. The tīpārātaṉai do not always begin punctually, but their timing with ucci nēram is a conscious goal. The importance of these "zenith times" is also underlined by the simultaneous pūjā to two minor deities: Ucci Kāttāṉ ("protector of the ucci") and Ucci Pali Māṭaṉ ("god/spirit of the ucci sacrific ").

19. The mēḷam, which plays at other temple functions, marriages, etc., consists of a long oboe (*nāgasvaram*), two large, double-headed drums (*taval*), and two smaller, double-headed drums, strapped on top of each other (*pampai*). The kuravai is a loud ululation produced by moving the tongue rapidly across an open mouth; it is at least as old as the Tamil epic *Cilappatikāram* (c. A.D. 500), in which the term seems to indicate a folk dance associated with the cry. On the kuravai in Ceylon, see Pālacuntaram 1976; Mathew 1931, xxxi; Raghavan 1969.

20. Possession also occurs outside the festival context, usually as an unwanted attack (*pēy piṭikkatu,* "caught by a malevolent spirit"); but within the koṭai festival, it is a beneficient visitation (*cāmi mēl varavatu,* "the god descends"). This distinction (see also p. 217) between attacks outside the festival and visitations inside the festival corresponds to Lewis' distinction (Lewis 1971) between "peripheral" and "central" possession cults; attacks by the malevolent Tamil pēy, however, do not

have the sociopolitical meanings given to peripheral cults by Lewis. On the complexity of possession in South Asia, see Claus 1979b; Obeyesekere 1981; Kakar 1982; Kapferer 1983.

21. Other terms for the dancer-medium are *cāmi koṇṭāṭi* ("god's celebrant") and *kōmarattāṭi* ("dancer with the royal staff"?); by itself, *kōmaram* means "spirit possession."

22. Some sections of the Piḷḷai caste select their dancers in another ritual called "picking the flower" (*pū eṭukkal*), in which the candidates attempt to pick a special flower from among a heap of flowers (M. Shanmukam Pillai, personal communication [letter], 1980).

23. The kuṟi, however, is not always spoken in the most easily understood idiom; some mediums use a garbled Malayalam (to indicate that they have contact with the powerful Malayali spirits). I was told that one dancer, possessed by the "White-Man god" (*veḷḷai-kāra cāmi*), speaks in English, even American English!

24. In particular, see Geertz 1973; also Schieffelin 1976.

25. For the meanings of *śakti*, see Wadley 1975, 55, and Egnor 1980.

26. In some large goddess temples another form of possession, *mañcal nīr āṭutal* ("dancing with turmeric water"), occurs just before the tīpārātaṉai in the center slot. For this, the possessed medium dips a bunch of margosa leaves into a pot of boiling water and turmeric powder, and then holds it on his head as he dances so that the scalding solution drips down his body. Nadar Christians, it is said, never attend these festivals because their lack of belief would leave them unprotected against the hot liquid when it sprays into the crowd.

27. Local people do recognize degrees of authentic possession, from "false dance" (*poy āṭṭam*) to "fierce dance" (*payaṅkara āṭṭam*), but generally it is accepted as a cultural given and not much discussed. Sometimes, however, possession can be both accepted and criticized: while one young man was dancing (in an unremarkable fashion) during a festival, some friends told me, "He's young; his father danced well, but he's just a kid. He wanted to dance, so we let him, but when the time came he just stood there. It was embarrassing, so we took him aside and told him, we showed him how to dance. You know, 'first this step, then that.' Now he's better, he goes to other festivals and watches dancers; he's learning."

28. Dumont (1957, 384) also found a tripartite structure to a local temple festival in a different Tamil region, but there the positions of worship to the goddess (first day) and to Śāstā (second day) are the reverse of the bow song sequence.

CHAPTER 4

1. This generic quality of the Śāstā story, its frequency in performance, and the fact that it is the first story learned by a singer have led to the conclusion that it is the original story from which the bow song tradition evolved (Kōmatināyakam 1979, 80–83; Paramēsvarayyar 1953, 292–93). However, since the story is widely known outside the tradition, I would speculate that it was adapted by the bow song as a counterpoint to the death stories that are the foundation of the tradition.

2. For references to both these stories, see O'Flaherty 1973, 228–29; 1980a, 321–22. Some South Indian texts combine the two stories in a manner similar to the

Vallarakkan̲ bow song text, except that the demon is known as Bhasmāsura (Elmore 1925, 52; Oppert 1893, 508). In the Rajastani epic of Pābūjī, the combined story (with Bhasmāsura) explains the birth of Hanumān (J. D. Smith, personal communication [letter], 1983); in Sri Lanka, it leads to the birth of Mahasona (Kapferer 1983, 121).

3. The pivotal role of Mōhin̲i was often pointed out by singers who explained that "the death of Vallarakan̲ brings the birth of Śāstā." Cf. the Tamil proverb: "Born by a woman, destroyed by a woman" (*āvatum peṇṇālē aḻivatum peṇṇālē*).

4. The "five-handed god" is Gaṇeśa; the "god with six faces" is Murukan̲ or Ār̲umukam (lit. "Six-Faced").

5. The following verses invoke the *kāval* ("watch" or "guardian") gods that some, but not all, performances set out in the cardinal directions.

6. With this sentence, the lead performer has shifted from song to speech in delivery style. See p. xxiv for an explanation of formatting in the translations.

7. These three "ancient books," attributed to the Tamil poetess Auvaiyār, are *Ar̲aner̲i* (or *Nalvaḻi*), *Kon̲r̲aivēntan̲*, and *Mūturai*.

8. "Fifty-six lands (or rajas)" is a folklore convention in South India (see Roghair 1982, 174–75; Buchanan 1807, 2:304–6).

9. Here one of the performers is making fun of another member of the group who failed to show up that day; his absence caused a minor panic until a substitute was recruited to play the cymbals.

10. A friendly rivalry exists between bow song performers and the mēḷam musicians; they play at the same festivals—the mēḷam for the tīpārātan̲ai, the bow singers for the stories—and sometimes cooperate at ritually critical moments in the narrative (see Blackburn 1986).

11. A Tamil proverb: *ēṭṭu curaikāy kar̲ikku utavā?* Literally, "Does a gourd drawn [on paper] help [to make] a curry?" That is, Śiva's words are as useless as a picture.

12. Any food item that does not fit into a meal can be added to a chutney sauce; cf. the American idiom, "You can always put it in the soup."

13. This proverb (*vaḷartta kīṭa mārpil payantatu pōl*) dramatizes the ingratitude shown by Vallarakkan̲ (the pet animal) to Śiva (its master).

14. A proverbial saying pointing out that Gaṇeśa's mount is even less agile than he.

15. Episodes from the Kṛṣṇa (Kaṇṇan̲) story are often used to introduce Viṣṇu into the Śāstā/Vallarakkan̲ story.

16. In Tamil mythology, Viṣṇu is Pārvati's brother and therefore Śiva's brother-in-law.

17. As part of their continual tête-à-tête, Viṣṇu here pokes fun at Śiva by citing some of his disreputable acts. In the *Tiruviḷaiyāṭal Purāṇam,* Śiva, disguised as a laborer, carries mud to help build a dike, but ends up dancing, singing, and throwing his basket into the river. Some South Indian myths that explain Gaṇeśa's elephant head suggest that he was sexually interested in his mother Pārvati; Vēlan̲'s (Murukan̲'s) marriage to Vaḷḷi (a Kur̲avar woman) is a popular theme in Tamil folk literature.

18. In most Tamil castes, the oldest son makes an offering of his hair at his father's funeral.

19. This is a fairly standard list of beauty marks (cf. the thirty-two "marks of a

Great Person" found on the Shakyamuni Buddha at his birth), but the inclusion of "prawn-like legs" is curious.

20. Here a male performer feigns ignorance of female ornaments, deliberately confusing *kuṭṭuvam* (a Malayalam word for pestle) with *kaṭṭuvam* (a Tamil word for a kind of necklace); this section of the performance thoroughly delighted the audience, especially women.

21. Indian women do not generally use their husband's name, and certainly not in public; instead, they call him "he" (respectful form) or "husband."

CHAPTER 5

1. A bow singer's description of death stories (interview with Taṅkaiya Nadar, 1979).

2. The patrilineal succession of the Tampimār also found support with the Tamil ruler of Madurai, and with the Muslim ruler of Arcot; both, however, were bought off by Mārttāṇṭa Varma.

3. See Ibrahim Kunju 1976; Nagam Aiya 1906, 1:333–38; Krishna Ayyar 1966, 99–100; Panikkar 1960, 234–35; Sreedhara Menon 1978, 22.

4. Beck 1982, 20–24, 35, 122–24, passim; Smith 1982, 13–14. Other Tamil narratives with a brother pair as heroes include the Marutu brothers of Civakaṅkai (Chandrasekharan 1954) and the Ciṉṉaṇṇaṉ-ciṉṉatampi story in the Koṅku area (Varatarāculu 1977). However, as Smith notes, many oral epics (and both Sanskrit epics) have a group (often five) rather than a pair of brothers as heroes.

5. Thompson 1955–1958, motifs L10, L100.

6. See pp. 133–34.

7. Here the story of Āṉantāci has incorporated the international tale-type AT 178; Emeneau (1967) has compiled and compared most of the versions reported from India.

8. Āṉantāci and her daughter are named White and Yellow Māriyammaṉ; they have no connection with the popular goddess Māriyammaṉ (Reṇukā) known throughout Tamil Nadu and parts of South India.

9. In other variants of this story (from northern Tamil Nadu), the Brahmin kills his wife (not his lover), and Nīli (Icakki) is a form of Pārvati; for a discussion of early literary versions (dating to the tenth century A.D.), see Shulman 1980, 194–97.

10. These two aspects of the Hindu goddess, the malign and the benign, have been considered by several scholars in psychosexual terms: male desire and fear of female sexuality leads to images of women as either passive and maternal, or aggressive (sexual) and dangerous. See O'Flaherty 1980a, 77–145; Shulman 1980, 138–316; Babb 1975, 215–26; Brubacker 1978; Ramanujan 1986.

11. This link between violence and deification is taken up again in Chapter 7. See also, Ramanujan 1986.

12. Other examples of this pattern, from other regions of India, are discussed in Blackburn 1986.

13. The events surrounding the Tampimār story have generated a second cult in the bow song tradition centered on the Eṭṭu Vīṭṭil Piḷḷaimār who were Nāyar chieftains opposed to Rajā Mārttāṇṭa Varma and allied with the Tampimār. They are still worshiped in a few temples, but their story is not sung.

14. For another comment on enjambement, see Chapter 2, note 11.

15. This incident, it should be pointed out, is highly unusual; most people in the audience know only the broad outline of the story.

16. Unfortunately, the song to Viṣṇu was not recorded on tape and therefore does not appear in the translation.

17. Kiṭṭiṇāttāḷ is the Tampimār's mother; she is called Apirāmi before she marries Rāma Varma. Her brother Krishna is also given a new name, Kocumara Piḷḷai.

18. "Taking . . . rang"—this pair of lines is often used in the bow song tradition to indicate a raja's just rule; the "bell of injustice" is a literary convention known also in medieval Tamil literature (e.g., the story of Maṇunītikaṇṭacōḻaṉ in the *Periya Purāṇam*). See also p. 118.

19. The places named in this line are in Tinnevelly district. This performance uses many such lines as streams of sound that move the characters over time and space. Two important place-names recur: Patmanāpapuram is the capital of Travancore and residence of both Rāma Varma (father of the Tampimār) and Mārttāṇṭa Varma (their enemy); nearby is the Vēmpaṭivāḷ palace at Ciṅkanallūr where Rāma Varma sometimes stayed and where the Tampimār lived.

20. The three-faced god at Cucīntiram is also known as Tāṇumālayyaṉ—a combination of Śiva (Tāṇu), Viṣṇu (Māl), and Śāstā (Ayyaṉ).

21. The "marriage cloth" (*paṭṭu kaccai*) was traditionally given by a man to his future wife at a betrothal ceremony.

22. A local legend holds that the *Mahābhārata* heroes lived in this forest outside Nagercoil during their twelve years in exile.

23. The conch and discus are emblems of Viṣṇu.

24. *Valiya* and *kuñcu* are Malayalam for "large" and "small"; in local Tamil speech, the Tampimār are also called Pāppu Tampi and Rāmaṉ Tampi.

25. The Travancore maharaja was annually purified by a ritual bath in the sea at Vāliyāṇpāṟai, a small village near Kanya Kumari.

26. A song that repeats the letters of the Tamil alphabet has been omitted here.

27. The *Koṉṟaivēntaṉ* is a text attributed to the early Tamil poetess Auvaiyār; see also Chapter 4, note 7.

28. Grantha is a Tamil script adapted for writing in Sanskrit.

29. Ammāṇṭiviḷai is the village in which this performance took place.

30. No details of this apparently important message and place are found in the texts or, as far as I could discover, in local tradition.

31. "The cut-hand village" (*kai kaṭika paṭṭiṇam*) is a folk etymology for Kaṭiyappaṭṭiṇam, the name of a village.

32. This curing ceremony (*nīrañcaṉam*) involves lighting a wick in a shallow bowl, adding margosa leaves, and waving it around the patient's head.

33. Danger is imminent when the maharaja, protector of the state, dies.

34. If there were no urgency, the brothers would bathe with hot water in a private place.

35. In most South Indian castes the preferred bride is the man's cross-cousin on his mother's side (his mother's brother's daughter). Mārttāṇṭa Varma's request conforms to standard practice because Koccumaṇi is his maternal uncle's daughter.

36. "House" (*illam*) refers to those kin with whom marriage was permitted, "distant house" (*turuvam*) to those with whom it was not; however, it is unclear why the

Āṟṟiṅkal family of Mārttāṇṭa Varma should be labeled "distant" because his mother was Rāma Varma's sister.

37. The possession dance for Perumāḷ Cāmi (Viṣṇu) began at this point; soon the Tampimār possessed their medium, who continued to dance until the end of the entire performance, one and one-half hours later. See pp. 95–96.

38. See p. 90.

39. Here the raja is needling the Tampimār by suggesting that since they have no father, the mercenary Aḻakappaṉ Mutaliyār has become their benefactor. Valiya Tampi counters by insinuating that the same Mutaliyār has even more control over the raja, since a maternal uncle (māma) is sometimes more influential (arranging marriages, for instance) than a father.

40. To summarize the remainder of the story: Kuñcu Tampi races to the palace, finds the gates locked, but kicks them down, bolts past the guards and raises his sword above the cowering Mārttāṇṭa Varma. When he brings down the sword, however, the blade strikes an overhead beam and breaks off; defenseless, he is captured and beheaded. Immediately, he and his brother are taken to Kailāsa, where their mother, sister, and uncle join them after committing suicide. The Tampimār receive boons from Śiva and return to earth as gods.

CHAPTER 6

1. In Tinnevelly and Kanya Kumari districts a hair tuft in front of the head is characteristic of Brahmins, a tuft in back of Untouchables. Sacred ash (*tiru nīr, vipūti*) is not worn exclusively by Brahmins, but is considered a sign of devotion.

2. I was able to locate two palm-leaf manuscripts of the story (both dating from the eighteenth century) in Kanya Kumari, and one (undated) in the Oriental Manuscripts Library, Kerala University, Trivandrum. The second variant of the story has no written texts in the tradition, although it is found in a few popular retellings in printed pamphlet form.

3. According to Vāṉamāmalai (1971, 9), Cakkiliyars first arrived in the area (traditionally called Āriya Nāṭu) as cobblers for invading Telugu armies.

4. A longer discussion of the substituted birth motif in Tamil folk narrative is found in Blackburn 1978.

5. Vāṉamāmalai (1971, 15–16) reports that the bow singer at the Corimuttu Ayyaṉ temple, the leading site of the cult, introduced the second variant in direct response to pressure from high-caste patrons. This temple, mentioned in the story (p. 152 and p. 166), is located in the mountains above the major Śaivite pilgrimage center at Pāpanācam; during the annual koṭai there Cakkiliyar families offer pairs of leather sandals to Muttuppaṭṭaṉ (as Paṭṭavaraiyar), commemorating his gift to Pakaṭai in the story. Nadars from Kanya Kumari, many of whom worship Muttuppaṭṭaṉ in house shrines, also make the pilgrimage to the temple at this time.

6. An even more ingenious way of viewing the story as a challenge to social hierarchy, while still maintaining that the Cakkiliyar women were in fact Brahmins, was contrived by a Piḷḷai singer: though Muttuppaṭṭaṉ and the sisters were Brahmins, their marriage still defied convention, he claimed, because they were not properly related (i.e., were not cross-cousins).

7. It may be the case that South Indian folklore and mythology is especially sympathetic to the theme of Brahmin-Untouchable union. Stories with the theme are cited in the following sources: Gopalakrishnan 1953, 154; Oppert 1893, 486; Whitehead 1976, 84–85, 118; Thurston 1975, 7:304; Moffatt 1979, 125; Elmore 1925, 119–21, 129. (One story in Elmore [pp. 119–20] closely follows the Muttuppaṭṭaṉ pattern—a Brahmin becomes an Untouchable—but the transformation is more violent: a sacrifice of the Brahmin to the goddess whom he refused to worship.) Of the forty-five goddess stories summarized in Elmore and Whitehead, Ramanujan (1980, 72) found that fourteen contained a Brahmin-Untouchable liaison; one of these is a folk version of the classical myth of Reṇukā (in which the heads of a Brahmin and an Untouchable are switched), the subject of Thomas Mann's novel *The Transposed Heads*.

8. On androgyny, see O'Flaherty 1980a, 282–334.

9. Paṟaiyaṉ is another Untouchable caste in Tamil Nadu, named for its traditional occupation of playing a *paṟai* drum on ceremonial occasions. A version of the proverb has been reported from Jaffna, Sri Lanka: "*nan paraiyan* [sic], *tampi pārpār:* I am a Paṟaiyaṉ, my younger brother is a Brahmin" (Pfaffenberger 1982, 54, citing David 1976, 189–90). This hidden identity between Brahmins and Untouchables has been pointed out also by Mateer (1884) and Dumont (1980, 54–55).

10. There are, of course, many other areas in which Brahmins and Untouchables do interact regularly; one area in Tamil Nadu is Tanjore district (see Gough 1955, 1973, 1981, 318–38; Beteille 1965, 5–7, 99–100).

11. Dubois 1978, 51, note 1; Thurston 1975, 6:88ff.; Gough 1981, 294; Hart 1980, 126, note 12; Dumont 1980:59, notes 25i, 25j.

12. An example of Nadar-Piḷḷai conflict is the Nāṭāṉ Cāmi story; see pp. 6–7.

13. Some versions of the story add still another task: a raja, angered at the cross-caste marriage, ordered Pakaṭai to stitch one thousand sandals overnight or be killed; Muttuppaṭṭaṉ calmly completed the order and saved his father-in-law.

14. With a single exception (pp. 160–61), these announcements have been omitted from the translation.

15. This particular point was clarified for me by V. Narayana Rao.

16. Although the death of Muttuppaṭṭaṉ is usually cited as the climax of the story, some people regard the lament by his young widows as more important. As one older, educated man put it, "The whole point of the story is that they [the wives] died without enjoying marriage; this is not just a story of death, but also of sorrow [*cōkam*]."

17. The Corimuttu Ayyaṉ (Śāstā) temple is regarded as the center of the Muttuppaṭṭaṉ cult; see also note 5 (this chapter).

18. See note 3 (this chapter).

19. Although singers (and texts) list only six brothers, they are consistent with a very widespread folk motif by claiming there are seven.

20. The remainder of this song, which continues through each sound in the Tamil alphabet, has been omitted.

21. It is also possible, as suggested to me by a local man, that he intentionally garbled the recitation to avoid the evil eye: if he recited the story well, he would draw attention, and thereby possible harm, to himself.

22. Kōṭṭārakarai is on the route from Tamil Nadu, through the Shencottah gap, to Kerala.

23. Janata ("common people") meals came into fashion after the Janata party defeated Indira Gandhi's Congress Party in 1977.

24. Feeding someone milk at the moment of death is considered auspicious because it removes any desires that might linger after death.

25. The sound of a cricket chirping, especially as one exits from a building, is considered auspicious in Nāñcil Nāṭu. Muttuppaṭṭaṉ's wish has been fulfilled: he is now worshiped at the Corimuttu Ayyaṉ temple (see also note 5).

26. The "short measure" (*kuṭṭaḷavu*), a measuring cup that falsely shows more than it actually holds, is a symbol for fraud in Tamil folklore.

27. These stone platforms, "load bearers" or *cumai tāṅki,* are built in a "T" shape—two slabs upright and a third across them. In Nāñcil Nāṭu they are memorials for women who die in childbirth ("bearing a load"), and sometimes evolve into temples with a festival and bow song performances.

28. Tamils in Nāñcil Nāṭu commonly believe that the most powerful *mantra vāti*s live in Kerala.

29. The Auvaiyār fast (*nōṉpu*) is popular among low- to middle-level castes in Kanya Kumari and Tinnevelly districts (Naṭarācaṉ 1977; Poṉṉaiya 1979, 35). Cf. *vrat* fasts in North India.

30. Auvaiyār, an ancient Tamil poetess, is today worshiped in several small temples in Nāñcil Nāṭu.

31. The uṭukkai is the hourglass-shaped drum used in bow song performances and other ritual singing (see p. 13; Chap. 2 notes 3 and 4).

32. "Ailasa, aiyelasa" is a semantically empty, rhyming phrase characteristic of some Tamil folksong genres, particularly fishermen songs.

33. This motif of the *liṅgam* washed away and tapas ruined is found also in the *Skanda Purāṇa* (O'Flaherty 1973, 11), where the male and female roles are reversed: Pārvati's *liṅgam* is washed away by Śiva.

34. Cross-cousins (especially mother's brother's daughter and father's sister's son) are preferred marriage partners in most South Indian castes. Cf. the use of this kin bond in the Tampimār story (Chapter 5, note 35).

35. The Tamil expression is *toṭṭāl tītu, niḻal paṭṭāl tōṣam.*

36. That is, since caste is prohibited by law, one might go to jail for mentioning it.

37. Crabs and "little fish" are not only impure (as meat); they are also very low-status since they are eaten by the poorest castes and tribes like the Kuṟavar, who ferret out the bitter crabs from bunds in rice fields.

38. "Child of a Kuṟavar" refers to Kaṇṇappar, the Śaiva saint who, in order to replace the eye that fell from Śiva's icon, cut out his own with an arrow; for the rest of the figures in these verse lines, refer to the glossary. Vyāsa's birth from a fisherwoman and Atri's son's (Vidura's) birth from a Cakkiliyar (or "commoner") accord with the *Mahābhārata;* Nārada's from a washerwoman and Kaṅkaiyaṉ's (Bhīṣma's) from a donkey do not.

39. Contact with dead or decaying substances (like a human or animal corpse, fermented liquor, or meat) is considered ritually polluting. Untouchable castes in South India play a ritual role in funerals, drag off dead animals, and then utilize their skins. Muttuppaṭṭaṉ's fine pair of sandals thus marks his nearly complete conversion from Brahmin to Untouchable.

40. Each line of this verse adds another polluting substance that would (in normal

circumstances) convert the feast into a disgrace. Serving betel nut in a cow's skull, in particular, is an extreme, almost absurd, symbol of the pollution that Muttuppaṭṭaṉ suffers in his new in-laws' home.

41. Food exchanges, and marriages, are very carefully regulated because they involve sharing substances. Thus, receiving meat cooked by an Untouchable is perhaps the most inherently polluting act possible.

42. The Tamil proverb is: *kai niṟaintu paṇattilum, kaṇ niṟaintu māppiḷḷaiyum.*

CHAPTER 7

1. For the cults on the southwest coast, see Kurup 1973 and Claus 1975; for related traditions in central Kerala, see Gough 1959. The Gujarati and Rajasthani cults are described in Kothari 1982, Fischer and Shah 1973; the Sri Lankan cults in Kapferer 1983 and Obeyesekere 1984. More material on cults of the dead in North India is found in Crooke 1978, vol. 1, chap. 4. See also Blackburn 1985.

2. The folk religions of South India and Sri Lanka may be even more closely related than Obeyesekere's detailed study indicates. Mahasona (see Kapferer 1983), for instance, is known in the bow song tradition (as Mahāṣana) with the same meaning ("God/demon of the Great Cemetery"). The torches carried by dancers in the Sri Lankan exorcisms (Kapferer 1983, 166, 167, passim), moreover, are also used by bow song dancers and are known by the same term (pantam). Finally, the Sri Lankan deity Sudalayi (Obeyesekere 1981, 151) is widely worshiped in the bow song tradition (as Cuṭalai Māṭaṉ) and is the central god in another oral tradition (*kaṇi āṭṭam,* "dance of the Kaṇiyaṉ") in Nāñcil Nāṭu and Tinnevelly district.

3. A similar development from a local (*bhomiyā*) story to a widespread folk epic (Pābūjī in Rajasthan) has been outlined by Smith (1980).

4. Notable exceptions include Wadley 1975; Claus 1975; Babb 1975; Dumont 1957; Harper 1964.

5. Worship of the deified dead appears to be a fundamental layer of religion among the indigenous "tribals" of India; see, for example, von Fürer-Haimendorf 1979, 363–93; Aiyappan 1976; Elwin 1955, esp. p. 81. Students of classical Hinduism have also noted the primacy of death themes: Long 1976; Knipe 1976; Parry 1982; Hiltebeitel 1976, chap. 10; and Kaushik 1976.

6. The sociological explanation for ancestor worship is stated most forcefully in Goody 1962; see also, Ahern 1973 and Middleton 1960. Interpretations of the worship of the dead from a psychological perspective include Freud 1918, 1950; Bradbury 1966; Obeyesekere 1981, 117–22; Opler 1958; Gough 1959.

7. The liminality theory (merged with Hertz's idea of the corpse as a metaphor for the dead soul) has been fruitfully applied in an analysis of mortuary rituals in Borneo (Metcalf 1982).

8. The case of the dangerous, liminal *preta* in Hinduism is clearly stated by Das (1977, chap. 5).

9. Notice, however, that karma has no bearing on the death of the hero or heroine, which is always unjust and undeserved.

10. Obeyesekere (1984, 277), for instance, mentions that the enactment of the death scene in the Pattini cults is thought to contain "ritual danger" (*vas*).

11. The extreme case—that ritual language is fixed and therefore has no propositional power—is stated by Bloch (1974) and critiqued by Tambiah (1985). For the Malinowskian background to the issue of ritual language, see Tambiah 1968. For individual studies, see Leach 1964, Bauman and Sherzer 1974, and Samarin 1976.

12. Gossen 1974 and Sherzer 1983, for example, are fine studies of ritual language (some of which is narrative), but they do not address the issue of narrative as ritual instrument. Wadley's study (1975) of North Indian village myths demonstrates how they act as exegeses for the accompanying ritual.

13. For references to studies of African "praise-poetry," see Opland 1983. Opland's statement (1983, 148) that Xhosa "praises of the dead are . . . invocations" applies equally well to the longer Tamil bow songs.

14. For this episode in a bow song performance, see p. 73.

Appendix: Temple Plans

Temple Plan A
Palavēcamcērvaikkārar Temple at Kuṇṭal
(Śāstā performance)

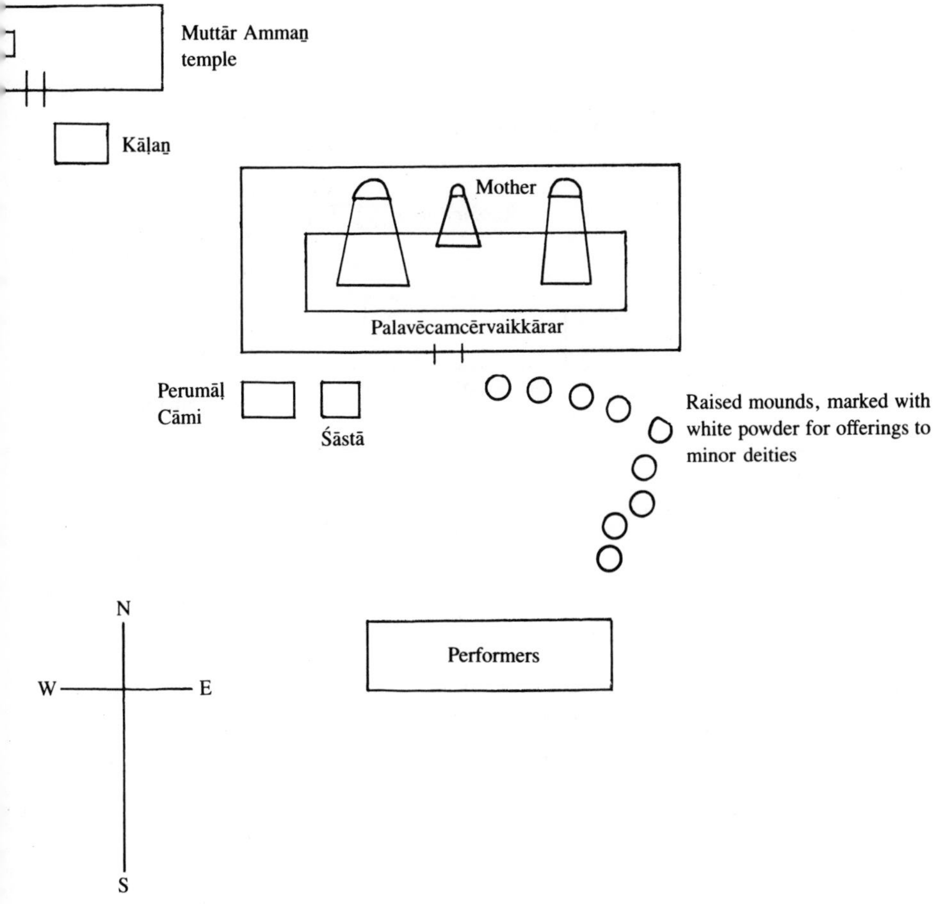

Temple Plan B
Tampimār Temple at Ammāṇṭiviḷai
(Tampimār performance)

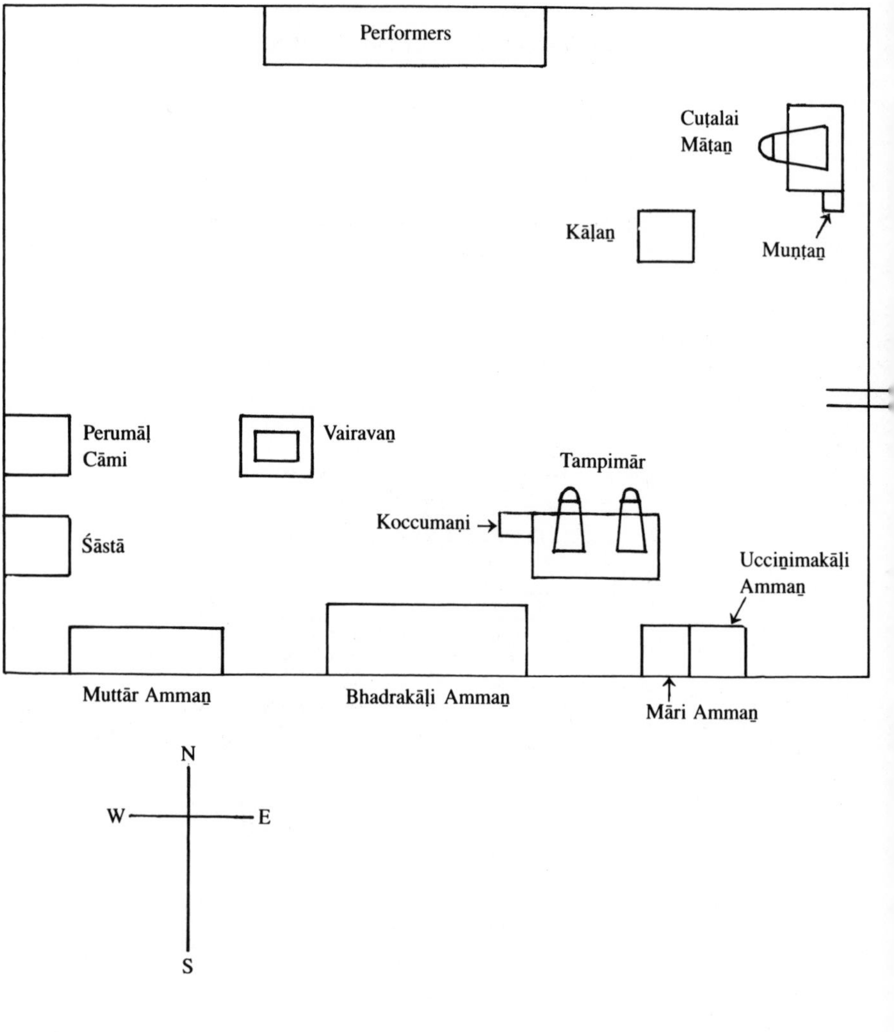

Temple Plan C
Pula Māṭaṉ Temple at Aralvāymoḻi
(Muttuppaṭṭaṉ performance)

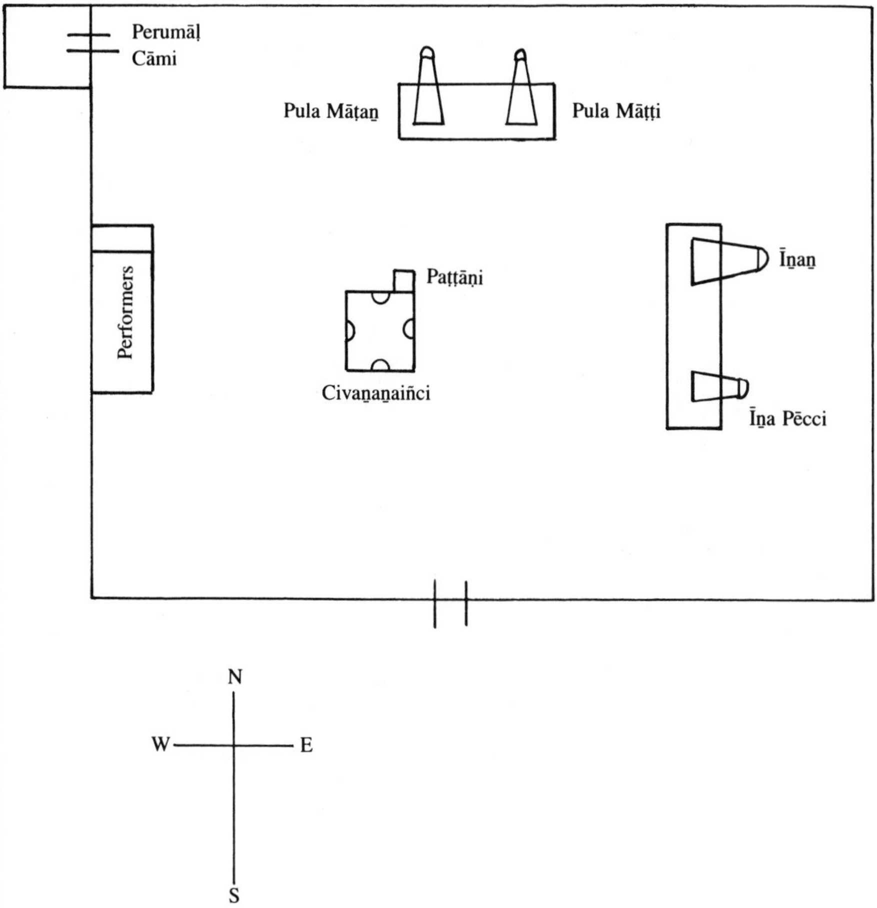

Glossary

abiṣēkam: consecration of an icon by bathing it with milk or ghee
agrahāram (*akkirakāram*): Brahmin settlement
Aiyaṉār: name for Śāstā common in central and northern Tamil Nadu
Ākamam: religious texts in Tamil
ammaṉ: goddess, "mother"
anna: unit of Indian money
aṇṇāvi: teacher, leader ("guru") of bow song group
Araṉ: Śiva (Sanskrit Hara)
arivāḷ: hooked knife for harvesting crops
Ariyaṉ Kāvu: mountain residence of Śāstā
Aruṇā: vocative to Śiva ("the Sun")
Ātipūrṇā: vocative to Śiva ("The Supreme-Complete")
Atri's son: Vidura, uncle to the heroes in the *Mahābhārata;* born from Kṛṣṇa Dvaipāyana's union with a "slave woman"
āṭṭam: dance
Auvaiyār: Tamil poetess, variously identified (see Zvelebil 1975, 169–71)
Ayodhyā: city of Rāma in the *Rāmāyaṇa*

Bhadrakāḷi: form of Kāḷi
Bhagavāṉ: supreme deity, usually Śiva
bhakti/bhakta: devotion/devotee
Bhīma: hero in the *Mahābhārata,* renowned for strength
Bhūtam (*pūtam*): ghost-like spirit, which often protects treasures, temples, and the like

Cakkiliyar: Untouchable cobbler caste; Telugu-speakers
cāmi: "god"; respectful form of address
carāyam: distilled liquor
cīr: unit of measurement
cōciyaṉ: astrologer, diviner
Cucīntiram: important temple complex near Kanya Kumari

darṣan: auspicious view of a god
dāsi: female temple dancer
dharma: duty, religious charity

gaṇa: celestial guardian; associated with Śiva
Gaṇapati: Śiva's older, elephant-faced son; Vināyaka
Gaṇeśa: Gaṇapati
ghat: watering place, bathing place near temple
Gōpis: cowherder girls who sport with Kṛṣṇa
Gōvinda: Viṣṇu

Hanumān: monkey ally of Rāma
Hara: Śiva
Hari: Viṣṇu

Indrāni: wife of Vedic god Indra

kali yuga: last and worst of the four time cycles in Indian cosmology
kaḷḷu: mildly intoxicating drink fermented from sap of palmyra tree
Kaṅkaiyaṉ (Sanskrit Gāṅgeya): Bhīṣma, great-uncle of the *Mahābhārata* heroes; son of the river Ganges
Kaṇṇaṉ: Kṛṣṇa, especially as a young boy
Kantaṉ: Skanda/Murukaṉ; younger son of Śiva
kāppu: invocatory verse(s); bracelet or string worn around the wrist as a protection against harm
Kaṟaikaṇṭaṉ: Śiva ("He [with] poison [in his] throat")
Karṇa: warrior in the *Mahābhārata*
Karppakam: wishing tree in heaven
Kāsi: city of Benares (North India)
Kausalyā: mother of Rāma
kōlam: geometric drawing made with rice flour at thresholds
koṭai: bow song festival; "offering"
Kṣetra Nātaṉ/Kṣetra Pālakaṉ: pair of minor deities associated with Viṣṇu
Kumarā: vocative to Murukaṉ
kumkum: vermilion powder worn by women on their forehead
kummi: folk song/dance, mostly by women
kuravai: ululation made at critical points in a bow song festival and other rituals
kuṟi: "omen," "mark"; words of a god spoken through possessed medium

liṅgam (*liṅkam*): phallic-shaped icon of Śiva

Mahābhārata: Sanskrit epic composed c. 400 B.C to A.D. 400
Mahādeva: Śiva ("Great-God")

Malayalam: language spoken in Kerala
Malayali: a speaker of Malayalam; also an adjective (e.g., Malayali culture)
māma: maternal uncle; potential or present father-in-law
maṇṭapam: outer hall of palace or temple
mantra (*mantiram*): words endowed with magical power
mantra vāti: specialist in mantra, black magic
māṭaṉ: class of male deities (both birth and death gods) in the bow song tradition
Māyaṉ: Viṣṇu
mēḷam: musical ensemble that plays in bow song festivals, marriages, and temple ceremonies
Mōhiṉi: Viṣṇu in his female form; "enchantress"
mokṣa: state of release from cycle of rebirth and redeath
muṇṭa: unit of measurement
Murukaṉ: younger son of Śiva; popular Tamil god

nāgasvaram (*nākacuvaram*): long, double-reeded aerophone used in *mēḷam* and other temple music
namaskāram: respectful greeting (with palms pressed together)
Nandavaṉam: garden where flowers for the gods' garlands are picked
Nandi: Śiva's mount; a bull
Nantaṉ: Untouchable Śaiva saint
Nārada: crafty sage of Hindu mythology
Nāthā: vocative to Śiva ("The Lord")
Nawab: Muslim ruler
Nellai: Tirunelveli city; Śiva in the temple there
Nīlakaṇṭaṉ: Śiva ("He [with] a dark throat")

pantal: a temporary thatch roof constructed for festivals, marriages, and other ceremonies
Pāpanācam: city and temple in western Tinnevelly district; literally "the destruction of sins"
Pārvati: wife of Śiva
Pātāḷam: underworld realm of demons
Paṭṭavaraiyar: form of Muttuppaṭṭaṉ worshiped in the bow song tradition
pāyacam: sweet, rice pudding
pēy/picācu: harmful spirit; sometimes a synonym for māṭaṉ
poṉṉuravi: long, iron whip; instrument of war
Potikai, Mt.: legendary mountain associated with Agastya (Akattiyar), a sage who brought northern Sanskritic culture to the Tamil land
poṭṭu: circular beauty mark worn on the forehead
pūjā: basic form of Hindu worship
purāṇas: mythological texts (c. A.D. 300–1500)

raja: king, ruler
Rāmāyaṇa: epic story of Rāma and Sītā; composed c. 200 B.C. to A.D. 200
Rāmesvaram: city and temple on Tamil seacoast, linked to the *Rāmāyaṇa*
ṛṣi: Vedic "seer"
rudrakṣa beads: rosary, associated with holy men

Sabari, Mt.: mountain associated with Śāstā (as Ayyappaṉ)
Sadāśivā: vocative to Śiva ("Eternal-Śiva")
sādhu: wandering ascetic; *sannyāsin*
śakti: energy, power; the goddess
Śaṅkara: medieval philosopher from South India
sannyāsin: sādhu
śāstra: Hindu text describing legal, social, and ritual laws
satī: woman cremated at the time of her husband's cremation
Śeṣa: Ananta; serpent upon which Viṣṇu reclines
Śivarāttiri: night of fasting in honor of Śiva
Śrī: Lakṣmī, wife of Viṣṇu; goddess of fortune and beauty

Tai Tīrttam: ritual bath taken by the Travancore maharaja in the month of Tai (January/February)
tāli: marriage pendant for women
Tāṇuliṅgam: Śiva at Cucīntiram
Tāṇumālayyaṉ: Śiva-Viṣṇu-Śāstā; central deity at Cucīntiram
tapas: acts of self-denial (fasting, continence, physical postures) to win a boon or expiate a wrongdoing
Teyvayāṉai: first wife (North Indian) of Skanda/Murukaṉ
tīpārātaṉai: special pūjā conducted at bow song festivals
tīrttam: pilgrimage spot for religious bathing and purification
Tiruccentūr: city; temple to Murukaṉ
Tiruppukaḻ: poems praising Śiva and Murukaṉ sung by Aruṇakirinātar (A.D. fifteenth century)

Ulakāṇṭāḷ: local goddess ("She who Rules the World")
Umā: Pārvati
urumi mēḷam: special mēḷam with the urumi (or *timukku*) drum
uṭukkai: hourglass-shaped drum played in bow song festivals and other rituals

vacaṉam: "speech" delivery style in bow song performance
Vaikuṇṭa: Viṣṇu's heaven
Vaḷḷi: second (Tamil) wife of Murukaṉ; a Kuṟavar (tribal) woman
Vaḷḷuvar: Untouchable diviner/astrologer
varalāṟu: "history"; portion of a bow song performance that follows the invocation (kāppu)

vaṭai: fried, donut-like food

vātai: class of deities worshiped in the bow song tradition; like the māṭaṉ, mostly harmful and probably borrowed from hill tribes

Vēlaṉ/Vēlavar: Murukaṉ ("He of the Spear")

veṭci: flower, emblem of victory

vēṭṭi: man's lower garment, wrapped around the waist

vīcukōl: pair of sticks used to strike bow string during performance

vil: bow

Vināyaka: Gaṇapati (Gaṇeśa)

Vyāsa: sage thought to have composed the *Mahābhārata*

Yama: lord of the dead

Bibliography

WORKS IN TAMIL (AND MALAYALAM)

Aruṇācalakavuṇṭar, Ku. 1968. Villu pāṭṭu. *Kalaikkaḷañciyam* 9:362–3. Madras: Tamiḻ Vaḷarcci Kaḻakam.

Chandrasekharan, T., ed. 1954. *Sivagangai-c-Carittira-k-Kummi and Ammāṉai*. Madras: Government Press.

Chantera, C. M. S. *Kaḷi Āṭṭam: Paṭhanavum Pāṭṭukaḷum*. Kottayam: National Book Stall.

Cilappatikāram, with a commentary by Aṭiyārkkunallār. Edited by Po. Vē. Cōmacuntaraṉār. Madras: Kaḻakam, 1969.

Kōmatināyakam, T. C. 1979. *Tamiḻ Villu Pāṭṭukaḷ*. Ceṉṉai: Tamiḻ Patippakam.

Makārācaṉ, S. 1962. *Oli Celvam*. Maturai: Maṉōṉmaṇi.

Mukkūṭal Paḷḷu. 1970. Edited by N. Cēturakunātaṉ. Madras: Kaḻakam.

Naṭarācaṉ, Centi. 1977. Auvai nōṉpu. *Ārāycci* 6, no. 1:17–27.

Nīlakaṇṭaṉ, A. P. 1973. *Kuruti Vayal*. Aḻakiyapāṇṭiyapuram: the author.

Pakṭavatcalaṉ, P. S. K. 1973. Teṉ Tiruvitāṅkūr tōlcilai pōrāṭṭum. *Ārāycci* 4, no. 1:83–94.

Pālacuntaram, E. 1976. Maṭṭakkaḷappu kuravai kūttu: paḻamaiyum putumaiyum. *Ārāycci* 5, no. 3:157–68.

Paramēsvarayyar, Uḷḷūr S. 1953. *Kēraḷa Sāhitya Caritram*. Trivandrum: University of Kerala (Kerala University Series, 30).

Piccai Kuṭṭi, Ca. Pa. 1969. Villicai. *Tamiḻ Vaṭṭam* 2:165–67.

Poṉṉaiya, Mōcas. 1979. *Nāṭār Varalāṟu*. Maturai: Nāṭār Makājaṉa Caṅkam.

Tamil Lexicon. 1982 (1926–1939). 6 vols. Reprint. Madras: University of Madras.

Tēcikavināyakam Piḷḷai, S. 1974 (1942). *Nāñcil Nāṭu Marumakkaḷvaḻi Māṉmiyam*. Ceṉṉai: Pāri Nilaiyam.

Umaitāṇu, Ci. 1966. *Pakavāṉ Vaikuṇṭa Cuvāmikaḷ Varalāṟu*. Nākarkōyil: Tāc Cāṉ.

Vāṉamāmalai, Na. 1959. Ciṉṉa Tampi villu pāṭṭu. *Tāmarai* 1, no. 2:24–31.

———, ed. 1971. *Muttuppaṭṭaṉ Katai*. Maturai: Maturai Palkalaikkaḻakam.

———, ed. 1974. *Aivar Rācakkaḷ Katai*. Maturai: Maturai Palkalaikkaḻakam.

———. 1976. Muruka vaṇakkam: iru paṇpāṭukaḷiṉ iṇaippu. *Ārāycci* 6, no. 4: 457–73.

Varatarāculu, S. 1977. Ciṉṉaṇṇaṉ-ciṉṉatampi katai. *Ārāycci* 5, no. 4:223–26.

Veḷḷaivaraṉār, K. 1961. Yāḻ. *Kalaikkaḷañciyam* 8:580–83. Madras: Tamiḻ Valarcci Kaḻakam.

Vināyakamūrtti, A. 1978. *Maturai Vīraṉ Ammāṉai*. Maturai: Kūṭal.

WORKS IN OTHER LANGUAGES

Abbs, John. 1870. *Twenty-two years' missionary experience in Travancore*. London: J. Snow.

Abrahams, Roger. 1968. Introductory remarks to a rhetorical theory of folklore. *Journal of American Folklore* 81:143–58.

———. 1970. A performance-centered approach to gossip. *Man* 5:290–301.

———. 1977. Toward an enactive-centered theory of folklore. In *Frontiers of Folklore,* ed. W. Bascom, 79–120. Boulder: Westview.

———. 1978. License to repeat and be predictable. *Folklore Preprint Series* 6, no. 3.

Ahern, Emily H. 1973. *The cult of the dead in a Chinese village*. Stanford: Stanford University Press.

Aiyappan, A. 1976. Deified men and humanized gods: Some folk bases of Hindu theology. In *The realm of extra-humans: Agents and audiences,* ed. A. Bharati, 139–48. The Hague: Mouton.

Aravamuthan, T. G. 1932. The Maturai chronicles and the Tamil academies. *Journal of Oriental Research* (Madras) 6:27–94.

Ashley, Wayne. 1979. *Teyyam kettu* of northern Kerala. *The Drama Review* 23: 99–112.

Asirvatham, Sheila. 1978. Villu pāṭṭu—a form of folk ballad. *Āyvu Kōvai. 10th Intiya Palkalaikkaḻakam Tamiḻ Āciriyar Maṉṟam*. Vol. 1, 639–44. Madras.

Babb, Lawrence. 1975. *The divine hierarchy: Popular Hinduism in central India*. New York: Columbia University Press.

Balfour, Henry. 1899. *The natural history of the musical bow.* Oxford: Clarendon Press.

Basgöz, Ilhan. 1975. The tale-singer and his audience. In *Folklore: Performance and communication,* ed. Dan Ben-Amos and Kenneth Goldstein, 143–203. The Hague: Mouton.

Basso, Keith H. 1974. The ethnography of writing. In *Explorations in the ethnography of speaking,* ed. Richard Bauman and Joel Sherzer, 425–32. New York: Cambridge University Press.

Bateson, Gregory. 1972 (1955). A theory of play and fantasy. In Bateson, *Steps to an ecology of mind,* pp. 177–93. New York: Ballantine.

Bauman, Richard. 1969. Towards a behavioral theory of folklore; a reply to Roger Welsch. *Journal of American Folklore* 82:167–70.

———. 1977. *Verbal art as performance*. Rowley, Mass.: Newbury House.

———. 1986. *Story, performance, and event.* Cambridge Studies in Oral and Literate Culture, no. 10. Cambridge: Cambridge University Press.

Bauman, Richard, and Joel Sherzer, eds. 1974. *Explorations in the ethnography of speaking*. Cambridge: Cambridge University Press.

Beck, Brenda E. F. 1972. *Peasant society in Koṅku*. Vancouver: University of British Columbia Press.

———. 1981. The goddess and the demon: A local South Indian festival and its wider context. *Puruṣārtha* 5:83–136.

———. 1982. *The three twins: The telling of a South Indian folk epic*. Bloomington: Indiana University Press.

Ben-Amos, Dan. 1972. Toward a definition of folklore in context. In *Toward new perspectives in folklore,* ed. Richard Bauman and Americo Paredes, 3–15. Austin: University of Texas Press.

———. 1975. *Sweet words: Storytelling events in Benin.* Philadelphia: Institute for the Study of Human Issues.

———. 1983. Introduction. *Research in African Literatures* 14, no. 3:277–82.

Berreman, Gerald. 1972 (1963). *Hindus of the Himalayas.* Revised. Berkeley: University of California Press.

Beteille, Andre. 1965. *Caste, class, and power.* Berkeley: University of California Press.

Bharati, S. S. 1935. Pre-deluge Pandinad and her southern frontier. *Journal of the Annamalai University* 5:64–88.

Blackburn, Stuart. 1978. The folk hero and class interests in Tamil heroic ballads. *Asian Folklore Studies* 37, no. 1:131–49.

———. 1981. Oral performance: Narrative and ritual in a Tamil tradition. *Journal of American Folklore* 94:207–27.

———. 1985. Death and deification: Folk cults in Hinduism. *History of Religions* 24:255–74.

———. 1986. Performance markers in the interpretation of an Indian story-type. In *Another harmony: New essays on the folklore of India,* ed. S. Blackburn and A. K. Ramanujan, 167–94. Berkeley: University of California Press.

Blacker, Carmen. 1975. *The Catalpa bow: A study of shamanistic practices in Japan.* London: George Allen and Unwin.

Bloch, Maurice. 1974. Symbols, song, dance, and features of articulation or is religion an extreme form of traditional authority? *Archives Européenes de Sociologie* 15, no. 1:55–81.

Bradbury, R. D. 1966. Father, elders, and ghosts in Edo religion. In *Anthropological approaches to the study of religion,* ed. Michael Banton, 127–53. London: Tavistock.

Brubacker, Richard. 1978. The ambivalent mistress. A study of South Indian goddesses and their religious meaning. Ph.D. diss., University of Chicago.

Buchanan, Francis. 1807. *A journey from Madras through the countries of Mysore, Canara, and Malabar.* 3 vols. London: Bulmer.

Burke, Kenneth. 1969. *A rhetoric of motives.* Berkeley: University of California Press.

Caldwell, Rev. Robert. 1849. *The Tinnevelly Shanars, a sketch of their religion, and their moral condition and characteristics as a caste.* Madras: Christian Knowledge Society.

Carstairs, Morris G. 1967 (1958). *The twice-born: A study of a community of high-caste Hindus.* Reprint. Bloomington: Indiana University Press.

Claus, Peter. 1975. The Siri myth and ritual: A mass possession cult of South India. *Ethnology* 14, no. 1:47–58.

———. 1979a. Mayndala: A legend and possession cult of Tulunad. *Asian Folklore Studies* 38, no. 2:95–129.

———. 1979b. Spirit possession and mediumship from the perspective of Tulu oral literature. *Culture, Medicine and Psychiatry* 3:29–52.

———. 1982. The significance of variation in the performance context of the Kordabbu epic. Paper presented at the Conference on Indian Oral Epics, Madison, Wisconsin.

Clothey, Fred. 1978. *The many faces of Murukan: The history and meaning of a South Indian god.* The Hague: Mouton.

Cohn, Bernard. 1955. The changing status of a depressed caste. In *Village India: Studies in the little community,* ed. McKim Marriott, 53–77. Chicago: University of Chicago Press.

Crooke, William. 1978 (1896). *The popular religion and folklore of northern India.* 2 vols. Reprint. New Delhi: Munshiram Manoharlal.

Daniel, Sheryl. 1980. Marriage in Tamil culture: The problem of conflicting "models." In *The powers of Tamil women,* ed. Susan S. Wadley, 61–91. Maxwell School of Citizenship and Public Affairs, Foreign and Comparative Studies, South Asian Series, no. 6. Syracuse: Syracuse University Press.

Das, Veena. 1977. *Structure and cognition.* Delhi: Oxford University Press.

David, Kenneth. 1976. Hierarchy and equivalence in Jaffna, North Ceylon: Normative codes as mediators. In *The new wind: Changing identities in South Asia,* ed. K. David, 179–226. The Hague: Mouton.

Desikavinayagam Pillai, S. 1931. The Mudaliyar manuscripts. *Kerala Society Papers* 7:19–40.

Dubois, Abbe J. A. 1978 (1825). *Hindu manners, customs and ceremonies.* Translated from the French by Henry K. Beauchamp. Reprint. Delhi: Oxford University Press.

Dumont, Louis. 1957. *Une sous-caste de L'Inde du sud: Organisation sociale et religion des Pramalai Kallar.* Paris: Mouton.

———. 1980 (1966). *Homo hierarchicus: The caste system and its implications.* Revised English ed. Chicago: University of Chicago Press.

Dundes, Alan. 1964. *The morphology of North American Indian folktales.* Folklore Fellows Communications no. 195. Helsinki: Suomalainen Tiedeakatemia.

Egnor, Margaret. 1980. On the meaning of *sakti* to women in Tamil Nadu. In *The powers of Tamil women,* ed. Susan S. Wadley, 1–34. Maxwell School of Citizenship and Public Affairs, Foreign and Comparative Studies, South Asian Series, no. 6. Syracuse: Syracuse University Press.

Elmore, Theodore W. 1925 (1915). *Dravidian gods in modern Hinduism.* Reprint. Madras: Christian Literature Society.

Elwin, Verrier. 1955. *The religion of an Indian tribe.* Bombay: Oxford University Press.

Emeneau, Murray B. 1967. A classical Indian folk-tale as a reported modern event: The brahman and the mongoose. In Emeneau, *Dravidian linguistics, ethnology, and folktales, collected papers,* 374–82. Annamalainagar: Annamalai University Press.

Finnegan, Ruth. 1974. How oral is oral literature? *Bulletin of the School of Oriental and African Studies* 37:52–64.

———. 1977. *Oral poetry: Its nature, significance, and social context.* Cambridge: Cambridge University Press.

Fischer, Eberhard, and Haku Shah. 1973. *Vetra ne Khambha, Memorials for the dead.* Ammedabad: Gujarat Vidyapith.

Freud, Sigmund. 1918. *Reflections on war and death.* Translated by A. A. Brill and A. B. Kuttner. New York: Moffat, Yard & Co.

———. 1950. *Totem and taboo.* Translated by J. Strachey. New York: W. W. Norton & Co.

Geertz, Clifford. 1973. Deep play: Notes on the Balinese cockfight. In Geertz, *The interpretation of culture,* 412–54. New York: Basic Books.

Gell, A. 1980. The gods at play: Vertigo and possession in Muria religion. *Man* 15, no. 2:219–48.

Gnanamuthu, S. 1975. On the place-name Kanya Kumari. In *Proceedings of the All-India conference of Dravidian linguistics, Tirupathi,* ed. G. N. Reddy and S. P. Nair, 40–50. Trivandrum: University of Kerala.

Goffman, Erving. 1974. *Frame analysis: An essay on the organization of experience.* New York: Harper Colophon.

Goldman, Robert. 1977. *Gods, priests, and warriors: The Bhṛgus of the Mahābhārata.* New York: Columbia University Press.

Goody, Jack. 1962. *Death, property and the ancestors.* Stanford: Stanford University Press.

———, ed. 1968. *Literacy in traditional societies.* Cambridge: Cambridge University Press.

Gopalakrishnan, M. S. 1953. Mother goddess: A regional study (Madras and Malabar). M. Litt. thesis. University of Madras.

Gossen, Gary. 1974. *Chamulas in the world of the sun: Time and space in a Maya oral tradition.* Cambridge: Harvard University Press.

Gough, Kathleen. 1955. The social structure of a Tanjore village. In *Village India: Studies in the little community,* ed. McKim Marriott, 36–52. Chicago: Chicago University Press.

———. 1959. Cults of the dead among the Nayar. In *Traditional India: Structure and change,* ed. Milton Singer, 24–72. Austin: University of Texas Press.

———. 1973. Harijans in Tanjavur. In *Imperialism and revolution in South Asia,* ed. Gough and H. Sharma, 222–45. New York: Monthly Review Press.

———. 1981. *Rural society in Southeast India.* New York: Cambridge University Press.

Hameed, K. P. S. 1956. Bow song: A folk art from South Travancore. *Tamil Culture* 5, no. 3:274–84.

Hardgrave, Robert. 1968. The breast-cloth controversy: Caste consciousness and social change in southern Travancore. *The Indian Economic and Social History Review* 5, no. 2:171–87.

———. 1969a. *The Nadars of Tamilnadu: The political culture of a community in change.* Berkeley: University of California Press.

———. 1969b. The new mythology of a caste in change. *Journal of Tamil Studies* 1, no. 1:61–87.

Harper, Edward. 1963. Spirit possession and social structure. In *Anthropology on the march,* ed. Bala Ratnam, 156–77. Madras: Book Centre.

———. 1964. Ritual pollution as an integrator of caste and religion. In *Religion in South Asia,* ed. Edward Harper, 151–96. Seattle: University of Washington Press.

Hart, George L. 1973. Women and the sacred in ancient Tamilnad. *Journal of Asian Studies* 32, no. 2:233–50.

———. 1975. *The poems of ancient Tamil: Their milieu and their Sanskrit counterparts.* Berkeley: University of California Press.

———. 1980. The theory of reincarnation among the Tamils. In *Karma and rebirth in classical Indian traditions,* ed. Wendy O'Flaherty, 116–33. Berkeley: University of California Press.

Hayavadana, C. Rao. 1915. The Vellalas of Nancil Nad, Travancore state, India. *Anthropos* 10:512–22.

Haymes, Edward R. 1973. *A bibliography of studies relating to Parry's and Lord's oral theory.* Cambridge: Harvard University Press.

Hiltebeitel, Alf. 1976. *The ritual of battle: Krishna in the Mahābhārata.* Ithaca: Cornell University Press.

Huntington, Richard, and Peter Metcalf, eds. 1979. *Celebrations of death: The Anthropology of mortuary ritual.* Cambridge: Cambridge University Press.

Hymes, Dell. 1975. Breakthrough into performance. In *Folklore: Performance and communication,* ed. Dan Ben-Amos and Kenneth Goldstein, 11–74. The Hague: Mouton.

Ibrahim Kunju, A. P. 1976. *The rise of Travancore, a study of the life and times of Martanda Varma.* Trivandrum: Kerala Historical Society.

India. 1903. *Census of Travancore, 1901.* Pt. 3. Trivandrum: Government Press.

———. 1912. *Census of Travancore, 1911.* Pt. 3. Provincial Tables. Trivandrum: Government Press.

———. 1965. *Census of India, 1961, Madras.* Vol. 9, pt. 6. Village Survey Monographs, no. 18. Kottuthal Azhamkulam. Madras: Government Press.

———. 1966. *Census of India, 1961, Madras.* Vol. 9, pt. 1-A. Madras: Government Press.

Jacobs, Melville. 1959. *The content and style of an oral literature: Clackamas Chinook myths and tales.* Chicago: University of Chicago Press.

Jeffrey, Robin. 1976. *The decline of Nayar dominance: Society and politics in Travancore, 1847–1908.* New York: Holmes and Meier.

Joseph, P. 1958. Lost Lemuria: Fresh evidence. *Tamil Culture* 7, no. 2:121–30.

Kailasapathy, K. 1968. *Tamil heroic poetry.* Oxford: Oxford University Press.

Kakar, Sudhir. 1982. *Shamans, mystics, and doctors.* New York: Alfred Knopf.

Kapferer, Bruce. 1983. *A celebration of demons: Exorcism and the aesthetics of healing in Sri Lanka.* Bloomington: Indiana University Press.

Karunakkaran, K. 1972. Language contact and linguistic interference in Dravidian. In *Third seminar on Dravidian linguistics,* ed. S. Agesthialingom and S. V. Shanmugam, 173–83. Annamalainagar: Annamalai University.

Kaushik, Meena. 1976. The symbolic representation of death. *Contributions to Indian Sociology* 10, no. 2:265–92.

Kerala Society Papers. 1928–1932. Trivandrum.

Kirshenblatt-Gimblett, Barbara. 1975. A parable in context. In *Folklore: Performance and communication,* eds. D. Ben-Amos and K. Goldstein, 105–30. The Hague: Mouton.

Knipe, David M. 1976. *Sapiṇḍikārana:* The Hindu rite of entry into heaven. In *Religious encounters with death: Insights from the history and anthropology of religions,* ed. Frank E. Reynolds and Earle H. Waugh, 111–124. University Park, Pa.: Pennsylvania State University Press.

Kothari, Komal. 1968. *Indian folk musical instruments.* Delhi: Sangeet Natak Akademi.

———. 1982. Oral epics of Rajasthan. Paper delivered at the Conference on Indian Oral Epics, Madison, Wisconsin.

Krishna Ayyar, K. V. 1966. *A short history of Kerala*. Ernakulam, India: Pai and Co.

Krishna Iyer, L. A. 1941. *The Travancore tribes and castes*. Vol. 3. Trivandrum: Government Press.

Kurup, K. K. N. 1973. *The cult of teyyam and hero-worship in Kerala*. Trivandrum: Kerala Historical Society.

———. 1977. *Aryan and Dravidian elements in Malabar folklore*. Trivandrum: Kerala Historical Society.

Leach, Edmund. 1964. Ritualization in man in relation to conceptual and social development. *Philosophical Transactions of the Royal Society of London* series B, no. 772, vol. 251:403–48.

Lévi-Strauss, Claude. 1955. The structural study of myth. *Journal of American Folklore* 78:428–44.

Lewis, I. M. 1971. *Ecstatic religion: An anthropological study of spirit possession and shamanism*. Harmondsworth, Eng.: Penguin.

Long, J. Bruce. 1976. Death as a necessity and gift in Hindu mythology: Dying to the world in medieval Hinduism. In *Religious encounters with death: Insights from the history and anthropology of religions,* ed. Frank E. Reynolds and Earle H. Waugh, 73–96. University Park, Pa.: Pennsylvania State University Press.

Lord, Albert B. 1960. *The singer of tales*. Cambridge: Harvard University Press.

———. 1974. Perspectives on recent work on oral literature. *Forum for Modern Language Studies* 10:187–210. Reprinted in *Oral literature: Seven essays,* ed. Joseph J. Duggan, 1–24. Edinburgh: Scottish Academic Press, 1975.

———. n.d. Characteristics of orality. (To appear in a Festschrift for Walter J. Ong.)

Losty, Jeremiah. 1982. *The art of the book in India*. London: British Museum.

Ludden, David. 1985. *Peasant society in South India*. Princeton: Princeton University Press.

Mahapatra, P. K. 1972. *The folk cults of Bengal*. Calcutta: Indian Publications.

Mandelbaum, David. 1960. Social trends and personal pressures. In *Anthropology of folk religion,* ed. Charles Leslie, 221–56. New York: Bantam Books.

Marcuse, Sibyl. 1975. *A survey of musical instruments*. New York: Harper and Row.

Mateer, Rev. Samuel. 1870. *The land of charity: An account of Travancore and its devil worship*. New York: Dodd and Mead.

———. 1883. *Native life in Travancore*. London: W. H. Allen.

———. 1884. The pariah caste in Travancore. *Journal of the Royal Asiatic Society of Great Britain and Ireland* n.s. 16:180–89.

Mathew, I. 1931. Travancore a hundred years ago. *Kerala Society Papers* 2, no. 8:123–33, i–xxxii.

Menon, Padmanabha K. P. 1983 (1924–1933). *A history of Kerala, written in the form of notes on Visscher's letters from Malabar.* 4 vols. Ernakulam, India: Cochin Government Press. Reprint. New Delhi: Asian Educational Services.

Merriam, Alan. 1973. The Bala musician. In *The traditional artist in African society,* ed. W. L. d'Azevedo, 250–81. Bloomington: Indiana University Press.

Metcalf, Peter. 1982. *A Borneo journey into death: Berawan eschatology from its rituals*. Philadelphia: University of Pennsylvania Press.

Middleton, John. 1960. *Lugbara religion.* London: Oxford University Press.

Moffatt, Michael. 1979. *An untouchable community in South India: Structure and consensus.* Princeton: Princeton University Press.

Murton, Brian. 1975. Geography and the study of South India. In *Essays on South India,* ed. Burton Stein, 92–120. Honolulu: University Press of Hawaii.

Nagam Aiya, V. 1891. *Report on the census of Travancore 1891.* Vol. 2. Trivandrum: Government Press.

———. 1906. *The Travancore state manual.* 3 vols. Trivandrum: Government Press.

Narayana Rao, Velcheru. 1986. Epics and ideologies: Six Telugu folk epics. In *Another harmony: New essays on the folklore of India,* ed. Stuart H. Blackburn and A. K. Ramanujan, 131–64. Berkeley: University of California Press.

Nicholas, Ralph. 1978. Sītalā and the art of printing: The transmission and propagation of the myth of the goddess of smallpox in rural West Bengal. In *Mass culture, language, and the arts in India,* ed. Mahadev Apte, 152–80. Bombay: Popular Prakashan.

Nketia, J. H. Kwabena. 1973. The musician in Akan society. In *The traditional artist in African society,* ed. W. L. d'Azevedo, 79–100. Bloomington: Indiana University Press.

Obeyesekere, Gannanath. 1969. The ritual drama of the Sanni demons: Collective representations of disease in Ceylon. *Comparative Studies in Society and History* 11, no. 2:174–216.

———. 1981. *Medusa's hair: An essay on personal symbols and religious experience.* Chicago: Chicago University Press.

———. 1984. *The cult of the goddess Pattini.* Chicago: University of Chicago Press.

O'Flaherty, Wendy D. 1973. *Asceticism and eroticism in the mythology of Śiva.* Oxford: Oxford University Press. (Reprinted as *Śiva: The erotic ascetic,* 1981.)

———. 1976. *The origins of evil in Hindu mythology.* Berkeley: University of California Press.

———. 1980a. *Women, androgynes, and other mythical beasts.* Chicago: Chicago University Press.

———. 1980b. Inside and outside the mouth of god: The boundary between myth and reality. *Daedalus* 109:93–125.

Opland, Jeff. 1983. *Xhosa oral poetry, aspects of a black South African tradition.* Cambridge Studies in Oral and Literate Culture, no. 7. Cambridge: Cambridge University Press.

Opler, Morris. 1958. An interpretation of ambivalence in two American Indian tribes. In *Reader in comparative religion* 2d ed., ed. William A. Lessa and Evon Z. Vogt, 421–31. New York: Harper and Row.

Oppert, Gustav. 1893. *On the inhabitants of Bharatavarsa or India.* Westminster, England: Archibald Constable.

Panikkar, K. M. 1960. *A history of Kerala 1498–1801.* Annamalainagar: Annamalai University.

Parry, Jonathan. 1982. Sacrificial death and the necrophagous ascetic. In *Death and the regeneration of life,* ed. J. Parry and Maurice Bloch, 74–110. New York: Cambridge University Press.

Parry, Jonathan, and Maurice Bloch, eds. 1982. *Death and the regeneration of life.* New York: Cambridge University Press.

Perinbanayakam, R. S. 1982. *The karmic theatre: Self, society, and astrology in Jaffna*. Amherst, Mass.: University of Massachusetts Press.

Perumal, A. N. 1982. *Folk arts of the Tamils*. Madras: International Institute of Tamil Studies.

Pfaffenberger, Bryan. 1982. *Caste in Tamil culture: The religious foundations of Sudra domination in Tamil Sri Lanka*. Maxwell School of Citizenship and Public Affairs, Foreign and Comparative Studies, South Asian Series, no. 7. Syracuse: Syracuse University Press.

Pillay, K. K. 1953. *The Sucindram temple*. Madras: Kalakshetra Publications.

Pillay, Lakshmana. 1918. Travancore music and musicians. In L. Pillay, *Essays*, 99–133. Trivandrum.

Propp, V. 1968 (1928). *The morphology of the folktale*. Translated from the Russian by Laurence Scott. Reprint. Austin: University of Texas Press.

Raghavan, V. 1969. The *koravai*—a folk custom of the Ceylon Tamils reminiscent of the art of the sangam age. In *Proceedings of the 1st international conference-seminar of Tamil Studies, Kuala Lumpur, 1966*, vol. 2, 450–52. Kuala Lumpur: International Association of Tamil Research.

Ramachandran, P. 1975. The history of Nancil Nadu, 1600–1800. M.A. thesis. University of Kerala, Trivandrum.

Ramakrishna Pillai, Thottakadu. 1911 (1891). Reprint. *Life in an Indian village*. London: T. F. Unwin.

Ramanujan, A. K. 1980. The relevance of folklore to South Asian studies. Paper delivered to the Conference on Models and Metaphors in South Asian Folklore, Berkeley.

———. 1981. *Hymns for the drowning: Hymns for Viṣṇu by Nammāḻvār*. Princeton: Princeton University Press.

———. 1986. Two realms of Kannada folklore. In *Another harmony: New essays on the folklore of India*, ed. Stuart H. Blackburn and A. K. Ramanujan, 41–75. Berkeley: University of California Press.

Reiniche, Marie-Louise. 1979. *Les dieux et les hommes, etude des cultes d'un village du Tirunelveli (Inde du Sud) (Cahiers de l'homme* n.s. 19). Paris: Mouton.

Reynolds, Frank, and Earle H. Waugh, eds. 1976. *Religious encounters with death: Insights from the history and anthropology of religions*. University Park, Pa.: Pennsylvania State University Press.

Robinson, William. 1908. *Ringletaube the rishi*. Madras: Christian Literature Society.

Roghair, Gene. 1982. *The epic of Palnāḍu: A study and translation of Palnāṭi Vīrula Katha*. New York: Oxford University Press.

Sachs, Curt. 1940. *The history of musical instruments*. New York: W. W. Norton.

Samarin, William, ed. 1976. *Language in religious practice*. Rowley, Mass.: Newbury House.

Schieffelin, Edward. 1976. *The sorrow of the lonely and the burning of the dancers*. New York: St. Martins.

Seitel, Peter. 1981. *See so that we may see: Performances and interpretations of traditional tales from Tanzania*. Bloomington: Indiana University Press.

Shah, A. M., and R. G. Shroff. 1959. The Vahīvancā Bārots of Gujarat, a caste of genealogists. In *Traditional India: Structure and change*, ed. Milton Singer, 40–72. Austin: University of Texas Press.

Shanmugam Pillai, M. 1960. Tamil—literary and colloquial. In *Linguistic diversity in South Asia,* ed. Charles Ferguson and John Gumperz, 27–42. Bloomington: Indiana University Press.

Sherzer, Joel. 1983. *Kuna ways of speaking: An ethnographic perspective.* Austin: University of Texas Press.

Shulman, David D. 1978. The Tamil flood myth and the *caṅkam* legend. *Journal of Tamil Studies* 14:14–31.

———. 1980. *Tamil temple myths: Sacrifice and divine marriage in the South Indian śaiva tradition.* Princeton: Princeton University Press.

———. 1986. Battle as metaphor in Tamil folk and classical traditions. In *Another harmony: New essays on the folklore of India,* eds. Stuart H. Blackburn and A. K. Ramanujan, 105–30. Berkeley: University of California Press.

Siegel, James. 1979. *Sound and shadow: The historical thought of a Sumatran people.* Chicago: University of Chicago Press.

Smith, J. D. 1977. The singer or the song? A reassessment of Lord's "oral theory." *Man* 12, no. 1:141–53.

———. 1980. Old Indian: The two Sanskrit epics. In *Traditions of heroic and epic poetry,* ed. A. T. Hatto, 48–78. London: The Modern Humanities Research Association.

———. 1982. The heroic theophany. Paper presented at the Conference on Indian Oral Epics, Madison, Wisconsin.

Sreedhara Menon, A. 1978. *Cultural heritage of Kerala, an introduction.* Cochin: East-West Publications.

Srinivas, M. N. 1966. *Social change in modern India.* Berkeley: University of California Press.

Stein, Burton. 1980. *Peasant state and society in medieval South India.* Delhi: Oxford University Press.

Stolz, Benjamin, and Richard Shannon, eds. 1976. *Oral literature and the formula.* Ann Arbor: Center for Ancient and Modern Studies.

Subramoniam, V. I. 1958. A descriptive analysis of a Tamil dialect. Ph.D. diss., Indiana University.

Sweeney, Amin. 1978. Three hours from three minutes: Oral composition in the Malay shadow-play. Paper presented at the Conference on Asian Puppet Theater, London.

Tambiah, Stanley J. 1968. The magical power of words. *Man* 3, no. 2:175–208.

———. 1985. A performative approach to ritual. In Tambiah, *Culture, thought and social action,* 123–66. Cambridge: Harvard University Press.

Tampy Pillai, V. J. 1913. An old tradition preserved. *The Tamilian Antiquary* (Trichinopoly) 2, no. 1:1–12.

Tedlock, Dennis. 1972. On the translation of style in oral narrative. In *Toward new perspectives in folklore,* ed. Richard Bauman and Americo Paredes, 114–33. Austin: University of Texas Press.

Thampuran, H. H. Kerala Varma. 1936. The Kali cult in Kerala. *Bulletin of the Sri Rama Varma Research Institute* (Trichur) 4:77–97.

Thompson, Stith. 1955–1958. *Motif-index of folk-literature.* 6 vols. Bloomington: Indiana University Press.

Thurston, Edgar. 1975 (1909). *Castes and tribes of southern India.* 7 vols. Reprint. Delhi: Cosmo Publications.

Turner, Victor. 1974. *Dramas, fields, and metaphors.* Ithaca: Cornell University Press.

———. 1982. *From ritual to theatre: The human seriousness of play.* New York: Performing Arts Publications.

von Fürer-Haimendorf, Christoph. 1979. *The Gonds of Andhra Pradesh: Tradition and change.* London: George Allen & Unwin.

Wadley, Susan S. 1975. *Shakti: Power in the conceptual structure of Karimpur religion.* University of Chicago Studies in Anthropology. Series in Social, Cultural, and Linguistic Anthropology no. 2. Chicago: Department of Anthropology, University of Chicago.

———. 1978. Texts in contexts: Oral traditions and the study of religion in Karimpur. In *American studies in the anthropology of India,* ed. Sylvia Vatuk, 309–41. New Delhi: Manohar.

———. n.d. Choosing a path: Performance strategies in Indian oral epics. Manuscript.

Whitehead, Henry. 1976 (1921). *The village of gods of South India.* Reprint. Delhi: Sumit Publications.

Zvelebil, Kamil. 1973a. *The smile of Murugan, on Tamil literature of South India.* Leiden: E. J. Brill.

———. 1973b. The earliest account of the Tamil academies. *Indo-Iranian Journal* 15:109–35.

———. 1975. *Tamil literature.* Leiden: E. J. Brill.

Index

Akactīcuvaram, 27
Ammāṇṭiviḷai, 93, 233n.29
Āṉantāci, 91–93, 232nn.7,8
Ancestor worship, 216–217, 237n.6
Animal sacrifice, 40, 51
Aṇṇaṉmār epic, 215–216, 219
Aṇṇāvi, 11, 14–17, 23, 25–26, 44
Auvaiyār, 178–181, 231n.7, 233n.27, 236nn.29,30

Bards, 26–27
Bauman, Richard, xvii–xviii, 223n.6
Birth deities, 33–34, 37, 42, 218
Birth stories, xviii–xix, 31–36, 44–46, 48–52, 143, 218–219, 228nn.2,3
Bow, use as musical instrument, 1–2, 11, 223n.2, 226n.1
Bow songs: composition of, xx–xxi, 23–26; delivery styles of, 16–23; geographic spread of, 2, 142, 224n.7, 228n.10; literary references to, 1, 223n.3; manuscripts, xviii, xxi, xxiii, 26–29, 227nn.15,19,22, 228n.25, 234n.2; memorization and improvisation of, xx–xxii, 10, 23–26, 94, 227nn.11–17; narrative patterns in, 31–36; narrative units in, 22–23; payment and patronage of, xx, 14, 37–38, 145–149, 226n.6, 228n.11; performing group, 11–16; recordings of, 224n.6; rhyme and repetition in, 18–21, 226–227nn.9,10; ritual role of narrative in, xviii–xix, xxi, 42–47, 141, 150, 214–215, 218–221, 238nn.11,12; speech styles in, 21; temples, 36–38, 228n.11, 229n.13; themes in, 23; women as performers, 9, 13–14. See also *Koṭai* festival; Performers of bow songs
Brahmin caste, xx, 6, 8, 27, 141–145, 225n.13, 228n.11, 232nn.1,6,7, 233nn.7,9,10
Breast cloth controversy, 7, 225n.19
Brothers, as heroes, 90, 232n.4
Burke, K., xvii

Cakkiliyar caste, 141–145, 234nn.3,5,6
Caldwell, Robert, 1–2
Caste system, xx, 5–9, 14, 141–145, 225–226nn.13–24, 229n.14, 234n.6, 235n.7. *See also* names of specific castes
Childlessness, 33, 40, 168–176, 183, 228n.4
Christianity, influence of, 1–2, 4, 7, 28, 224n.10, 226n.24, 230n.26
Ciṟappu festival, 51, 229n.16
Cōciyaṉ, (diviner/astrologer), 34, 101–105
Composition, models of in oral literature, 23–24
Cucīntiram, 3, 27
Cults of the dead, xix, 34, 214–220, 237nn.1,2,5, 238n.13
Cuṭalai Māṭaṉ, 45, 228n.6

Death deities, 34, 37, 42, 217–218
Death stories, xviii–xxi, 31–36, 44–46, 48, 89–96, 141–145, 148–150, 214–220, 228nn.2,3
Deification of the dead, 36, 91–93, 215–220, 232n.11
Dharma, 57, 115, 146, 169–170, 174

Etukai, 18–20, 226n.9
Exorcisms, Sri Lankan, 215, 237n.2

Fasting, 40, 178–180
Finnegan, Ruth, 23
Flood myth, Tamil, 3, 224n.11

Gaṇeśa, 15, 44, 50
Geerts, Clifford, xx
Gennep, Arnold van, 46
"God-stories," 228n.2
Gods and goddesses: birth deities, 33–34, 37, 42, 218; icons of, 37–38, 41–42,

Gods and goddesses (*continued*) 93, 95; temple deities, 37, 39–45, 51, 229n.17. *See also* names of specific gods and goddesses
Goffman, E., xvii
Gorky, S. M., 228n.10

Hariharaputra, 48

Icakki Ammaṉ, 92–93, 218, 232n.9, plates 5, 6
Iconic theory of language, 221
Icons, 37–38, 41–42, 93, 95
Inheritance, systems of, 5, 91, 225n.14
Itāmoḻi, 27

Kailāsa, 5, 33–34, 36, 42, 45, 48–50, 92, 143
Kāḷi Ammaṉ, 33, 92, 147–149
Kanya Kumari, 2–4, 8, 27, 51, 223n.8
"King-stories," 228n.2
Koccumaṇi, 90
Koṭai festival, xviii, 9, 36–47, 141, 214, 219, 223n.1, 229nn.15,16, 230n.28
Kuravai, 39, 41, 43–44, 95, 229n.19
Kuṟi, 41–43, 230n.23, plate 14

Liminality-*preta* theory, 217–218, 237nn.7,8
Lingam, 142, 168, 195, 205, 236n.33
"Little brothers" story. *See* Tampimār story
Lullaby, 33, 35, 92, 102–103, 186–189

Mahābhārata, 14, 60, 233n.22, 236n.38
Malayalis, 2–6, 9, 224n.7, 225nn.13,16, 230n.23
Māma (maternal uncle), 137, 145, 199
Marriage: caste system and, 143–145, 225n.16, 234n.6, 235n.7; cross-cousin, 121–122, 197, 233–234nn.35,36; represented in bow songs, 45–48, 90–91
Mārttāṇṭa Varma, 89–91, 95, 232nn.2,13
Mēḷam, 39, 41, 44, 95, 229n.19
Missionaries. *See* Christianity, influence of
Mōhiṉi, 48–50, 92
Mōṉai, 18–20, 226n.9
Muttār Ammaṉ, 33–36, 51
Muttuppaṭṭaṉ story, xx, 45–46, 141–145, 148–150, 219, 226n.8, 234n.5, 235nn.13,16,17, plate 9

Nadar caste, xx, 5–9, 14, 27, 89, 93, 144, 225nn.17–19, 226nn.23,24, 227n.20, 235n.12
Nagercoil, xxii, 2, 7, 28, 227n.24
Nāñcil Nāṭu, xxiii, 2–9, 14, 89, 223n.1,8, 224n.10
Nāṭāṉ Cāmi story, 6–7, 34, 91, 235n.12
Nērccai (vow), 40
Nīli, 92, 232n.9

Obeyesekere, Gananath, 215
Omen, 121, 166
Oral formula, theory of, 23–25, 227n.11

Palavēcam Brothers, 51
Palm-leaf manuscripts, xviii, xxi, xxiii, 26–29, 227nn.15,19,22, 228n.25, 234n.2
Palnāḍu epic, 216
Pamphlets, of bow song texts, xxi, xxiii, 29, 227n.24, 234n.2
Pārvati, 33–35, 232n.9
Pātāḷam, 50
Patmanāpapuram, 3, 27, 93
Patronage, xx, 14–15, 145–147, 226n.23, 228n.11, 234n.5
Performance, theories of, xvii–xviii, xxii
Performers of bow songs, 11–17, 21, 226n.2,7; apprenticeship and training of, 14–16, 23, 25; choral singers, 11, 16–17; lead singer, xxii, 9, 11–17, 21, 23, 50; payment to, 14, 38, 145–147; pot player, 11, 13, 21, 50; women as, 9, 13–14
Perumāḷ, 27, 95
Piḷḷai caste, xx, 5–9, 14, 27, 93, 144, 225nn.16,19, 226n.23, 230n.22, 235n.12
Pītam (bow song icon), 37–38, 229n.12, plates 2, 4
Portuguese influence, 3–4
Pot player, 11, 13, 21, 50
Proverbs, 66–68, 144, 155–156, 199, 211, 231n.3
Pūjā (worship), 34, 39–40, 51, 224n.10
Pūlaṅkoṇṭal, story of, 35, 93
Pulavar (scholar), 27, 226n.23
Purāṇas, 14, 36, 227n.15

Rāmāyaṇa, xxiii, 14, 45, 141, 145, 154–155, 168, 228n.2
Ringletaube, Tobias, 224n.10
Ritual depth, 41–46
Ritual naming, 220–221
Russian literature, performed as bow song, 224n.7

Śakti, 42, 230n.25
Śāstā story, 15, 23, 33–34, 39, 42, 44–46,

48–52, 92, 219, 223n.2, 230–231nn.1–3
Seven brothers, 153
Singer of Tales, xviii, 24
Singers. *See* Performers of bow songs
Sītā, 45
Śiva, 5, 33–35, 48–50, 90, 92, 143, 220
Spirit possession, xviii, 13, 41–46, 51, 95–96, 141, 219, 229–230nn.20–27

Tambiah, Stanley, 221
Tamil Nadu, xxii
Tamils, 2–9, 17, 224n.7, 225n.13,16
Tampimār ("Little Brothers") story, 23, 46, 89–91, 93–96, 217, 219, 232nn.2,13
Temple deities, 37, 39–45, 51, 229n.17
Temples, 9, 36–38, 228n.11, 229n.13
Texts, of bow songs. *See* Bow songs, manuscripts
Textualization, 149
Tinnevelly district, 14, 142, 223n.8, 224n.10, 228n.10
Tīpārātaṉai, 38–44, 219, 229n.18
Tōṭṭukkāri Ammaṉ, 5, 24
Travancore, xx, 3–5, 27, 89, 225n.14, 227nn.21,22
Trivandrum, 3, 7, 224n.7, 234n.2
Turner, Victor, xvii, 31, 219, 228n.1

Uncle, maternal, 137, 145, 199
Untouchable castes, xx, 6–8, 141–145, 225n.21, 234nn.1,3,5,6, 235nn.7,9,10

Vacaṉam, 16, 21, 25
Vallarakkaṉ, 33, 45, 49–51, 92–93, 219, 230–231nn.2,3
Vaḷḷuvar (astrologer), 208
Vāṉamamālai, Na., xxii, 223–224n.3, 234nn.3,5
Viṣṇu, 33, 36, 48–51, 95, 233n.16

Women as performers of bow songs, 9, 13–14

Yugoslav epics, composition of, 24